Modern C++ Programming
Orhan Gazi, PhD

Copyright Information

Orhan Gazi
Electrical and Electronics Engineering Department
Ankara Medipol University
Ankara, Turkey

Preface

C++ programming language was developed in 1980. In time, the language have been improved with the introduction of standards, C++11, C++14, C++17, C++20, and C++23, and the current C++ language is much more improved considering its versions before the year of 2010, and a new name "Modern C++" is adopted in literature for the current C++. Although new features are added to the C++ language by the introduction of new standards, the skeleton of the language stays the same.

In this book, we explain modern C++ programming language. In chapters 1-7, we explain basic programming concepts which are data types, conditional statements, loops, functions, arrays and type conversion. In chapter-6, we included lambda functions which are introduced in modern C++ programming. Besides, automatic data definition which is covered in chapter-2 is also a topic of modern C++ language. It should be never forgotten that in digital devices 2's complement representation is used for signed number. For this reason, we covered fundamentals concepts like binary, hexadecimal numbers and number representation in chapter-1. It is critical to have good knowledge of binary number representations when studying the pointers which are covered in chapter-9. For this reason, we strongly advise the reader to study the chapter-1 before processing with the other chapters.

C programming language is usually considered for embedded software engineering; on the other hand, due to the object oriented ability of the C++ language its application scope is vaster considering the C language. Both C and C++ languages are the most adopted programming languages. According to the TIOBE index, C and C++ languages have always been in the top three places for the last 40 years, among 100 programming languages considering the reference year 2024. As every technology, programming languages improve in time. There is an increasing competition among programming languages over the last few decades. Although python language showed a tremendous incline in the recent years, C and C++ languages are still in the top three popularity places. Due to the tough computation among programming languages, C++ had to update itself with a number of recent published standards. In these standards, either new features are introduced or some weak parts of the C++ language are improved. For instance, with the introduction of smarts pointers in C++11 standard, automatic de-allocation is enabled for dynamically allocated memory spaces, and memory leakage problem is alleviated.

The object oriented programming using C++ is covered in chapters 13, 14, 15 and 17. Object oriented programming is not a simple subject for new beginners. For this reason, while explaining the subjects, classes, inheritance, operator overloading, and templates, we paid attention to be as simple as possible and we focused on the main concepts avoiding complex programming notation. We avoided using long variable and object names, and we tried to keep the programming lines in its minimum number. From our years of experience, we realized that providing complicated or long expressions even for variable names tires the human brain and brakes the learning speed, for this reason we just aimed to give the target information and avoided long lines and class or object names.

Complex numbers are very widely used for electrical and computer engineers. In chapter-8, we explain how to use the complex numbers in C++ programming. Chapter-16 covers parallel programming, or concurrency in C++ programming. The speed of a computer is determined by the clock frequency of its processor, and the frequency of a clock source cannot go beyond a certain limit, since, at very huge frequencies electrons are converted to photons and electronic devices burn. To decrease the computation time of high complex operations parallel processing can be employed and for this purpose electronic devices can contain multiple processors and each processor deal with a specific part of the computation. In C++ programming, we use threads for parallel processing operations, and to prevent race condition which arises when multiple threads try to access a shared resource, we use either mutex functions or atomic variables. These concepts are explained in details in Chapter-16.

This is the first edition of the book, and the book will be updated and new examples will be added whenever it is needed. Lastly, for new programmers, we want to give a piece of advice, there is no difficult subject in science and engineering; something is difficult if it is not divided into sufficient number of pieces. If you follow the divide and conquer policy in your learning, your learning speed will be faster and your learning quality will be better.

I dedicate this book to my lovely sister Seviye Gür, and to those people who like to teach something to the people.

Prof. Dr. Orhan Gazi
Electrical and Electronics Engineering Department
Ankara Medipol University
Saturday, February 17, 2024

Chapter-1

Representation of Numbers and Characters in Computer

Abstract: This chapter covers the computer representation of numbers and characters. Computer uses binary number system. Everything is represented by binary numbers in computer. Information is expressed using symbols which include characters, numbers and symbols other than characters. Every symbol and number is represented by 7-bit ASCII codes. ASCII representation of positive numbers is the same as their binary representation. However, negative numbers are represented in 2's complement form in most of the electronic devices including computers.

1.1 Number Bases

Number base is a positive integer, and a number with base N can contain digits less than N.

1.1.1 Decimal Numbers

If base equals to 10, then all the digits forming a number should be less than or equal to 9. The numbers under base 10 are called decimal numbers.

Example-1.1: We can write a few decimal numbers as

    456   99988   67890   45433

In fact, in our daily life we use decimal numbers

1.1.2 Binary Numbers

If the base equals 2, then the numbers are called binary numbers and binary numbers can be formed using the digits 0 and 1.

Example-1.2: We can write a few binary numbers as

    1011   10111101   101101010   11111111

1.1.3 Octal Numbers

If the base equals 8, then the numbers formed under this base are called octal numbers and an octal number can be formed using the digits

$$0, \quad 1, \quad 2, \quad 3, \quad 4, \quad 5, \quad 6, \quad 7$$

Example-1.3: We can write a few octal numbers as

76403   22334   54634

1.1.4 Hexadecimal Numbers

If the base equals16, then the numbers formed under this base are called hexadecimal numbers and a hexadecimal number can be formed using the digits

$$0, \quad 1, \quad 2, \quad 3, \quad 4, \quad 5, \quad 6, \quad 7, \quad 8, \quad 9,$$
$$A, \quad B, \quad C, \quad D, \quad E, \quad F$$

where the letters A, B, C, D, E and F denote the numbers

$$10, \quad 11, \quad 12, \quad 13, \quad 14, \quad 15.$$

Example-1.4: We can write a few octal numbers as

AB04   FF0A   456FEA09

We can use $0x$ or 0X prefix in front of the hexadecimal numbers. The hexadecimal number in the previous example can be written either as

0xAB04   0xFF0A   0x456FEA09

or as

0XAB04   0XFF0A   0X456FEA09

but usually small x, i.e., $0x$, is preferred.

1.2 Conversion between Bases

Assume that we have a number under a base. The equivalent of this number in another base can be calculated. This procedure is called conversion between bases.

1.2.1 Binary to Decimal Conversion

The n-bit binary number

$$b_{n-1}b_{n-2}\ldots b_1 b_0$$

can be converted to decimal as

$$b_{n-1}2^{n-1} + b_{n-2}2^{n-2} + \ldots + b_1 2^1 + b_0 2^0$$

Example-1.5: The decimal equivalent of

$$10110$$

can be calculated as

$$2^4 + 0 \times 2^3 + 1 \times 2^2 + 1 \times 2^1 + 0 \times 2^0$$

which is equal to

$$22$$

1.2.2 Binary to Octal Conversion

To convert a binary number to octal, starting from the right most position we first divide the binary string into groups having 3 bits, and then convert each 3 bits to an octal number.

Example-1.6: Convert the binary number

```
1010001101011
```

to a number in octal base.

Solution-1.6: Starting from the right most position we first divide the binary string into groups having 3 bits

as

where the left most bit can be left padded by zeros to make a group of three bits as

and we convert each group to an octal number as in

Thus, the equivalent octal number is

```
12153
```

1.2.3 Binary to Hexadecimal Conversion

To convert a binary number to octal, starting from the right most position we first divide the binary string into groups having 4 bits, and then convert each 4 bits to a hexadecimal number.

Example-1.7: Convert the binary number

11010001101011

to a number in hexadecimal base.

Solution-1.7: Starting from the right most position we first divide the binary string into groups having 3 bits as

where the left most bit can be left padded by zeros to make a group of three bits as

and we convert each group to an octal number as in

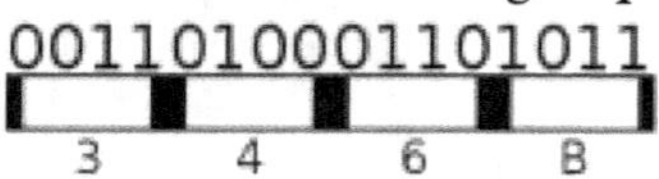

Thus, the equivalent hexadecimal number is

346B

1.2.4 Decimal to Binary Conversion

A decimal number can be converted to a binary number using successive division operation. In this method, the decimal number is divided by 2 and the remainder is recorded, the dividend is again divided by 2 and the remainder is recorded. This procedure is repeated with dividends until no more division operation can be achieved.

Example-1.8: Convert the decimal number 351 to binary.

Solution-1.8: We divide 351 by 2 and remainder equals 1 and dividend equal 350. We indicate this division operation as on the right hand side of Figure-1.1.

$$
\begin{array}{r|l}
351 & 2 \\
\underline{350} & 175 \\
1 &
\end{array}
\quad\longrightarrow\quad
\begin{array}{r|l}
351 & 1 \\
175 &
\end{array}
$$

Figure-1.1 Decimal to binary conversion for Example-1.8.

If we continue division operation in a successive manner we obtain Figure-1.2.

$$
\begin{array}{r|l}
351 & 1 \\
175 & 1 \\
87 & 1 \\
43 & 1 \\
21 & 1 \\
10 & 0 \\
5 & 1 \\
2 & 0 \\
1 &
\end{array}
$$

Figure-1.2 Successive division for Example-1.8.

Finally, we collect the binary numbers from bottom to top as depicted in Figure-1.3, and obtain

`101011111`

$$
\begin{array}{r|l}
351 & 1 \\
175 & 1 \\
87 & 1 \\
43 & 1 \\
21 & 1 \\
10 & 0 \\
5 & 1 \\
2 & 0 \\
1 &
\end{array}
$$

Figure-1.3 Bits are collected from bottom to top.

Exercise: Find the decimal equivalent of the binary number

`101011111`

1.2.5 Octal to Binary Conversion

To convert an octal number to binary, we first convert each octal digit to a binary string having three bits, then concatenate all the bits and obtain the binary equivalent of the octal number.

Example-1.9: Convert the octal number 763015 to binary.

Solution-1.9: We first express each octal digit by three bits as shown in

7	6	3	0	1	5
↓	↓	↓	↓	↓	↓
111	110	011	000	001	101

then we concatenate the bits and obtain the binary equivalent number as

111 110 011 000 001 101

where removing spaces we get

111110011000001101

1.2.6 Hexadecimal to Binary Conversion

To convert a hexadecimal number to binary, we first convert each hexadecimal digit to a binary string having four bits, then concatenate all the bits and obtain the binary equivalent of the hexadecimal number.

Example-1.10: Convert the hexadecimal number $0x$1AF39502 to binary.

Solution-1.10: We first express each octal digit by three bits as shown in

7	6	3	0	1	5
111	110	011	000	001	101

then we concatenate the bits and obtain the binary equivalent number as

111 110 011 000 001 101

where removing spaces we get

111110011000001101

1.2.7 Hexadecimal to Decimal Conversion

The n-digit hexadecimal number

$$h_{n-1}h_{n-2}\ldots h_1 h_0$$

is converted to decimal as

$$h_{n-1}16^{n-1} + h_{n-2}16^{n-2} + \ldots + h_1 16^1 + h_0 16^0$$

Example-1.11: The decimal equivalent of

```
0xFF
```

can be calculated as

$$15 \times 16^1 + 15 \times 16^0$$

which is equal to

```
255
```

Example-1.12: The decimal equivalent of

```
0xFFF
```

can be calculated as

$$15 \times 16^2 + 15 \times 16^1 + 15 \times 16^0$$

which is equal to

```
4095
```

1.3 Positive Integers

Positive integers are also called unsigned integers, and in computer positive integers are represented by their binary equivalents.

Example-1.13: The hexadecimal number $\texttt{0xFF}$ equals to the decimal number 255 which is represented in computer by $\texttt{1111 1111}$

1.4 Two's Complement Form

To find the 2's complement of a binary string, i.e., binary number, we start from the right most position and proceed to the left until we meet the first 1, and after meeting the first one, we go on proceeding to the left but we flip each bit to its complement form, i.e., 1 is converted to 0, and 0 is converted to 1.

Example-1.14: Find the 2's complement of
10101110001000

Solution-1.14: We start from the left-most bit and proceed to the left until we meet the first 1 as shown in Figure-1.4.

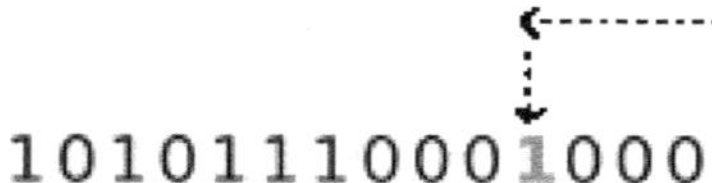

$$10101110001000$$

Figure-1.4 Location of the first '1'.

Next, we go on proceeding to the left, and take the complement of each bit as shown in Figure -1.5.

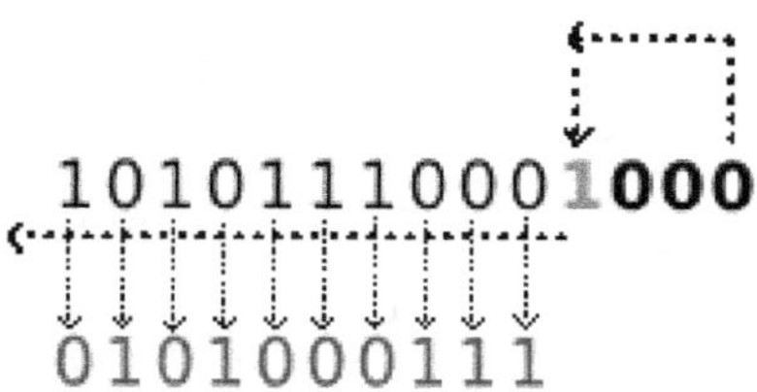

Figure-1.5 Take the complement of each bit after first '1'.

and the 2's complement form is obtained as

$$0101\ 0001111\ \mathbf{000}$$

where removing the spaces we obtain
01010001111000

Example-1.15: Find the 2's complement of
11111111

Solution-1.15: We start from the left-most bit and proceed to the left until we meet the first 1, however, for this string the first 1 is at the first position as shown in Figure-1.6.

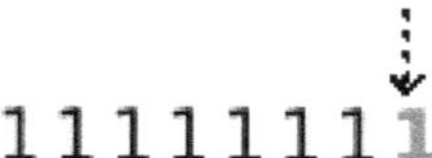

$$11111111$$

Figure-1.6 Location of first '1'.

Next, we go on proceeding to the left, and take the complement of each bit as shown in Figure-1.7.

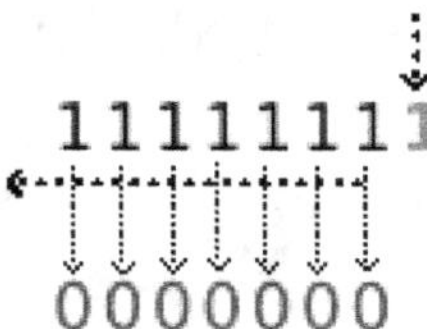

Figure-1.7 Complemented ones.

and the 2's complement form is obtained as

00000001

where removing the spaces we obtain

00000001

Example-1.16: 2's complement of

11111111

is   00000001

What is the 2's complement of

00000001

Solution-1.16: 2's complement of   00000001
is

11111111

Hence, we can write that

If **d** is the 2's complement of **a,** i.e., **d** = 2's comp(**a**)

then 2's complement of **d** is **a,** i.e., **a** = 2's comp(**d**)

1.5 Negative Integers

Assume that **a** is a positive integer, in computer the positive integer **a** is represented by a binary string which is obtained by converting **a** into binary. That is

a is represented by **d** which is obtained by converting **a** into binary

Negative integers in digital devices are represented in 2's complement form.

That is

if **a** is represented by **d,** then **−a** is represented by 2's complement of **d**

Example-1.17: How are the numbers 17 and -17 are represented in computer? Use 8 bits for the representation.

Solution-1.17: Using 8 bits, we can write the binary equivalent of 17 as

00010001

Then, in computer the string

00010001

represents the number 17.

If the string 00010001 represents 17, then -17 is represented by

2's complement of 00010001

which is

11101111

Thus, in computer

the string 00010001 represents 17

and

the string 11101111 represents -17

In 2's complement form the most significant bit is always 1.

Example-1.18: The string 11111111 represents a negative integer in computer. What is the decimal equivalent of the number?

Solution-1.18: Negative integers are represented by 2's complement of the binary representation of the it's opposite sign integer, i.e., positive integer. We know that

If d=2's complement of a, then a = 2's complement of d

To find the value of negative integer, we first take the 2's complement of the binary string which represents the negative integer, then convert the result to decimal and put a negative sign in front of it, accordingly, 2's complement of

11111111

is   00000001

and the decimal equivalent of this string is 1, then we can say that the string

11111111

represents -1.

Example-1.19: The string 11111001 represents a negative integer in computer. What is the decimal equivalent of the number?

Solution-1.19: Decimal equivalent of the negative integer can be calculated as

$- 2\text{'s comp}(11111001) \rightarrow\ \ - 00000111\ \ \rightarrow - 7$

Thus, the string 11111001 is used to represent -7.

1.6 Registers

Registers are memory building blocks of memory units. A register is capable of holding a number of bits. A register is usually called number of cells it contains. Each cell can hold only 1-bit information.

Example-1.20: 8-bit register contains 8 cells and can hold 8-bit of information.

1.7 Memory Units

A memory is composed of a number of registers, and each register has an address. Address values of the registers are kept in another set of registers. Register addresses are usually expressed using hexadecimal numbers. In Figure-1.8, a memory unit is depicted.

Address	Content
0x000000000065FE18	0x78
0x000000000065FE19	0x56
0x000000000065FE1A	0x34
0x000000000065FE1B	0x12
0x000000000065FE1C	0x94
0x000000000065FE1D	0xEF
0x000000000065FE1E	0xCD
0x000000000065FE1F	0xAB

Figure-1.8 A typical memory unit with 16-bit register addresses.

1.8 How are the Integers Stored in Computer Memory, Big-Endian and Little-Endian?

Numbers are stored in registers. Each register has an address. There are 2 types of data storage; these are little-endian and big-endian methods. In the little-endian method the least significant byte is written to the memory first, whereas, the big-endian method, the most significant byte is written to the memory first. In Figure-1.9, little-endian and big-endian methods are explained.

```
int a = 0x1245A78F
```

Little-Endian

Address	Content
0x000000000065FE14	0x8F
0x000000000065FE15	0xA7
0x000000000065FE16	0x45
0x000000000065FE17	0x12

Big-Endian

Address	Content
0x000000000065FE14	0x12
0x000000000065FE15	0x45
0x000000000065FE16	0xA7
0x000000000065FE17	0x8F

Figure-1.9 Little-endian and big-endian memory storage.

In this book, we will use little-endian method in our examples.

Assume that 8-bit registers are used for storing number. The most significant byte of the integer is stored the **highest** address and the others are stored consecutive lower addresses. Note that a 32-bit integer variable is stored into 4 consecutive registers.

A typical resister is illustrated in Figure 1-10.

Address	Content

Figure-1.10 A typical register.

Problems

1) Convert the following decimal numbers to binary

456   255   89   567   123

2) Convert the following binary number to decimal, octal, hexadecimal

101010111100111110011

3) Convert the hexadecimal number 0xA467B to decimal.

4) Find the representation of the following positive numbers in computer, use 16-bit for representation:

255   1024   4096   30000

5) Find the representation of the following negative numbers in computer, use 16-bit for representation:

-255   - 1   - 32768   - 4095   - 154

6) The following strings represent some negative integers in computer; find the decimal equivalents of these integers

1100111100000111   1011111100111111   11001100

7) How is the hexadecimal number 0 × ABCDE789AA56 stored in memory according to little-endian and big-endian conventions?

Chapter-2

Data Types and Operators

Abstract: In this chapter we first will explain primary data types used in C++ programming and then explain the use of arithmetic, logical and shift operators for these data types. The primary data types of C++ language are **char**, **int**, **float**, **double** and their **unsigned** counterparts. To comprehend the subjects explained in this chapter very well, the reader should have a good knowledge of representation of numbers in computer-like systems. For this reason, we advise the reader to study the topics explained in chapter-1 before proceeding with this chapter.

2.1 How to Start Writing a C++ Program?

To write a C++ program, we should first form the main function of the program. For this purpose, we first write the word 'int' as in Code-2. 1.

Code 2.1
```
int
```

Then, next to 'int' we write 'main(void)' as in Code-2.2.

Code 2.2
```
int main(void)
```

We add curly brackets as in Code-2.3.

Code 2.3
```
int main(void) {

}
```

The statement 'return 0;' is written before the closing curly bracket. Note that there is a semicolon after 'return 0'.

Code 2.4
```
int main(void) {

return 0;
}
```

Semicolon can also be written after '}', but is it not required.

Code 2.5
```
int main(void) {

return 0;
};
```

The C++ program lines called statements are written in main function of the program and we get the template of the main function as in Code-2.6.

Code 2.6
```
int main(void) {

// statements

return 0;
```

```
}
```

A return value of 0 indicates the successful completion of program, while any other value indicates an error. The template can be simplified. The word 'void' in 'main' can be omitted as in Code-2.7.

Code 2.7
```
int main() {

// statements

return 0;
}
```

We can also omit return 0; statement as in Code-2.8.

Code 2.8
```
int main() {

// statements

}
```

Even, we can omit 'int' word before main, and we get Code-2.9.

Code 2.9
```
main() {

// statements
}
```

In this case, compiler issues warning, but it does not have any operational effect. We can start the curly parenthesis after main as in Code-2.10.

Code 2.10
```
main()
{

// statements
}
```

In this case, compiler issues warning, but it does not have any operational effect.

2.2 Comments in C++ Programming

Single line comments can be written using after // as in Code-2.11.

Code 2.11
```cpp
int main() {

// Single line comment

}
```

Multi line comments can be written using between the characters /* and */ as in Code-2.12.

Code 2.12
```cpp
int main() {

/* This is a multiple line
comment in C++ */

// This is single line comment in C++

}
```

2.3 The first C++ Program

C++ programs usually use built-in library functions, and these functions are included using header directives as in Code-2.13.

```
Code 2.13
#include <iostream>

using namespace std

int main() {

// statements

}
```

In this program <iostream> is the name of the header file, the brackets < > indicate the library directory where header file exists, and the sign # is used to write the directives.

Our first C++ program is shown in Code-2.14.

```
Code 2.14
#include <iostream>

using namespace std;

int main() {

cout << "Hello World!";
};
```

where **cout** object is used to display the string on console. The output of the program is "Hello World."

Example-2.1: The **cout** is used twice in Code-2.15.

```
Code 2.15
#include <iostream>

using namespace std;

int main() {

cout << "Hello World!";
cout << "How are You.";
};
```

Output(s): Hello World.How are You.

Example-2.2: To print the next sentence to a new line, we can use new line character **\n** or **endl** manipulator as in Code-2.16.

Code 2.16
```cpp
#include <iostream>

using namespace std;

int main() {

cout << "Hello World!" << endl;
cout << "How are You.";
};
```

Output(s):
Hello World.
How are You.
The new line character \n can be used at any place inside a sentence as in Code-2.17.

Code 2.17
```cpp
#include <iostream>

using namespace std;

int main() {

cout << "Hello \n World.\n";
cout << "How \n are You.";
};
```

Output(s):
Hello
World.
How
are You

2.4 Variable and Data Types

A variable as its name implies can take a variety of values. But these values belong to a single data type. For instance if x is an integer than x can have many different integer values, but it cannot have a fractional value.

A variable is declared as

dataType variable_name;

Primary data types are:

char 8 bit signed numbers usually used to represent characters,

int 32 bit singed integers used to represent integers,

float 32 bit signed numbers used to represent single precision fractional real numbers,

double 32 bit signed numbers used to represent double precision fractional real numbers.

auto this specifier is used for automatic type detection

The variables belonging to the same data type can be defined on the same line

dataType variable_name1, variable_name2;

Different data types should be separated by semicolon as in Code-2.18.

Code 2.18

```
#include <iostream>

using namespace std;

int main() {

char ch1 ='A', ch2;

int num1, num2 = 14; double num3, num4 = 6.8;

auto num5 = 8.7;
}
```

To print the values of variable to the screen we use cout object which is used as

cout << variable_name;

To print more than one variable value to the screen, we use the format

cout << variable_name1 << variable_name2;

Example-2.3: We define four variables using both specific and auto type qualifiers, and we print the values using **cout** object in Code-2.19.

Code 2.19

```
#include <iostream>

using namespace std;
```

```cpp
int main() {
char ch1 = 'A';
auto ch2 = 'B';

int num1 = 25;
auto num2 = 45;

cout << "ch1 = " << ch1 << endl;
cout << "ch2 = " << ch2 << endl;
cout << "num1 = " << num1 << endl;
cout << "num2 = " << num2 << endl;
}
```

The code can be written using a single cout as in Code-2.20.

Code 2.20
```cpp
#include <iostream>
using namespace std;
int main() {
char ch1 = 'A';
int num1 = 25;
auto num2 = 45;
auto ch2 = 'B';
cout << "ch1 = " << ch1 << endl << "ch2 = " << ch2 << endl;
cout << "num1 = " << num1 << endl << "num2 = " << num2 << endl;
}
```
Output(s):
```
ch1 = A
ch2 = B
num1 = 25
num2 = 45
```
The 8-bit data type char can take integer values between -128 and +127.

Example-2.4: The tilde symbol ~ has the ASCII value 126. Tilde symbol and its ASCII value can be printed as in Code-2.21.

Code 2.21
```cpp
#include <iostream>

using namespace std;

int main() {
char ch = 'A';
int num = 25;

cout << "Letter is " << ch << endl;
cout << "Number is " << num;
};
```

Output(s):
Letter representation is ~
Number value is 126

2.5 Binary number representation in Modern C

Binary numbers can be expressed using **0b** or **0B** prefix.

> **Example-2.5:** The previous code can also be written using binary number representation as in Code-2.26.

Code 2.22

```cpp
#include <iostream>

using namespace std;

int main() {

char ch = 0b01111110;

cout << "Letter representation is " << ch;

cout << "\nNumber value is " << (int) ch;
}
```

Output(s):

```
Letter representation is ~
Number value is 126
```

Example-2.6: The numbers outside the rage $-128...127$ can be assigned to a char variable. In this case the assigned number is converted to binary and only the least 8 bits are used for the variable. In Code-2.23, this concept is illustrated.

Code 2.23

```cpp
#include <iostream>
using namespace std;
int main() {
char ch1 = 0b01111110;
char ch2 = 0b11001101111110; // the least significant 8 bits are taken
char ch3 = 126; // its binary representation is 01111110
cout << "Letter representations are " << ch1 << ch2 << ch3 << endl;
cout <<"Number values are " << (int) ch1 << (int) ch2 << (int) ch3;
}
```

Output(s):

```
Letter representations are ~ ~ ~
Number values are 126 126 126
```

In embedded hardware programming binary assignment is preferred to the char variables to see the contents of the registers clearly.

2.6 sizeof operator in C++

The **sizeof** operator can be used to get the number of bytes occupied by a data type in C++ programming. The data type char holds 1 byte size in memory.

 Example-2.7: sizeof operator can be used both with the variable name and data type name.

Code 2.24

```cpp
#include <iostream>
using namespace std;
int main() {
char ch = -100;
cout << "Size of char is " << sizeof(char) << endl;
cout << "Size of ch is " << sizeof(ch);
}
```

Output(s):

```
Size of char is 1
Size of ch is 1
```

Example-2.8:

Code 2.25

```cpp
#include <iostream>
using namespace std;
int main() {
// - 100 is repsesented by 10011100 in 2s complement form
char ch1 = 0b10011100;
char ch2 = 0b11001110011100; // the least significant 8 bits are taken
char ch3 = 13212; // its binary representation is 11001110011100
char ch4 = -100;
cout << sizeof(ch1) << sizeof(ch2)
<< sizeof(ch3) << sizeof(ch4);
}
```

Output(s): 1 1 1 1

2.7 Unsigned Char Data Type

Variables using **unsigned char** data type can have 8-bit non-negative integer values. The minimum value of unsigned char is

```
00000000
```

which equals decimal 0 and the maximum value of unsigned char is

```
11111111
```

and when this number is converted to integer we get

$$2^0 + 2^1 + \ldots + 2^7 = \frac{2^8 - 1}{2 - 1} \rightarrow 255$$

Hence, unsigned char data type can represent the numbers in the set

```
[0...255]
```

Example-2.9: In Code-2.26, maximum value of unsigned char data type is printed in **decimal**, **hexadecimal** and **octal** forms.

Code 2.26

```cpp
#include <iostream>
#include <limits> // #include <climits>

using namespace std;

int main() {

unsigned char uc_max = UCHAR_MAX;
cout << "Maximum unsigned char: ";

cout << "decimal: " << (int) uc_max << ", ";

cout << oct << "octal:" << (int) uc_max << ", "
<< "hexadecimal: " << hex << (int) uc_max;
}
```

Output(s): Maximum unsigned char: decimal: 255, octal:377, hexadecimal: ff

Example-2.10: What happens if the negative number −100 is assigned to an **unsigned char** variable.

Solution-2.10: In computer negative numbers are represented in 2's complement form. The number -100 is represented in 2's complement form as

```
10011011
```

If we type

$$\text{unsigned char } \mathbf{num = -100}$$

then the 2's complement representation of -100 will be assigned to variable num, i.e., we will have

$$\mathbf{num = 0B10011011}$$

and the binary string is assumed to represent a non-negative number, and when this number is converted to unsigned integer we get

$$2^0 + 2^1 + 2^3 + 2^4 + 2^7 \rightarrow 156$$

Hence, num has decimal value 156.

Code 2.27

```cpp
#include <iostream>

using namespace std;

int main() {

unsigned char num = -100;
cout << "Number is: " << (unsigned) num;
}
```

Output(s): Number is: 156

2.8 Left and Right Shift Operators in C

The left shift and right shift operators are << and >>. In left shift operations, the bits are shifted to the left and new locations are filled with zeros. On the other hand, for the right shift operation, the bits are shifted to the right and **new positions are filled with 0 if the number is a positive number**, or the **new positions are filled with 1 if the number is a negative number**.

That is the in right shift operation, all the bits are shifted to the right and the new positions are filled with the sign bit.

Example-2.11: This example illustrates left shift operation.

Code 2.28

```cpp
#include <iostream>
using namespace std;
int main() {
// a = 5(00000101), b = 9(00001001), c = 255(11111111)
unsigned char a = 5, b = 9, c = 255;
unsigned char d = a << 2; //d = 00010100—> decimal 20
unsigned char e = b << 3; //e = 01001000—> decimal 72
unsigned char f = c << 2; //f = 11111100—> decimal 252
cout << "d is " << (unsigned) d << endl;
cout << "e is " << (unsigned) e << endl;
cout << "f is " << (unsigned) f << endl;
}
```

Output(s):

```
d is 20
e is 72
f is 252
```

Example-2.12: This example illustrates right shift operation.

Code 2.29

```cpp
#include <iostream>
using namespace std;
int main() {
signed char a = -5; // binary representation is 11111011
signed char b = a >> 3; //b = 11111111—> decimal -1
cout << "a is " << (int) a << ",";
cout << "a >> 3 is " << (int) b;
}
```

Output(s): a is -5, a >> 3 is -1

2.9 Integer Data Type

Integer variables can take values of whole number which have no fractional parts. An integer variable is defined as

int **var_name;**

The size of the integer data can be determined using the **sizeof** operator. The return type of the **sizeof** operator is **long unsigned**.

Example-2.13:

Code 2.30
```
#include <iostream>

using namespace std;

int main() {

int num;

cout << sizeof(num);
}
```

Output(s): 4

In my computer, integer size is 4 bytes. This means that an integer is represented by $4 \times 8 = 32$ bits.

Signed representation is used for integer data type. This means that for positive numbers the most significant bit is 0, and for negative numbers the most siginifactn bit is 1 and for negative numbers 2's complement representation is used.

The largest whole number that can be represented by 32-bit integer data type is

01111111111111111111111111111111

and when this number is converted to decimal we get

$$2^0 + 2^1 + \ldots + 2^{31} = \frac{2^{32} - 1}{2 - 1} \to 2.147.483.647$$

that can be considered as 2 billion to keep in the mind.

The smallest negative number is

10000000000000000000000000000000

which is in 2's complement form. To find the decimal equivalent of this number we take its 2's complement, convert it to decimal and put a – sign in front of it. The 2's complement of this number equals itself. Then the smallest negative number is

$$-2^{32} = -2.147.483.648$$

Thus, 32 bit integer data type can represent the numbers in the range

$$[\ -2.147.483.648 \quad \ldots \quad 2.147.483.647\ ]$$

If an integer value outside this range is assigned to an integer variable, the least significant 32 bits are taken into account from the binary representation of the value, and the rest is truncated.

If you forget how to calculate the maximum and minimum integer values, keep in your mind that they can be displayed using INT_MIN and INT_MAX constant parameters, or you can consider hexadecimal values of the maximum and minimum values, the minimum value in hexadecimal is

```
0 x 80000000
```

and the maximum value in hexadecimal is

```
0 x 7FFFFFFF
```

Example-2.14:

Code 2.31

```cpp
#include <iostream>
#include <climits> // #include <limits>
using namespace std;
int main() {
int num;
cout << "Minimum integer value is " << INT_MIN << endl;
cout << "Maximum integer value is " << INT_MAX;
}
```

Output(s):

Minimum integer value is -2147483648

Maximum integer value is 2147483647

2.10 Hexadecimal and Octal Numbers

Consider the decimal number 15. The binary representation of this number in C++ language is

```
0B1111    or    0b1111
```

Octal representation is

```
017
```

and hexadecimal representation can be one of these

```
0XF     0xF     0xf     0Xf     0X0F     0x0F     0x0f     0X0f
```

Example-2.15:

Code 2.32

```cpp
#include <iostream>
#include <iomanip>
using namespace std;
int main() {
int num1 = 0xF; // this is a 4-bit number,
// F indicates 1111 in binary,
int num2 = 15; // decimal assigment
int num3 = 0B1111; // binary assigment
int num4 = 017; // octal assigment
cout << "Numbers are "
<< num1 << " " << num2 << " " << num3 << " " << num4;
}
```

Output(s): Numbers are 15 15 15 15

The integer numbers can be displayed in hexadecimal format using

cout << hex;

Example-2.16:

Code 2.33

```cpp
#include <iostream>
#include <iomanip>

using namespace std;

int main() {

int num1 = 0xF; // this is a 4-bit number,
// F indicates 1111 in binary,

int num2 = 15; // decimal assigment
int num3 = 0B1111; // binary assigment
int num4 = 017; // octal assigment
```

```
    cout << "Numbers are "
    << hex << num1 << " " << num2 << " "
    << num3 << " " << num4;
}
```

Output(s): Numbers are f f f f

2.11 How are Integers are Stored in Computer Memory

Refer to the chapter-1for little-endian and big-endian storage explanations. In this book, we will use little-endian method in our examples.

The address of an integer variable can be obtained using the & symbol in front of the variable name, i.e., as

&variable_name

Example-2.17: Consider the 32-bit integer $0x12345678$. When this value is assigned to an integer variable, the address of the stored register can be displayed using Code-2.34.

Code 2.34

```
#include <iostream>

using namespace std;

int main() {

int num = 0x12345678;

cout << "Adress is " << &num;
}
```

In our computer the output is 0x7ffecea72a54 and this is the address of the most significant byte, i.e., at this location we have the number $0x12$.

That means that the 32-bit integer is stored in the memory as shown in Table-2.1.

Table-2.1 Memory Locations

Address	Content
0x7ffecea72a54	12
0x7ffecea72a55	34
0x7ffecea72a56	56
0x7ffecea72a57	78

2.11.1 Short Integer Data Type

Short integers are defined either as

short int **variable_name;**

or as

short **variable_name;**

Short integers are 16-bit integers, i.e., 2-byte integers. They are used to represent positive and negative whole numbers. For negative numbers 2's complement representation is used.

The maximum number that can be represented by short integer data type is

0111111111111111

and when this number is converted to decimal, we get

$$2^0 + 2^2 + \ldots + 2^{14} = \frac{2^{15} - 1}{2 - 1} \to 32767$$

and the smallest negative number that can be represented by short integer is

1000000000000000

and this number corresponds to the negative number

$$-2^{15} = -32768$$

Thus, short integer data type can represent the integers in the range

[-32768...32767]

If a number outside this range is assigned to a short integer variable, in this case, only the least significant 16-bits are taken into account and the rest is truncated. Minimum and maximum short integer values are defined as SHRT_MIN and SHRT_MAX.

Example-2.18:

Code 2.35

```cpp
#include <iostream>
#include <climits> // #include <limits>
using namespace std;
int main() {
int num;
cout << "Minimum short integer value is " << SHRT_MIN << endl;
cout << "Maximum short integer value is " << SHRT_MAX;
}
```

Output(s):

Minimum short integer value is -32768

Maximum short integer value is 32767

2.12 Why do we have both integer and short integer data types?

C++ language is very widely used in embedded hardware programming. The code written by C++ language is converted to assembly code and hardware is programmed by the assembly code. If we are dealing with small integer numbers and use integer data type for the variables, this wastes memory use. Each integer value consumes 4 byte memory locations. If all the 4 byte memory locations are used, it is a waste use of memory.

2.13 Long Integer and Long-Long Integer Data Types

Long integers are defined either as

long int variable_name;

or as

long variable_name;

Long integers are assumed to be 64-bit integers, i.e., 8-byte integers. However, depending on the computer, long integers can be 32-bit integers. In this case, there is no difference between an integer and long integer data type.

Long-long integers are defined either as

long long int variable_name;

or as

long long variable_name;

Example-2.19: In Code-2.36, we use sizeof operator for integer data types.

Code 2.36

```cpp
#include <iostream>
using namespace std;
int main() {
cout << "Size of short integer is " << sizeof(short) << endl;
cout << "Size of integer is " << sizeof(int) << endl;
cout << "Size of long integer is " << sizeof(long) << endl;
cout << "Size of long-long integer is " << sizeof(long long);
}
```

Typical outputs are:

```
Size of short integer is 2
Size of integer is 4
Size of long integer is 8
Size of long-long integer is 8
```

In our computer long-long integers are 64-bit integers. The minimum and maximum numbers that can be represented by long-long integers are

$$-2^{63} \quad \text{and} \quad 2^{63} - 1$$

Example-2.20:

Code 2.37

```cpp
#include <iostream>
using namespace std;
int main() {
short num1 = 0x1234; // 2 bytes in my computer
int num2 = 0x12345678; // 4 bytes in my computer
long num3 = 0x12345678; // 4 bytes in my computer
long long num4 = 0x1234567890ABCDEF; // 8 bytes in my computer
cout << hex;
cout << "Short integer is " << num1 << endl;
cout << "Integer is " << num2 << endl;
cout << "Long integer is " << num3 << endl;
```

```
cout << "Long-long integer is " << num4 << endl;
}
```
Output(s):
Short integer is 1234
Integer is 12345678
Long integer is 12345678
Long-long integer is 1234567890abcdef

2.14 Unsigned Integer Data Type

Unsigned integers data types are used for non-negative numbers, i.e., the numbers greater than or equal to zero. Variables for unsigned integer data types can be declared as

unsigned int **variable_name; or** unsigned **variable_name**

unsigned short **variable_name;** unsigned long **variable_name;**

unsigned long long **variable_name;**

Size of unsigned int and unsigned long int variables are 4 bytes, and size of unsigned short variables, or are 2 bytes. However, these numbers may change on some computers.

The unsigned short data types are 16-bit numbers. The smallest number that can be represented by unsigned data type is

0000000000000000

which equals decimal number 0. And the maximum unsigned short integer number is

1111111111111111

and when this number is converted to decimal, we obtain

$$2^0 + 2^1 + \ldots + 2^{15} = \frac{2^{16} - 1}{2 - 1} \rightarrow 65535$$

Thus unsigned short int data type can represent numbers in the range

[0...65535]

In a similar manner, we can calculate the range of number that can be represented by unsigned int data type as

$[0...2^{32} - 1] \rightarrow [0...4.294.967.295]$

which is also the range for unsigned long int data type for my computer. For unsigned long long int data type, the range is

$[0...2^{64} - 1] \rightarrow [0...18.446.744.073.709.551.615]$

Example-2.21:

Code 2.38

```cpp
#include <iostream>
using namespace std;
int main() {
unsigned short int num1 = 0x1234; // 2 bytes
unsigned int num2 = 0x12345678; // 4 bytes
unsigned long int num3 = 0x12345678; // 4 bytes
unsigned long long int num4 = 0x1234567890ABCDEF; // 8 bytes
cout << hex;
cout << "Unsigned short number is " << num1 << endl;
cout << "Unsigned integer number is " << num2 << endl;
cout << "Unsigned long integer number is " << num3 << endl;
cout << "Unsigned long-long integer number is " << num4;
}
```

Output(s):

Unsigned short number is 1234

Unsigned integer number is 12345678

Unsigned long integer number is 12345678

Unsigned long-long integer number is 1234567890abcdef

Example-2.22: The integer -1 is represented in 2's complement form as

```
11111111111111111111111111111111
```

That is, 32 ones in computer represent -1. Its hexadecimal representation is

```
0xFFFFFFFF
```

That is, 8 F letters represent -1 in hexadecimal base in 2's complement form.

Example-2.23: Find the output of Code-2.39.

Code 2.39
```cpp
#include <iostream>

using namespace std;

int main() {

unsigned int a = -1;

cout << hex;
cout << "a is " << a << endl;

cout << dec;
cout << "a is " << a << endl;

cout << "a is " << (int)a;
}
```

The integer -1 which is represented by 32 ones in 2's complement form is assigned to an unsigned integer variable. The assigned 32 ones is accepted as representing an unsigned number.

The statements

```cpp
cout << hex;
cout << "a is " << a << endl;
```

print the hexadecimal number
0xFFFFFFFF

The statements

```cpp
cout << dec;
cout << "a is " << a << endl;
```

print the decimal equivalent of   0xFFFFFFFF
which equals
4294967295

In the last statement

```cpp
cout << "a is " << (int)a
```

the casting interprets it as a negative number, since the most significant bit is 1, the output of the last statement is -1. Thus, the outputs are:

a is 0xFFFFFFFF

a is 4294967295

a is -1

Example-2.24: What is the output of Code-2.40.

Code 2.40
```cpp
#include <iostream>

using namespace std;

int main() {

unsigned char a = -1;

cout << hex;
cout << "a is " << (int)a << endl;

cout << dec;
cout << "a is " << (unsigned int)a << endl;

cout << "a is " << (int)a;
}
```

Unsigned char is 8-bit data type, and -1 is represented by 8 ones in 2's complement form
`11111111`

The statements

```cpp
cout << hex;
cout << "a is " << (int)a << endl;
```

interprets the value as signed 32-bit integer and the binary representation is expanded as
`00000000000000000000000011111111`

and the cout operator prints the hexadecimal number
`0xFF`

The statements

```cpp
cout << dec;
cout << "a is " << (unsigned int)a << endl;
```

interprets the value as signed 32-bit unsigned integer and the binary representation is expanded as
`00000000000000000000000011111111`

and the cout operator prints the decimal number
`255`

In the last statement

```cpp
cout << "a is " << (int)a;
```

the number is considered as a negative number, since the most significant bit is 0, the output of the last statement is `255`.

Thus, outputs are:

a is `0xff`

a is `255`

a is 255

2.15 Floating-Point Number in C

For real numbers two data types which are **float** and **double** used in C++ programming. For my computer, size of float is 4 bytes and size of double is 8 bytes.

2.15.1 IEEE 754 Floating Point Standard (Single Precision)

The format of the 32-bit floating point number is

whose value is calculated as

$$\text{value} = (-2S + 1)(2^{127-\text{Exponent in Decimal}})(1 + \text{Fraction Value in Decimal})$$

32-bit floating point data type is called single precision data type, and 64-bit floating point data type is called double precision data type.

For 64-bit floating number, sign has 1 bit, exponent has 11 bits, and fractional part has 52 bits, and the decimal value of the number is calculated using

$$\text{value} = (-2S + 1)(2^{1023-\text{Exponent in Decimal}})(1 + \text{Fraction Value in Decimal})$$

The floating point binary strings that represent negative numbers have 1 at their most significant bit.

Example-2.25: Calculate the value of the 32-bit floating point number

```
1    01111110    11111111111111111111001
```

Solution-2.25: Here the sign bit is 1, and this indicates that the string represents a negative number, and the string is in 2's complement form. To find the real value of the number, we first take the 2's complement of the string

```
0    10000001    00000000000000000000111
```

and using the formula

$$\text{value} = (-2S + 1)(2^{127-\text{Exponent in Decimal}})(1 + \text{Fraction Value in Decimal})$$

we obtain

$$\text{value} = -(2^{127-129})(1 + 2^{-1} + 2^{-2} + 2^{-3}) \rightarrow$$

$$\text{value} = -0.25(1 + 0.5 + 0.25 + 0.125) \rightarrow$$

$$\text{value} = -0.46875$$

Example-2.26:

Code 2.41

```cpp
#include <iostream>
using namespace std;
int main() {
cout << "Size of float is " << sizeof(float) << endl;
cout << "Size of double is " << sizeof(double) << endl;
cout << "Size of long double is " << sizeof(long double);
}
```

Output(s):

Size of float is 4

Size of double is 8

Size of long double is 16

Example-2.27:

Code 2.42

```cpp
#include <iostream>
```

```cpp
using namespace std;
int main() {
float num1 = 12.34;
double num2 = 34.67;
long double num3 = 34755.6798;
cout << num1 << " " << num2 << " " << num3 << endl;
}
```

Output(s): 12.34 34.67 34755.7

Note that in C++ programming default precision is 6.

2.16 Keyboard Input Using cin in C++

The C++ operator **cin** is used to get input from use via keyboard. Its use is

$$\textbf{cin} >> variableName1 >> variableName2;$$

Example-2.28: This program inputs two integers from the user and prints them to the screen.

Code 2.43

```cpp
#include <iostream>
using namespace std;
int main() {
int num1, num2;
cout << "Please enter the first integer number: ";
cin >> num1;
cout << "Please enter the second integer number: ";
cin >> num2;
cout << "You entered " << num1 << " and " << num2;
}
```

Output(s):

```
Please enter first integer number: 23
Please enter second integer number: 45
You entered 23 and 45
```

This code can also be written as

Code 2.44

```cpp
#include <iostream>
using namespace std;
int main() {
int num1, num2;
cout << "Please enter the first and the second integer numbers:";
cin >> num1 >> num2;
cout << "You entered " << num1 << " and " << num2;
}
```

Output(s):

```
Please enter the first and the second integer numbers: 45 56
You entered 45 and 56
```

2.17 Operators in C++ Programming

Operators can be classified as binary and unary operators. A binary operator operates on two parameters, for instance + is a binary operator, it is used as

    x + y

where x is called left operand, and y is called right operand.

The operators used in C++ programming can be classified as

Arithmetic operators

Logical operators

Relational operators

Assignment operators

Cast operators

2.17.1 Arithmetic Operators

Arithmetic Operators are used to perform mathematical operations and these operators and their functions can be outlined as

+ addition

- subtraction

* multiplication

/ division

% remainder

Example-2.29: Write a C++ program which gets two real numbers from user and displays the sum of these two numbers.

Code 2.45

```cpp
#include <iostream>
using namespace std;
int main() {
float num1, num2, result;
cout << "Please enter the first real number: ";
cin >> num1;
cout << "Please enter the second real number: ";
cin >> num2;
result = num1 + num2;
cout << "Sum of the numbers is: " << result;
}
```

Output(s):

Please enter the first real number: 45.7

Please enter the second real number: 12.9

Sum of the numbers is: 58.6

Example-2.30: Write a C++ program which gets two real numbers from user and displays the subtraction, multiplication and division results of these two numbers.

Code 2.46

```cpp
#include <iostream>
using namespace std;
int main() {
float num1, num2, result;
cout << "Please enter the first real number: ";
cin >> num1;
cout << "Please enter the second real number: ";
cin >> num2;
cout << "Results are: " << num1 - num2 << " " << num1 /num2
<< " " << num1 * num2;
}
```

Output(s):

Please enter the first real number: 34.9

Please enter the second real number: 45.4
Results are: -10.5 0.768722 1584.46

Division by Integer Numbers

If two integers are involved in a division operation, then the result is also an integer, otherwise, if one of the operands is a real number then the result is also a real number. For example

$$\frac{7}{2} \rightarrow 3 \qquad\qquad \frac{7}{2.0} \rightarrow 3.5 \qquad\qquad \frac{7.0}{2} \rightarrow 3.5$$

Example-2.31:

Code 2.47

```cpp
#include <iostream>
using namespace std;
int main() {
int a = 7, b = 2;
float c = 7.0, d = 2.0;
cout << "Results are: " << a / b << "," << a / d
<< "," << c / b;
}
```

Output(s): Results are: 3 3.5 3.5

If two integers are involved in a multiplication operation, then the result is also an integer, otherwise, it one of the operands is a real number then the result is a real number. For example

Example-2.32:

Code 2.48

```cpp
#include <iostream>
using namespace std;
int main() {
int a = 7, b = 2;
float c = 7.0, d = 2.0;
cout << "Results are: " << a * b << "," << a * d
<< "," << c * b;
}
```

Output(s): Results are: 14, 14, 14

2.17.2 Remainder Operator %

The remainder or modulus operator is used to find the remaining number after the division of two integers

Example-2.33:

Code 2.49
```cpp
#include <iostream>

using namespace std;

int main() {

int a = 14, b = 3;

cout << "Remainder is: " << a % b;
}
```

Output(s):
Remainder is: 2
The sign of the remainder for

$$a\%b$$

is the same as the sign of a.

Example-2.34:

Code 2.50
```cpp
#include <iostream>
using namespace std;
int main() {
int a = 14, b = 3;
cout << "Remainders are: " << a % b << ", " << a % -b << " "
<< -a % b << " " << -a % -b;
}
```
Output(s): Remainders are 2 2 -2 -2

2.17.3 Augmented Assignment Operators

The augmented assignment operators used in C++ programming are

$$+= \quad -= \quad *= \quad /= \quad \%=$$

and

a += b equals a = a + b

a -= b equals a = a - b

a *= b equals a = a * b

a /= b equals a = a / b

a %= b equals a = a % b

Example-2.35:

Code 2.51

```cpp
#include <iostream>
using namespace std;
int main() {
int a = 14, b = 3;
cout << "a, b are " << a << ", " << b << endl;
a += b;
cout << "after a += b, a is " << a;
}
```

Output(s):

```
a, b are 14 3
after a += b, a is 17
```

2.17.4 Logical Operators

Boolean Data Type

Boolean data type **bool** can be used to declare variables as in Code-2.52.

Example-2.36:

Code 2.52

```cpp
#include <iostream>
using namespace std;
int main() {
bool a = true;
bool b = false;
cout << "a, b are " << a << ", " << b << endl;
}
```

Output(s):

a, b are 1, 0

Example-2.37:

Code 2.53

```cpp
#include <iostream>

using namespace std;

int main() {

bool a = true;

if (a == true) {
cout << "True";
}
else {
cout << "False";
}

}
```

Output(s): True

The Boolean equivalent of non-zero numbers is **true** or 1, and the only **false** value is the zero number.

Example-2.38:

Code 2.54

```
#include <iostream>

using namespace std;

int main() {

int a = 36;
int b = 48;
int c = 0;

cout << "a, b, and c are " << (bool)(a) << ", "
<< (bool)(b) << ", " << (bool)(c);
}
```

Output(s): a, b, and c are 1 1 0

The logical operators can be listed as

&& logical AND operator
|| logical OR operator
! unary complement operator

When logical operators are operated on operands, each operand is converted to its Boolean equivalent value and the results are calculated according to

for AND operation

true && true ⇨ true
true && false ⇨ false
false && false ⇨ false

for OR operation

true || true ⇨ true
true || false ⇨ true
false || false ⇨ false

for complement operation

!true ⇨ false
!false ⇨ true

Example-2.39:

Code 2.55

```
#include <iostream>
```

```cpp
using namespace std;

int main() {

int a = 36;
int b = 48;
int c = 0;

bool r1 = a && b;
bool r2 = a && c;

cout << "AND results are " << r1 << ", " << r2;
}
```

Output(s): AND results are 1, 0

In Code-2.57, the variables a and b have nonzero values and each of them are evaluated as **true** and the result of the AND operation for a and b is **true.** The variable c has zero value, and it is evaluated as **false**. The result of the AND operation for a and c is zero.

2.17.5 Bitwise Operators in C++

Bitwise operators are completely different operators than logical operators we covered in the previous section.

Bitwise operators are very frequently used by the embedded software engineers. They are used in hardware programming, such as in microprocessor, and chip programming.

The bitwise operators are

bitwise AND: &

it operates on two bits, and the result is 1 if both bits are 1

bitwise OR: |

it operates on two bits, and the result is 1 if one of the bits is 1

bitwise XOR: ^

it operates on two bits, and the result is 1 if bits are different from each other

bitwise left shift: <<

it has two operands, the bits of the first operand are left shifted, and the second operand decides the number of places to shift.

bitwise right shift: >>

it has two operands, the bits of the first operand are right shifted, and the second operand decides the number of places to shift.

bitwise complement: ~

it takes one number and inverts all bits of it.

Example-2.40: Let's define the variable a and b as

$$\text{unsigned char } \mathbf{a} = 5, \mathbf{b} = 9, \mathbf{c};$$

Since unsigned char data type uses 8 bits, the binary representations of these variables are

$$\mathbf{a} = 00000101 \ \mathbf{b} = 00001001$$

Now consider

$$\mathbf{c} = a \ \& \ b$$

The corresponding bits of a and b at the same positions are **AND**ed, the result is assigned to c. The binary value of c happens to be

$$\mathbf{c} = 00000001$$

whose decimal value if 1.

Code 2.56

```cpp
#include <iostream>
using namespace std;
int main() {
unsigned char a = 5, b = 9, c;
cout << "a = " << (int)a << ", " << "b = " << (int)b << endl;
c = a & b;
cout << "c = " << (int)c;
}
```

Output(s):

```
a = 5, b = 9
c = 1
```

Example-2.41: Again let's define the variable a and b as

$$\text{unsigned char } \mathbf{a} = 5, \mathbf{b} = 9, \mathbf{c};$$

Since unsigned char data type uses 8 bits, the binary representations of these variables are

$$\mathbf{a} = 00000101 \ \mathbf{b} = 00001001$$

Now consider

$$\mathbf{c} = a \mid b$$

The corresponding bits of a and b at the same positions are **OR**ed, the result is assigned to c. The binary value of c happens to be

$$\mathbf{a} = 00000101$$
$$\mathbf{b} = 00001001$$
$$\mathbf{c} = 00001101$$

whose decimal value if 13.

Example-2.42:

Code 2.57

```cpp
#include <iostream>
using namespace std;
int main() {
unsigned char a = 5, b = 9, c;
cout << "a = " << (int)a << ", " << "b = " << (int)b << endl;
c = a | b;
cout << "c = " << (int)c;
}
```

Output(s):

```
a = 5, b = 9
c = 13
```

Example-2.43: Let's define the variable a and b as

$$\text{char } \mathbf{a} = -6, \mathbf{b} = 9, \mathbf{c};$$

The 8-bit representation of -6 in 2's complement form is 11111010. char data type uses 8 bits signed representation. The binary representations of the variables are

$$\mathbf{a} = 11111010$$
$$\mathbf{b} = 00001001$$

Now consider

$$\mathbf{c} = a \mid b$$

The corresponding bits of a and b at the same positions are **OR**ed, the result is assigned to c. The binary value of c happens to be

$$\mathbf{c} = 11111011$$

which represents a negative number in 2's complement form. The decimal value of this number is

- 2's complement $(11111011) = -00000101$ which is -5

Using Code-2.58, we get the same results.

Code 2.58

```cpp
#include <iostream>
using namespace std;
int main() {
char a = -6, b = 9, c;
```

```cpp
cout << "a = " << (int)a << ", " << "b = " << (int)b << endl;
c = a | b;
cout << "c = " << (int)c;
}
```

Output(s):

a =- 6, b = 9

c = -5

Example-2.44: Let's define the variable a as

$$\text{char } \mathbf{a} = -6;$$

The 8-bit representation of -6 in 2's complement form is 11111010.

What is the is displayed with

$$\text{cout} << \text{(unsigned) a;}$$

Answer:

The negative number -6 is represented by 8-bit string 11111010.

In the statement

$$\text{cout} << \text{(unsigned) a;}$$

The number is considered to be a 32 bit integer. Then, -6 is represented by 32-bit string

$$11111111111111111111111\ 11111010$$

and this string is accepted as an unsigned number, i.e., positive number, and it decimal equivalent is printed by

$$\text{cout} << \text{(unsigned) a;}$$

The decimal equivalent of

$$11111111111111111111111\ 11111010$$

can be calculated as

$$2^{31} + 2^{30} + \ldots + 2^3 + 2^1$$

which is

$$4294967290$$

Code-2.61 gives the same results.

Code 2.59

```cpp
#include <iostream>

using namespace std;

int main() {

char a = -6;

cout << "a = " << (unsigned)a;
}
```

Output(s): a = 4294967290

Example-2.45:

Code 2.60

```cpp
#include <iostream>
using namespace std;
```

```
int main() {
char a = 0b01101010;
char b = 0b00011001;
// a^b = 0b00110001
cout << "a XOR b is " << char(a ^ b) << endl;
cout << "a XOR b is " << (a ^ b) << endl;
}
```

Output(s):

a XOR b is : s

a XOR b is : 115

bitwise left shift: <<

The bitwise left shift operator is used as

$$a << b;$$

where a is the first operand whose bits are shifted to the left by b times, and b is the second operand.

Example-2.46:

Code 2.61
```
#include <iostream>

using namespace std;

int main() {

char a = 0b10000001;

char b = a << 2;

cout << "a is " << (int)a << endl;
cout << "b is " << (int)b;
}
```

Output(s):

a is -127

b is 4

The variable a has binary value 10000001 whose most significant bit is 1, and it indicates a negative number in 2's complement form. The decimal value of this value is

$$- \text{2's complement} (10000001) \rightarrow -01111111 \rightarrow -127$$

When char **b** = **a** << 2 is performed, the bits of a are shifted to the left by two places and b happens to be

```
00000100
```

whose decimal value is 4.

We get the same results using Code-2.64.

Code 2.62
```
#include <iostream>

using namespace std;
```

```
int main() {

char a = 0b10000001;

cout << "a is " << (int)a << endl;
cout << "a << 2 is " << (int)(a << 2) << endl;
}
```

Output(s):

a is -127

a << 2 is -508

In the statement

$$\text{cout} << \text{"a << 2 is "} << (\text{int})(a << 2) << \text{endl;}$$

the value **a** << 2 is accepted as 32-bit integer. It is not truncated to 8-bit as in the previous example, and shifting operation is performed on 32 bits. The value of a is written using 32 bits as

11111111111111111111111 **10000001**

and when this string is shifted to the left by 2 places we get

1111111111111111111111 **1000000100**

which represents a negative integer in 2's complement form, and the decimal equivalent of this integer is -508.

Example-2.47:

Code 2.63

```
#include <iostream>
using namespace std;
int main() {
int a = 0b10000000000000000000000000000011; // 32-bit integer
cout << "a is " << a << endl;
cout << "a << 2 is " << (a << 2) << endl;
}
```

Output(s):

a is -2147483645

a << is 12

The 32-bit integer a has binary value

10000000000000000000000000000011

which represents a negative number in 2's complement form since the most significant bit is 1. The decimal equivalent of this negative number is calculated as

$$-11111111111111111111111111111100 \rightarrow -2147483645$$

When the operation a << 2 is performed, we get

00000000000000000000000000001100

and this string represents a positive number and decimal equivalent of this number is 12.

bitwise right shift: >>

The bitwise left shift operator is used as

$$a >> b;$$

where a is the first operand whose bits are shifted to the right by b times, and b is the second operand.

Example-2.48:

Code 2.64

```cpp
#include <iostream>

using namespace std;

int main() {

char a = 0b10000000;

char b = a >> 2;

cout << "a is " << (int)a << endl;
cout << "b is " << (int)b;
}
```

Output(s):

a is -128
b is -32

The variable a has binary value 10000000 whose most significant bit is 1, and it indicates a negative number in 2's complement form. The decimal value of this value is

- 2's complement (10000000) → - 10000000 → - 128

When char b = a >> 2 is performed, the bits of a are shifted to the right by two places, and in this shifting operation the left most bit is for the new positions, and the shifted bit string happens to be

11100000

which represents a negative number in 2's complement form and the decimal equivalent of this number is

- 2's complement(11100000) →   - 00100000 →   - 32

Example-2.49:

Code 2.65

```cpp
#include <iostream>

using namespace std;

int main() {

char a = 0b10000000;

cout << "a is " << (int)a << endl;
cout << "a >> 2 is " << (int)(a >> 2);
}
```

Output(s):

a is -128
a >> 2 is -32
In the statement

$$\text{cout} << \text{"a >> 2 is "} << (\text{int})(\text{a >> 2});$$

the value **a** >> 2 is accepted as 32-bit integer. It is not truncated to 8-bit as in the previous example, and shifting operation is performed on 32 bits. The value of a is written using 32 bits as

11111111111111111111111 **10000000**

and when this string is shifted to the left by 2 places we get

111111111111111111111111 **100000**

which represents a negative integer in 2's complement form, and the decimal equivalent of this integer is -32.

bitwise complement: ~

The bitwise complement operator is a unary operator. When bitwise operator is applied on a bit of string then, all the 1's become 0's and vice versa.

For instance

```
~ 0000 0111 → 1111 1000
```

Example-2.50:

Code 2.66

```cpp
#include <iostream>
using namespace std;
int main() {
int num = 4;
cout << "Bitwise complement of " << num << " is " << ~num;
}
```

Output(s): Bitwise complement of 4 is -5

The 32-bit representation of the integer 4 is

```
00000000000000000000000000000100
```

and the complement of this string is

```
11111111111111111111111111111011
```

which represents a number in 2's complement form, and the number represented by this string is

```
- 2's comp (11111111111111111111111111111011)
```

which is

```
-00000000000000000000000000000101 → - 5
```

2.17.6 Increment and Decrement Operators

The prefix increment and decrement operators are used as

$$++variable\_name \quad —variable\_name$$

The postfix increment and decrement operators are used as

$$variable\_name++ \quad variable\_name—$$

The expression with prefix increment

result = ++var_name;

equals to

var_name = var_name + 1;

result = var_name;

The expression with postfix increment

result = var_name++;

equals to

result = var_name;

var_name = var_name + 1;

Example-2.51:

Code 2.67
```cpp
#include <iostream>

using namespace std;

int main() {

int a = 12, b;

b = a++;

cout << "a = " << a << ", b = " << b;
}
```

Output(s): a = 13, b = 12

Example-2.52:

Code 2.68
```cpp
#include <iostream>
```

```cpp
using namespace std;

int main() {

int a = 12, b;

b = ++a;

cout << "a = " << a << ", b = " << b;
}
```

Output(s): a = 13, b = 13

Example-2.53:

Code 2.69
```cpp
#include <iostream>

using namespace std;

int main() {

int a = 12, b;

b = a—;

cout << "a = " << a << ", b = " << b;
}
```

Output(s): a = 11, b = 12

Example-2.54:

Code 2.70
```cpp
#include <iostream>

using namespace std;

int main() {

int a = 12, b;

b =—a;

cout << "a = " << a << ", b = " << b;
}
```

Output(s): a = 11, b = 11

2.18 Operator Precedence

The precedence of the operators from highest to lowest is shown in Table-2.2.

Table-2.2 Operator Precedence

Precedence	Operator	Description	Associativity
	[]	Array subscripting	
	()	Function call or parentheses	
1	++ ,—	Postfix increment and decrement	Left-to-Right
	->	Member access through pointer	
	.	Structure and union member access	
	++ /—	Prefix increment, decrement	
	+ / –	Unary plus, minus	
	(type)	Cast Operator	
2	!, ~	Logical NOT and bitwise NOT	Right-to-Left
	*	Dereference operator	
	&	Address of operator	
	sizeof	Determine size in bytes	
	_Alignof	Alignment requirement	
3	* / %	Multiplication, division and remainder	Left-to-Right
4	+ -	Addition and subtraction	Left-to-Right
5	<< >>	Bitwise shift left and bitwise shift right	Left-to-Right
6	< <=	Relational operators < and <=	Left-to-Right
	> >=	Relational operators > and >=	
7	== !=	Relational operators == and !=	Left-to-Right
8	&	Bitwise AND	Left-to-Right
9	^	Bitwise XOR, i.e., exclusive OR	Left-to-Right
10	|	Bitwise OR or inclusive OR	Left-to-Right
11	&&	Logical AND	Left-to-Right
12	||	Logical OR	Left-to-Right
13	?:	Ternary conditional	Right-to-Left
	=	Assignment	
	+= -=	Augmented addition and subtraction	
	*= /=	Augmented multiplication and division	
14	%= &=	Augmented remainder and bitwise AND	Right-to-Left
	^= |=	Augmented bitwise exclusive and inclusive OR	
	<<= >>=	Augmented bitwise shift left and augmented bitwise shift right	
15	,	comma (expression separator)	Left-to-Right

Example-2.55:

Code 2.71

```cpp
#include <iostream>
using namespace std;
int main() {
int a = 7, b = 5, c = -1, d = 15;
if (a < b > c < d) // evaluated as (((a < b)> c) < d)
cout << "Result is TRUE.";
else
cout << "Result is FALSE.";
}
```

Output(s): Result is TRUE.

2.19 Manipulators

In this section we will explain manipulators which are used to format the output.

2.19.1 setw(), setprecision()

These manipulators can be used if the header file iomanip is included.

The **setw()** manipulator sets the width of the output field width.

The **setfill(c)** manipulator sets the fill character to c.

Example-2.56: In Code-2.72, setw() and setfill() manipulators are used.

Code 2.72

```cpp
#include <iostream>
#include <iomanip>

using namespace std;

int main() {

cout<< setw(5)<< "A" << endl;

cout << setfill('-');

cout<< setw(5)<< "B";
};
```

Output(s):
```
A
——B
```

Example-2.57: In Code-2.73, we explain the of setw() manipulator by forming a product table.

Code 2.73

```cpp
#include<iomanip>
using namespace std;

int main() {

int num = 8;

for(int indx = 1; indx <= 4; indx++) {

cout << num;
cout << setw(3) << "*";
cout << setw(3) << indx;
cout << setw(3) << "=";
cout << setw(4) << num * indx << endl;
}
}
```

Output(s):

```
8 * 1 = 8
8 * 2 = 16
8 * 3 = 24
8 * 4 = 32
```

2.19.2 right, left, and internal

These manipulators are used to justify the output to the left, to the right or to the center. The internal manipulator separates the negative sign bit from number and displays it at the first position.

Example-2.58: In Code-2.74, we illustrate the use of the right, left and internal manipulators.

Code 2.74

```cpp
#include<iostream>
#include<iomanip>
using namespace std;

int main() {

double num = -8.6;
cout << setfill('x');
cout << setw(6);

cout << left;
cout << num << endl;

cout << setfill('x');
cout << setw(6);
cout << right;
cout << num << endl;

cout << setfill('x');
cout << setw(6);
cout << internal;
cout << num << endl;
}
```

Output(s):
```
-8.6xx
xx-8.6
-xx8.6
```

2.19.3 showpoint

This manipulator displays the floating point number with decimal point and trailing zeros even if the fractional part contains all zeros.

Example-2.59: In Code-2.75, the use of showpoint manipulator is illustrated.

Code 2.75

```cpp
#include<iostream>
#include<iomanip>
using namespace std;

int main() {
double num = 23.0000;
cout << "num = " << num << endl;

cout << showpoint;
cout << "num = " << num << endl;

cout << noshowpoint;
cout << "num = " << num << endl;
}
```

Output(s):

```
num = 23
num = 23.0000
num = 23
```

2.19.4 setprecision(n)

The **setprecision** manipulator is used to set the total number of integers to be displayed exactly to **n** integers. The **default** precision is **6**. The **setprecision** manipulator is usually used with the **showpoint** and **fixed** manipulators.

Example-2.60: In Code-2.76, the use of setprecision() manipulator is illustrated.

```
Code 2.76
#include<iostream>
#include<iomanip>
using namespace std;

int main() {

double num = 234.12345678;

cout << "num = " << num << endl;

cout << setprecision(4);
cout << "num = " << num << endl;

cout << setprecision(5);
cout << "num = " << num << endl;

cout << setprecision(6);
cout << "num = " << num << endl;

cout << setprecision(8);
cout << "num = " << num << endl;
}
```

Output(s):
```
num = 234.123
num = 234.1
num = 234.12
num = 234.123
num = 234.12346
```

Example-2.61: In Code-2.77, the use of showpoint manipulator is illustrated for a number which has a single digit after dot.

```
Code 2.77
#include<iostream>
#include<iomanip>
using namespace std;

int main() {
```

```cpp
double num = 157.2;

cout << showpoint;

cout << "num = " << num << endl;

cout << setprecision(4);
cout << "num = " << num << endl;

cout << setprecision(5);
cout << "num = " << num << endl;

cout << setprecision(6);
cout << "num = " << num << endl;

cout << setprecision(8);
cout << "num = " << num << endl;
}
```

Output(s):
```
num = 157.200
num = 157.2
num = 157.20
num = 157.200
num = 157.20000
```

2.19.5 fixed, scientific, hexfloat, defaultfloat

The manipulator **fixed** sets the precision for the right hand side of the decimal point instead of the entire number.

The manipulator **scientific** is used to display the number in scientific "E" notation.

The manipulator **hexfloat** is used to display the number in hexadecimal floating-point format.

The manipulator **defaultfloat** resets the settings back to the default floating point format.

Example-2.62: In Code-2.78, the use of fixed, scientific, hexfloat, defaultfloat manipulators are illustrated.

Code 2.78
```cpp
#include <iostream>
#include<iomanip>
using namespace std;

int main() {

double num = 809.123456789;

cout << "default format, num = ";
cout << num << endl;

cout << fixed;
cout << setprecision(7);
cout << "fixed format, num = ";
cout << num << endl;

cout << hexfloat;
cout << "hexfloat format, num = ";
cout << num << endl;

cout << scientific;
cout << "scientific format, num = ";
cout << num << endl;

cout << defaultfloat;
cout << "defaultfloat, num = ";
cout << num << endl;
}
```

Output(s):
default format, num = 809.123
fixed format, num = 809.1234568
hexfloat format, num = 0x1.948fcd6e9b9cbp+9
scientific format, num = 8.0912346e+02
defaultfloat, num = 809.1235
In the output

fixed format, num = 809.1234568

the right of the decimal point contains 7 digits, whereas in the output

defaultfloat, num = 809.1235

in total there are 7 digits used to display the number.

2.19.6 showpos

The manipulator **showpos** is used to display a leading plus sign before positive values.

Example-2.63: In Code-2.79, we use showpos manipulator.

Code 2.79

```cpp
#include<iostream>
#include<iomanip>

using namespace std;

int main() {

double num = 5.7;

cout << showpos;

cout << setfill('x');
cout << setw(6);
cout << left;
cout << num << endl;

cout << setfill('x');
cout << setw(6);
cout << right;
cout << num << endl;
}
```

Output(s):
```
+5.7xx
xx+5.7
```

2.19.7 uppercase, lowercase, nouppercase

The manipulators **uppercase** and **lowercase** are used to print hexadecimal numbers using uppercase and lowercase letter, by default lowercase letters are used. The manipulator **nouppercase** is used to switch off the effect of uppercase.

Example-2.64: In Code-2.80, the use of uppercase, lowercase, nouppercase manipulators are illustrated.

Code 2.80
```cpp
#include<iostream>
#include<iomanip>

using namespace std;

int main() {

int num = 0xabcdef;

cout << hex;
cout << "num = " << num << endl;

cout << uppercase;
cout << "num = " << num << endl;

cout << "num = " << num << endl;

cout << nouppercase;
cout << "num = " << num << endl;
}
```

Output(s):
num = abcdef
num = ABCDEF
num = ABCDEF
num = abcdef

2.19.8 Formats for Integers

For the display of the octal, hexadecimal, and decimal numbers we use the manipulators **oct**, **hex**, and **dec**. If a manipulator is used for the integers its effect stays until we change it. We can define **octal**, **hex**, and decimal numbers using the prefixes, '0', ' 0x', ans '0b'

The manipulator **showbase** is used to indicate the base used, such as 8, 10 or 16.

The manipulator **noshowbase** is used to switch off the effect of **showbase**.

The binary numbers can be displayed using the function **bitset<n> (number)** where **n** is the number of bits in the binary representation.

Example-2.65: In Code-2.81, we display the numbers using different bases.

Code 2.81

```cpp
#include <iostream>
#include <bitset>

using namespace std;

int main() {

int num1 = 04574; // octal number
int num2 = 0xAB34; // hexadecimal number
int num3 = 0b10101011; // binary number

cout << showbase;

cout << oct;
cout << "num1 = " << num1 << endl;

cout << hex;
cout << "num2 = " << num2 << endl;

cout << "num3 = " << bitset<8> (num3) << endl;
}
```

Output(s):

```
num1 = 04574
num2 = 0xab34
num3 = 10101011
```

2.19.9 Formats for bool Values

The manipulator **boolalpha** is used to print a Boolean value as 'true' or 'false'.

The manipulator **noboolalpha** switches off the effects of **boolalpha.**

Example-2.66: In Code-2.82, the use of boolalpha and noboolalpha manipulators is illustrated.

Code 2.82
```cpp
#include <iostream>
using namespace std;

int main() {
bool a = true;
cout << "a = " << a << endl;

cout << boolalpha;
cout << "a = " << a << endl;
cout << noboolalpha;
cout << "a = " << a << endl;
}
```

Output(s):
```
a = 1
a = true
a = 1
```

2.19.10 cout with Member Functions

The cout object can also be used with functions such as put(), write(), etc.

cout.put(char& ch)

is used to display the character ch.

cout.write(char* str, int n);

is used to display the first n characters of the string str.

cout.setf(option);

is used to set a manipulator such as are left, right, scientific, fixed, etc.

cout.unsetf(option);

is used to disable a manipulator such as are left, right, scientific, fixed, etc.

cout.precision(int n);

is used to set the decimal precision to n for displaying floating-point values, it is the same as

cout << setprecision(n);

Example-2.67: In Code-2.83, we use the manipulators as member function of **cout**.

Code 2.83

```cpp
#include <iostream>
#include<iomanip>

using namespace std;

int main() {

double a = 23.48765;

cout << a << endl;

cout.precision(2);
cout << a << endl;

cout.precision(3);
cout << a << endl;

cout << setprecision(3);
cout << a << endl;

cout.precision(4);
cout << a << endl;

cout.precision(5);
cout << a << endl;

cout.precision(6);
cout << a << endl;
}
```

Output(s):
23.4876
23
23.5
23.5
23.49
23.488
23.4876

Example-2.68: In Code-2.84,

Code 2.84

```cpp
#include <iostream>

using namespace std;

int main() {

char a[] = "Hello_World";
char ch = 'X';

cout.write(a, 4);

cout.put(ch);
}
```

Output(s): HellX

2.19.11 Alternate notation

Although the specifiers listed above are normally used with cout, it is also possible to set any of these with actual function calls, as in:

```
cout.setf(ios_base::oct, ios_base::basefield);
cout.setf(ios_base::scientific, ios_base::floatfield);
cout.precision(4);
cout.width(7);
cout.setf(ios_base::left, ios_base::adjustfield);
cout.fill('?');
cout.flush();
```

Here:

- "adjustfield" refers to flags related to field adjustment
- "basefield" refers to flags related to the integer base
- "floatfield" refers to flags related to floating-point output

Problems:

1) Write a program that declares four variables of type char, int, float, and double, respectively:

2) Define two variables for float and int data types, initialize them, and print their values using cout.

3) What is the output of Code-2.85.

Code 2.85
```cpp
#include <iostream>

using namespace std;

int main() {

char ch = 0b11011101;

cout << "ch = " << (int)ch;
}
```

4) What is the output of Code-2.86.

Code 2.86
```cpp
#include <iostream>

using namespace std;

int main() {

char ch = 0b11001111111100;

cout << "ch = " << (int)ch;
}
```

5) Write a program that displays the decimal number -100 in octal, hexadecimal formats.

6) By drawing explain how are the values
$$\text{int } \textbf{num} = 0x12345678$$
are stored in memory

7) The binary representation of a **short int** type number is 1111011100000001. Write the binary representation of an **int** type number having the same decimal value.

8) What is the maximum value of a **long long int** number?

9) What is the size of a **long long int** data types?

10) What is the output of Code-2.87?

Code 2.87
```cpp
#include <iostream>

using namespace std;
```

```cpp
int main() {

unsigned char a =-8;

cout << hex;

cout << "a is " << (unsigned)a << endl;
cout << "a is " << (int)a;
}
```

11) What is the output of Code-2.88?

Code 2.88
```cpp
#include <iostream>

using namespace std;

int main() {

int a = 9, b = 2;

float c = 11.0, d = 2.0;

cout << "Results are " << a/b << ","
<< a/d << ", " << c/b;
}
```

12) What is the output of Code-2.89?

Code 2.89
```cpp
#include <iostream>

using namespace std;

int main() {

unsigned char a = 8, b = 17, c;

cout << "a = " << (int)a << ", b = " << (int)b << endl;

c = a | b;

cout << "c = " << (int)c;
}
```

13) What is the output of Code-2.90?
Code 2.90
```cpp
#include <iostream>
using namespace std;
```

```cpp
int main() {
char a = -13, b = 18, c;
cout << "a = " << (int)a << ", b = " << (int)b << endl;
c = a | b;
cout << "c = " << (int)c;
}
```

14) What is the output of Code-2.91?

Code 2.91

```cpp
#include <iostream>
using namespace std;
int main() {
char a = 0b11000011;
cout << "a is " << (int)a << endl;
cout << "a >> 2 is " << (int)(a >> 2);
}
```

14) What is the output of Code-2.92?

Code 2.92

```cpp
#include <iostream>
using namespace std;
int main() {
int num = -1;
cout << "Bitwise complement of " << num << " is " << ~num;
}
```

Chapter-3

Type Conversion in C++

Abstract: In this chapter, we explain the type conversion in C++ programming. Type conversion is a useful property of the C++ programming language. A good programmer should know how to efficiently benefit from the type-conversion utility. Insufficient knowledge of type-conversion may lead to inadequate programming which may result in erroneous programming.

3.1 Type Conversion Methods

There are two types of conversion in C++ which are:

implicit conversion (automatic)
explicit conversion (manual)

Explicit type conversion can be achieved using either

C style explicit typecasting

or

C++ style typecasting

3.1.1 Implicit Conversion

Implicit conversion is performed automatically by the compiler whenever a value of one type to is assigned to another type. For example, if you assign an integer value to a character type or vice versa.

Implicit type conversion also known as 'automatic type conversion'.

All the data types of the variables are upgraded to the data type of the variable with largest data type.

bool -> char -> short int -> int ->

-> unsigned int -> long -> unsigned ->

-> long long -> float -> double -> long double

Example-3.1: The Code-3.1 illustrates integer to float implicit conversion.

Code 3.1

```cpp
#include <iostream>

using namespace std;

int main() {

float myFloat = 18; // 18 is converted to 18.0000
cout << showpoint;
cout << myFloat;
}
```

Output(s): 18.0000

Example-3.2: Automatic conversion is illustrated in this example.

Code 3.2

```cpp
#include <iostream>

using namespace std;

int main() {

// Automatic conversion: float to int
int a = 23.45;
cout << a;
}
```

Output(s): 23

Example-3.3: We use showpoint manipulator in Code-3.3.

Code 3.3

```cpp
#include <iostream>
using namespace std;

int main() {

int a = 7 / 2;
double b = 7 / 2;

cout << showpoint;
cout << a << ", " << b;
}
```

Note that the default precision size is 6 for cout object.
Output(s): 3, 3.00000
In the statement

$$double\ b = 7 / 2;$$

the integer division 7/2 results in 3 and this is interpreted as a double result, i.e., implicit conversion is performed.

Example-3.4: Characters have ASCII values.

Code 3.4

```cpp
#include <iostream>
using namespace std;
int main() {
int x = 12; // integer x
char y = 'a'; // character y, ASCII value of 'a' is 97
x = x + y; // y is implicitly converted to integer
cout << "x = " << x;
}
```

Output(s): x = 109
Example-3.5: This example illustrates the implicit double to integer conversion.

Code 3.5

```cpp
#include <iostream>
using namespace std;

int main() {

// a is double variable
double a = 6754.38;

cout << "a = " << a << endl;

// implicit conversion from double to integer
int b = a;

cout << "b = " << b << endl;
```

```
}
```

Output(s):

```
a = 6754.38
b = 6754
```

Example-3.6: This example illustrates the implicit character to integer conversion.

Code 3.6
```cpp
#include <iostream>
using namespace std;

int main() {

// character variable
char x = 'a';

cout << "Character is: " << x << endl;

// assign character value to integer variable
int y = x;

cout << "Integer (ASCII) value: " << y << endl;
}
```

Output(s):

```
Character is: a
Integer (ASCII) value: 97
```

Example-3.7:

Code 3.7
```cpp
#include <iostream>
using namespace std;

int main() {

int a = 15;
char c = 'k'; /* ASCII value is 107 */
float s;

s = a + c;

cout << showpoint;
cout << "s = " << s;
}
```

Output(s): s = 122.000

Example-3.8: In Code-3.8, implicit conversion operations are illustrated.

Code 3.8

```cpp
#include <iostream>
using namespace std;

int main() {

int x = 10; // integer x
char y = 'a'; // character c

// y implicitly converted to int. ASCII
// value of 'a' is 97
x = x + y;

// x is implicitly converted to float
float z = x + 1.0;

cout << "x = " << x << endl
<< "y = " << y << endl
<< "z = " << z << endl;
}
```

Output(s):

```
x = 107
y = a
z = 108
```

Since in Code-3.8 no showpoint manipulator is used, the zero after dot is not displayed.

3.1.2 Static Cast

The explicit conversion can be performed using the **C style typecasting**

$$(\textbf{type})\ \text{expression}$$

or function style typecasting

$$\textbf{type}\ (\text{expression})$$

or **C++ style typecasting**

$$\textbf{static\_cast <type>}\ \text{expression}$$

The C++ style

$$\textbf{static\_cast <type>}\ \text{expression}$$

is a **compile-time** cast whereas the C style

$$(\textbf{type})\ \text{expression}$$

is **run-time** cast.

static_cast is less powerful than **C-style cast**, and this is done intentionally to limit erroneous conversions. The data-type to be static type-casted must be compatible with the new data type, otherwise, error arises.

Example-3.9: This example illustrates explicit conversion of integer to float.

Code 3.9
```cpp
#include <iostream>
using namespace std;

int main() {

// Explicit conversion of int to float
float a = (float) 7 / 2;

cout << "a = " << a;
}
```

Output(s): a = 3.5

In the statement

$$\text{float } \textbf{a} = (\text{float})\ 7\ /\ 2;$$

the integer 7 is converted to float data type, i.e., it becomes 7.0, and when this number is divided by 2 we get 3.5.

Example-3.10:

Code 3.10
```cpp
#include <iostream>
using namespace std;

int main() {

// Explicit conversion of int to float
```

```cpp
float a = (float) 7 / 2;

cout << "7 / 2 = " << 7 / 2 << endl;
cout << "a = " << a;
}
```

Output(s):

7 / 2 = 3
a = 3.5

Example-3.11: This example illustrates explicit conversion of integer to double.

Code 3.11
```cpp
#include <iostream>
using namespace std;

int main() {

// Explicit conversion of int to float
int a = 5;
int b = 2;
double c = (double) a / b;

cout << "c = " << c;
}
```

Output(s): c = 2.5

Example-3.12: This example illustrates explicit conversion of float to integer.

Code 3.12
```cpp
#include <iostream>
using namespace std;

int main() {

float a = 4.7;
int b = (int)a;

cout << "a = " << a << endl;
cout << "b = " << b;
}
```

Output(s):

a = 4.7
b = 4

Example-3.13: This example illustrates explicit conversion of double to integer.

Code 3.13

```cpp
#include <iostream>
using namespace std;

int main() {

double a = 3.7;

// Explicit conversion from double to int
int b = (int)a + 1;

cout << "b = " << b;
}
```

Output(s): b = 4

Example-3.14: In Code-3.14, C++ style explicit conversion is performed using static_cast operator.

Code 3.14
```cpp
#include <iostream>
using namespace std;

int main() {

double x = 78.56;

int y = static_cast<int>(x);

cout << y;
}
```

Output(s): 78

Example-3.15: In Code-3.15, Char to int explicit conversion is performed using static_cast.

Code 3.15
```cpp
#include <iostream>
using namespace std;

int main() {

char ch {'X'};

cout << ch << " = " << static_cast<int>(ch);
}
```

Output(s): X = 88

Example-3.16: Data types can be displayed using typid(..).name() function.

Code 3.16
```cpp
#include <iostream>
using namespace std;
```

```cpp
int main() {
char ch {'X'};
int a = static_cast<int>(ch);
cout << typeid(ch).name() << endl; // print data type
cout << typeid(a).name() << endl; // print data type
}
```

Output(s):

```
c
i
```

Example-3.17: static_cast() can be used to convert a derived class to a base class.

Code 3.17

```cpp
#include <iostream>

using namespace std;

int main() {

class Base{};

class Derived: public Base{};

Derived* d_ptr = new Derived;

Base* b_ptr = static_cast<Base*>(d_ptr);
}
```

Example-3.18:

Code 3.18

```cpp
#include <iostream>
using namespace std;

int main() {

char ch = 'X';

int* ptr = static_cast <int*> (&ch);

// error, not compatible conversion
}
```

3.1.3 Dynamic Cast

We use dynamic_cast operator only with pointers and references to objects. dynamic_cast is always successful when a pointer of a derived class is casted to a base class pointer, however the reverse is not always successfully unless virtual function is used in the base class.

Example-3.19:

Code 3.19
```cpp
#include <iostream>
using namespace std;

class Base{
};

class Derived: public Base {
};

int main() {

Base* bp;
Derived* dp = new Derived;

bp = dynamic_cast <Base*> (dp); // ok
}
```

Example-3.20:

Code 3.20
```cpp
#include <iostream>
using namespace std;

class Base{
};

class Derived: public Base {
};

int main() {

Base* btr = new Derived;
Derived* dtr;

dtr = dynamic_cast <Derived*> (btr); // error
}
```

Example-3.21:

Code 3.21

```cpp
#include <iostream>
using namespace std;

class Base{

public:
virtual void print() { }
};

class Derived: public Base {
};

int main() {

Base* btr = new Derived;

Derived* dtr;

dtr = dynamic_cast <Derived*> (btr); // ok
}
```

3.1.4 const_cast

Using const_cast, we can temporarily remove the constancy of an object and change the values of the object. The syntax of the const_cast is as

const_cast <newDataType> (expresisons);

Example-3.22: In Code-3.22, the pointer points to a constant value.

Code 3.22

```cpp
#include <iostream>
using namespace std;

int main() {

int a = 23;

const int* ptr = &a;

*ptr = 20; // error
}
```

When we compile Code-3.22, we get the error
main.cpp:10:8: error: assignment of read-only location '* ptr'
Since, the content of the address is a constant value and it cannot be changed. However, we can remove the constancy temporarily as in Code-3.23.

Code 3.23

```cpp
#include <iostream>
using namespace std;

int main() {

int a = 45;

const int* ptr = &a;

int* ptr2 = const_cast<int*>(ptr); // remove constancy

*ptr2 = 36;

cout << "*ptr = " << *ptr << endl;
cout << "*ptr2 = " << *ptr << endl;
cout << "a = " << a << endl;

//*ptr = 36; // still error
}
```

Output(s):

```
*ptr = 36
*ptr2 = 36
a = 36
```

3.1.5 reinterpret_cast

The reinterpret_cast is used to convert one pointer type to another type. It does not check whether the pointer type and converted pointer type are the same or compatible or not. The syntax of the reinterpret_cast is as

reinterpret_cast <newDataType> (expressions)

Example-3.23:

Code 3.24

```cpp
#include <iostream>
using namespace std;
int main() {
int* i_ptr = new int(109);
char* c_ptr = reinterpret_cast <char*> (i_ptr);
float* d_ptr = reinterpret_cast <float*> (i_ptr);
cout << "The value of *i_ptr is: " << *i_ptr << endl;
cout << "The value of i_ptr is: " << i_ptr << endl;
cout << "The value of *c_ptr is: " << *c_ptr << endl;
cout << "The value of c_ptr is: " << c_ptr << endl;
cout << "The value of *d_ptr is: " << *d_ptr << endl;
cout << "The value of d_ptr is: " << d_ptr << endl;
}
```

Output(s):

```
The value of *i_ptr is: 109
The value of i_ptr is: 0x556a54df9eb0
The value of *c_ptr is: m
The value of c_ptr is: m
The value of *d_ptr is: 1.52742e-43
The value of d_ptr is: 0x556a54df9eb0
```

Example-3.24:

Code 3.25

```cpp
// dynamic_cast
class B { };
class C : public B { };
class D : public C { };
void f(D* pd) {
C* pc = dynamic_cast<C*>(pd); // ok: C is a direct base class
// pc points to C subobject of pd
B* pb = dynamic_cast<B*>(pd); // ok: B is an indirect base class
// pb points to B subobject of pd
}
```

3.1.6 The returned characters of typeid(dataType).name() function

Depending on the type of the data typeid(dataTye).name() function retuns the characters shown in Table-3.1.

Table-3.1 Returned values for typeid(dataTye).name() function

Data Type	name() return tag
bool	b
char	c
signed char	a
unsigned char	h
signed short int	s
unsigned short int	t
signed int	i
unsigned int	j
signed long int	l
unsigned long int	m
signed long long int	x
unsigned long long int	y
float	f
double	d
long double	e

Example-3.25:

typeid(bool).name() returns b

typeid(signed long long int).name() returns x

3.2 Information Loss When a Higher Order Data is Converted to a Lower Order Data

Data loss may occur when conversion is performed between different data types. In general, when a higher order data is converted to a lower order data as shown in Figure-3.1 information loss can occur.

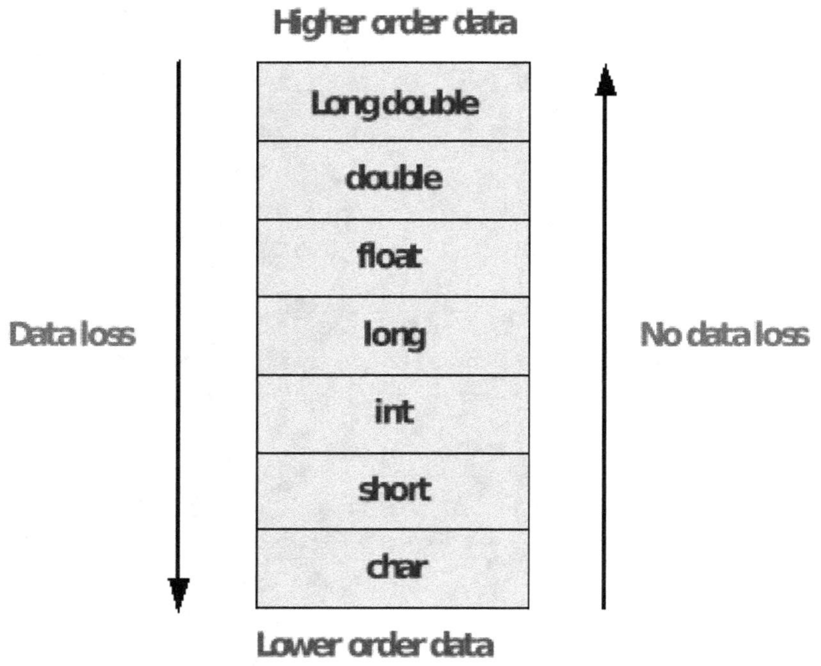

Figure-3.1 Information loss order.

Example-3.26: In Code-3.26, when an integer value is assigned to a short variable data loss occurs.

```
Code 3.26
#include <iostream>
using namespace std;

int main() {

int a = 0B01111111111111111110000000000000000;

short b = a;

cout << "a = " << a << endl;

cout << "b = " << b;
}
```

Output(s):

a = 2147418112

b = 0

In this code the integer variable 'a' has a 32-bit value, and the decimal equivalent of this value is 2147418112. Short integer data type is a 16-bit data type. When the assignment

$$\text{short } \mathbf{b} = \mathbf{a};$$

is performed only the first 16 bits of a is assigned to b, the first 16 bits of b are all 0's. Then the decimal equivalent of b is 0.

3.3 Information Loss When Conversion is Performed Between Signed and Unsigned Data Types

When unsigned and signed integers are mixed in arithmetic operations, unexpected results may be obtained.

Example-3.27: In Code-3.27, the binary string representing c in two's complement from is reinterpreted as representing an unsigned short integer.

Code 3.27

```cpp
#include <iostream>
using namespace std;

int main() {

short int a = -8;

unsigned short int b = 4;

unsigned short int c = a + b;

cout << "a = " << a << endl;

cout << "b = " << b << endl;

cout << "c = " << c << endl;
}
```

Output(s):
```
a = -8
b = 4
c = 65532
```
In the statement

$$\text{short int } \mathbf{a} = \text{-8;}$$

the short integer a is represented by 16-bits in 2's complement for as

1111111111111000

When the statement

$$\text{unsigned short int } \mathbf{c} = \mathbf{a} + \mathbf{b};$$

is performed the value of the variable a is converted to unsigned short int data type, i.e., the bit string is accepted representing an unsigned short integer, and the decimal equivalent of the bit string is

$$1111111111111000 \rightarrow 2^{15} + 2^{14} + \ldots 2^3 \rightarrow 65528$$

and when this number is summed by 4 we obtain 65532.

Problems

1) What are the outputs of Code-3.28.

Code 3.28
```cpp
#include <iostream>
using namespace std;

int main() {

char a = 0B11100101;

unsigned short b = a;

cout << "a = " << a;

cout << "b = " << b;
}
```

2) What is the output of Code-3.29.

Code 3.29
```cpp
#include <iostream>
using namespace std;

int main() {

char a = -64;

unsigned char b = a;

cout << "a = " << a;

cout << "b = " << b;
}
```

3) What is the output of Code-3.30.

Code 3.30
```cpp
#include <iostream>
using namespace std;

int main() {

cout << 9/2 << endl;

cout << (float)9/2 << endl;
```

```cpp
cout << (float)(9/2) << endl;
}
```

4) What is the output of Code-3.31.

Code 3.31
```cpp
#include <iostream>
using namespace std;

int main() {

int cnt = 0;

for(short int indx = 65535; indx > 0; indx—) {
cnt++;
}

cout << "cnt = " << cnt;
}
```

5) What is the output of Code-3.32.
Code 3.32
```cpp
#include <iostream>
using namespace std;
int main() {
short int x = 65530; // integer x
char y = 'a'; // character y, ASCII value of 'a' is 97
x = x + y; // y is implicitly converted to short integer
cout << "x = " << x;
}
```

Chapter-4

Conditional Statements

Abstract: In this chapter, we explain conditional statements used in C++ programming. A conditional statement is used when a decision is to be made considering a Boolean expression called a condition. A condition may depend only a single factor or it can be the combination of a number of factors.

4.1 Conditional Structure

The conditional statements are the statements which are executed when the condition is true. The syntax of the conditional statement containing the word **if** is a

if(condition) {

// Statements to be executed
// when condition is true

}

The syntax of the conditional statement containing the words **if-else** is as

if(condition) {

// Statements to be executed
// when condition is true

}
else {

// Statements to be executed
// when condition is false

}

A condition is accepted true if it has a non-zero value, or if it is a Boolean expression with true value.

Example-4.1: Any integer value different than zero is accepted as true.

Code 4.1
```cpp
#include <iostream>
using namespace std;

int main() {

int a = 10;

if(a) {
cout << "Inside if part";
}
else {
cout << "Inside else part";
}
}
```

Output(s): Inside if part

Example-4.2: Any float value different than zero is accepted as true.

Code 4.2
```cpp
#include <iostream>
using namespace std;

int main() {

float a = -2.5;

if(a) {
cout << "Inside if part" ;
}
else {
cout << "Inside else part";
}

}
```

Output(s): Inside if part

Example-4.3: Any double value different than zero is accepted as true.

Code 4.3
```cpp
#include <iostream>
using namespace std;

int main() {

double a = 0.0001;

if(a) {
cout << "Inside if part";
}
else {
cout << "Inside else part";
}

}
```

Output(s): Inside if part

Example-4.4: A zero value is accepted as false.

Code 4.4
```cpp
#include <iostream>
using namespace std;

int main() {

int b = 0;

if(b) {
cout << "Inside if part";
}
else {
cout << "Inside else part";
}

}
```

Output(s): Inside else part

Example-4.5: In Code-4.5 we use a Boolean value in the if statement.

```cpp
Code 4.5
#include <iostream>
using namespace std;

int main() {

bool a = true;

if(a) {
cout << "Inside if part";
}
else {
cout << "Inside else part";
}

}
```

Output(s): Inside if part

Example-4.6:

```cpp
Code 4.6
#include <iostream>
using namespace std;

int main() {

bool b = false;

if(b) {
cout << "Inside if part";
}
else {
cout << "Inside else part";
}

}
```

Output(s): Inside else part

Example-4.7: Logical comparisons produce Boolean results.

Code 4.7

```cpp
#include <iostream>
using namespace std;

int main() {

int a = 5;

if (a < 10) {

cout << "a < 10—> " << (a < 10) << endl;
cout << "a is less than 10 ";
}
else {
cout << "a is greater than 10";
}

}
```

Output(s):

a < 10 —> 1

a is less than 10

Example-4.8: In this example after cout, return 0 is written. When return 0 is met, the program terminates.

Code 4.8

```cpp
#include <iostream>
using namespace std;

int main() {

int a = 14;

if (a % 2 == 0) {
cout << a << " is even number";

return 0;
}

if (a % 2 == 1) {
cout << a << " is odd number";

return 0;
}
}
```

Output(s): 14 is even number

Example-4.9: Logical comparisons produce Boolean values.

Code 4.9

```cpp
#include <iostream>
using namespace std;

int main() {

int num = 23;

if (num > 35)
cout << "Inside if part";

cout << "Outside if part";

}
```

Output(s): Outside if part

4.2 Conditional Ladder Structure (if else if ladder)

The template for the conditional ladder structure is shown in Code-4.10.

Code 4.10

```
if(condition-1) {

statements-1;
}
else if(condition-2) {
statements-2;
}
else if(condition-3) {
statements-3;
}
.

.

else {
statements;
}
```

Example-4.10: This example illustrates the use of the conditional ladder structure.

Code 4.11

```cpp
#include <iostream>
using namespace std;

int main() {

int num;

cout << "Please enter an integer : ";

cin >> num;

if(num > 0) {

cout << "You entered a positive integer.";
}
else if(num < 0) {

cout << "You entered a negative integer.";
}
else {
cout << "You entered zero.";
}

}
```

Output(s):
Please enter an integer : -13
You entered a negative integer.

Example-4.11: This example illustrates the use of the conditional ladder structure with combined conditional expressions.

Code 4.12

```cpp
#include <iostream>
using namespace std;

int main() {

int avg_mark = 83;

if (avg_mark <= 100 && avg_mark >= 90)

cout << "A+ Grade";

else if (avg_mark < 90 && avg_mark >= 80)
```

```cpp
cout << "A Grade";

else if (avg_mark < 80 && avg_mark >= 70)

cout << "B Grade";

else if (avg_mark < 70 && avg_mark >= 60)

cout << "C Grade";

else if (avg_mark < 60 && avg_mark >= 50)

cout << "D Grade";

else

cout << "F Failed";
}
```

Output(s): A Grade

Example-4.12: This example illustrates the use of the combined conditional expressions in the ladder structure.

Code 4.13

```cpp
#include <iostream>
using namespace std;
int main() {
int num = 66;
cout << "Please enter an integer between 0 and 100 : ";
cin >> num;
// Check if num is between 0 and 25
if (num >= 0 && num <= 25)
cout << "You entered a number between 0 and 25";
// Since entered num is not between 0 and 25
// Check if num is between 26 and 50
else if (num >= 26 && num <= 50)
cout << "You entered a number between 26 and 50";
// Since entered num is not between 26 and 50
// Check if num is between 51 and 75
else if (num >= 51 && num <= 75)
cout << "You entered a number between 51 and 75";
// Since entered num is not between 51 and 75
// It means num is greater than 75
else
cout << "You entered a number between greater than 75";
}
```

Output(s):
Please enter an integer between 0 and 100 : 64

You entered a number between 51 and 75

4.3 Multi Conditional Structures

Multiple conditions can be checked using the logical AND, and OR operators

&& ||

The AND operator gives true result if all the conditions are true, on the other hand the OR operator gives true if one of the conditions is true.

Example-4.13: In Code-4.14 we combine three logical value using && operation.

Code 4.14
```cpp
#include <iostream>
using namespace std;

int main() {

int a = 4, b = -1, c = 13;

int and_result = (a == 4) && (b < 0) && (c > 10);

cout << "and_result = " << and_result;
}
```

Output(s):
and_result = 1

Example-4.14:

Code 4.15
```cpp
#include <iostream>
using namespace std;

int main() {

bool a = true;
bool b = false;

int c = 12;

bool and_result = a && (!b) && (c > 10);

cout << "and_result = " << and_result;

}
```

Output(s): and_result = 1

Example-4.15:

Code 4.16
```cpp
#include <iostream>
using namespace std;
```

```cpp
int main() {
bool a = true;
bool b = false;
int c = 12;
bool result1 = a && b || (c>10);
bool result2 = a || b && (c>10);
cout << "result1 = " << result1 << endl;
cout << "result2 = " << result2;
}
```

Output(s):

result1 = 1

result2 = 1

Note that AND operator has higher precedence than the OR operator

Example-4.16:

Code 4.17

```cpp
#include <iostream>
using namespace std;
int main() {
int num1, num2;
cout << "Please enter two integers : \n");
cin >> num1 >> num2;
if (num1 > 0 && num2 > 0 ) {
cout << "You entered two positive integers.");
}
else if (num1 < 0 && num2 < 0 ) {
cout << "You entered one positive and one negative integer.");
}
else if ((num1 > 0 && num2 < 0) || (num1 < 0 && num2 > 0)) {
cout << "You entered one positive and one negative integer.");
}
else if(num1 == 0 && num2==0) {
cout << "You entered two zeros.");
}
else {
cout << "One of the numbers is zero.");
}
}
```

Output(s):

Please enter two integers : 5 -12

You entered one positive and one negative integer.

4.4 Syntax of Nested if-else

The syntax of the nested if-else is shown in Code-4.18 where nesting is done in only if-part.

Code 4.18

```
if (condition-1) {
// Executed when condition-1 is true
if (condition-2) {
// Executed when condition-2 is true
}
else {
// Executed when condition-2 is false
}
}
else {
// Executed when condition-1 is false
}
```

The syntax of the nested if-else where nesting is done both in if-part and else part is shown in Code-4.19.

Code 4.19

```
if (condition-1) {
// Executed when condition-1 is true
if (condition-2) {
// Executed when condition-2 is true
}
else {
// Executes when condition-2 is false
}
}
else {
// Executed when condition-1 is false
if (condition-3) {
// Executed when condition-3 is true
}
else {
// Executes when condition-3 is false
}
}
```

Example-4.17: This example illustrates the use of nested if-else structure.

Code 4.20

```
#include <iostream>
using namespace std;
int main() {
int num;
```

```cpp
cout << "Please enter an integer between 0 and 100 : ";
cin >> num;
if (num < 50) {
cout << "You entered a number smaller than 50." << endl;
if (num < 25)
cout << "You entered a number smaller than 25.";
else
cout << "You entered a number greater than 25.";
}
else {
cout << "You entered a number greater than 49." << endl;
if (num > 75 )
cout << "You entered a number greater than 75.";
else
cout << "You entered a number smaller than 75.";
}
}
```

Output(s):

Please enter an integer between 0 and 100 : 67

You entered a number greater than 49.

You entered a number smaller than 74.

4.5 Conditional Operator in C++

The syntax of the conditional operator is as

(a) ? [executed if a is true] : [executed if a is false];

Note that every value other than zero is accepted as true.

The conditional operator can also be used as

variable = condition ? valueT : valueF;

which is equivalent to

(condition) ? (variable = valueT) : (variable = valueF);

which means

if(condition) {

variable = valueT;

}
else {

variable = valueF;

}

Example-4.18: In Code-4.21, the variable 'a' has value of 7 which is accepted as true.

Code 4.21
```cpp
#include <iostream>
using namespace std;

int main() {

int a = 7;
int b;

b = (a) ? 6 : 8;

cout << "b is " << b;
}
```

Output(s):
b is 6

Example-4.19: In Code-4.22, the variable 'a' has value of 0 which is accepted false.

Code 4.22

```cpp
#include <iostream>
using namespace std;

int main() {

int a = 0;
int b;

b = (a) ? 6 : 8;

cout << "b is " << b;
}
```

Output(s): b is 8

Example-4.20: Alternative form of the conditional operator is illustrated in Code-4.23.

Code 4.23
```cpp
#include <iostream>
using namespace std;

int main() {

int a = 5;

int b;

(a) ? (b = 6): (b = 8);

cout << "b is " << b;
}
```

Output(s): b is 6

Example-4.21:

Code 4.24
```cpp
#include <iostream>
using namespace std;

int main() {

int a = 0;
int b;

(a) ? (b = 6): (b = 8);

cout << "b is " << b;
}
```

Output(s): b is 8

Example-4.22: Not those, parentheses are necessary when conditional operator is used in the format **(condition) ? (variable = valueT) : (variable = valueF);** If parantheses are not used, error arises.

Code 4.25
```cpp
#include <iostream>
using namespace std;

int main() {

int a = 0;

int b;

(a) ? b = 6: b = 8;

cout << "b is " << b;
}
```

Output(s):
main.cpp: In function 'main':
main.cpp:9:20: error: lvalue required as left operand of assignment

Example-4.23:

Code 4.26
```cpp
#include <iostream>
using namespace std;

int main() {

int a = 8, b = 5;

(a > b) ? cout << "a > b" : cout << "a < b";
}
```

Output(s): a > b

Example-4.24: The code in the previous example can be written as in Code-4.27.

Code 4.27
```cpp
#include <iostream>
using namespace std;

int main() {

int a = 8, b = 5;

(a > b) ?
```

```
    cout << "a > b" :
    cout << "a < b";
}
```

Output(s): a > b

Example-4.25: Second alternative form of the conditional operator is illustrated in Code-4.28.

```
Code 4.28
#include <iostream>
using namespace std;

int main() {

int a = 8, b = 5;

int larger;

larger = (a > b) ? a : b;

cout << "Larger number is :" << larger;
}
```

Output(s): Larger number is : 8

4.6 switch Statement

The syntax of the switch statement is shown in Code-4.29.

```
Code 4.29
switch(variable-name) {
case value-1: statements-1;
break;

case value-2: statements-2;
break;
.
.
.
case value-N: statements-N;
break;

default: statements;
}
```

In Code-4.30, when the value of the variable matches one of the listed values, the corresponding statements are executed.

Example-4.26: In this example, an integer is entered by the user and a message is printed according to the entered value.

```
Code 4.30
#include <iostream>
using namespace std;

int main() {

int num;

cout << "Enter an integer between 1 and 4, \n"
<< "1 and 4 are included: ";

cin >> num;

switch (num) {
case 1:
cout << "You entered 1.";
break;

case 2:
cout << "You entered 2.";
break;

case 3:
cout << "You entered 3.";
```

```
break;

default:
cout << "You entered 4.";
break;
}
}
```

Output(s):

Enter an integer between 1 and 4,

1 and 4 are included: 3

You entered 3

Example-4.27: Between **case** and **break** keywords, more than one line can be written.

Code 4.31
```
#include <iostream>
using namespace std;

int main() {

int num;

cout << "Enter an integer between 1 and 4, \n"
<< "1 and 4 are included: ";

cin >> num;

switch (num) {
case 1:
cout << "You entered 1.";
break;

case 2:
cout << "You entered 2.";
break;

case 3:
cout << "You entered 3.";
break;

default:
cout << "You entered 4.";
break;
}
}
```

Output(s):

Enter an integer between 1 and 4,

1 and 4 are included: 3
You entered 3.
Thank you.

Example-4.28: We can use curly parentheses between **case** and **break** keywords.

Code 4.32

```cpp
#include <iostream>
using namespace std;

int main() {

int num;

cout << "Enter an integer between 1 and 4, \n"
<< "1 and 4 are included: ";

cin >> num;

switch (num) {

case 1: {
cout << "You entered 1.\n";
cout << "Thank you.";
break;
}

case 2: {
cout << "You entered 2.\n";
cout << "Thank you.";
break;
}

case 3: {
cout << "You entered 3.\n";
cout << "Thank you.";
break;
}

default: {
cout << "You entered 4.\n";
cout << "Thank you.";
break;
}
} // end of switch
}
```

Output(s):
Enter an integer between 1 and 4,
1 and 4 are included : 3
You entered 3.
Thank you.

Example-4.29: If **break** of a **case** is not written, the next line is also executed.

Code 4.33
```cpp
#include <iostream>
using namespace std;

int main() {

int num;

cout << "Enter an integer between 1 and 4, \n"
<< "1 and 4 are included: ";

cin >> num;

switch (num) {
case 1:
cout << "You entered 1.\n";
break;

case 2:
cout << "You entered 2.\n";

case 3:
cout << "You entered 3.\n";
break;

default:
cout << "You entered 4.\n";
break;
}
}
```

Output(s):
Enter an integer between 1 and 4,
1 and 4 are included: 2
You entered 2.
You entered 3.

Example-4.30: If **break** of a **case** is not written, the rest of the code is executed until **break** keyword is met.

Code 4.34
```cpp
#include <iostream>
```

```cpp
using namespace std;

int main() {

int num;

cout << "Enter an integer between 1 and 4, \n"
<< "1 and 4 are included: ";

cin >> num;

switch (num) {
case 1:
cout << "You entered 1.\n";
break;

case 2:
cout << "You entered 2.\n";

case 3:
cout << "You entered 3.\n";

default:
cout << "You entered 4.\n";
break;
}
}
```

Output(s):
Enter an integer between 1 and 4,
1 and 4 are included: 2
You entered 2.
You entered 3.
You entered 4.

Problems

1) What is the output of Code-4.35?

```cpp
Code 4.35
#include <iostream>
using namespace std;

int main() {

char a = '0';

if(a) {
cout << "Inside if part";
}
else {
cout << "Inside else part";
}
}
```

2) What is the output of Code-4.36?

```cpp
Code 4.36
#include <iostream>
using namespace std;

int main() {

if(6 < 7 > -5) {
cout << "Inside if part";
}
else {
cout << "Inside else part";
}
}
```

3) Write C++ program takes inputs an integer from the user and determines if the number is even or odd.

4) Write C++ program takes inputs an integer from the user and displays 1-digit number if it is a 1 digit integer, and it displays 2-digit number is it is a 2 digit integer, and it displays 3-digit number if it is a 3 digit integer, otherwise it displays a larger number.

5) Write a program that inputs an integer from a user and determines if the number is a prime number or not.

6) Write a C++ program which inputs 3 numbers from the user and determines and displays the largest of three numbers.

7) Write a C++ program which inputs 5 numbers from the user and determines and displays the largest of three numbers.

8) Write a C++ program which determines whether a triangle is equilateral, isosceles or scalene. Input the side lengths from the user.

9) What is the output of Code-4.37.

Code 4.37

```cpp
#include <iostream>
using namespace std;

int main() {

int a = -3;

int b;

b = (a) ? 9 : 17;

cout << "b is " << b;
}
```

10) What is the output of Code-4.38?

Code 4.38

```cpp
#include <iostream>
using namespace std;

int main() {

int a = 0;

int b;

(a) ? (b = 45): (b = 92);

cout << "b is " << b;
}
```

11) Write a program using the switch statement which inputs a digit from 1 to 5 and displays the digit entered by the user.

Chapter-5

Loop Statements

Abstract: In this chapter we explain the loop statements. Loop statements are used when a segment of the program needs to be run for a number of times. There different loop expressions are available in C++ programming, and these expressions are for-loop, while-loop, and do-while-loop. The goto statement can also be used to form loop expressions but it is not as frequently used as the other ones.

5.1 for-Loop

The structure of the for-loop is as

```
for(st0; st1; st2) {

st3

}
```

where st0, st1, st2, and st3 are the statements, and they are executed in row-wise as

```
st0, st1, st2, st3
st1, st2, st3
st1, st2, st3
st1, st2, st3
.....
```

until the loop terminates.

The formal syntax of the for-loop is as

```
for(initialization statements; loop execution condition; update statements) {
// Loop statements
}
```

where at initialization statements we have variable initialization expressions, such as

$$\text{int } a = 0;$$

loop execution condition is a Boolean expression, for example

$$a < 3$$

update statements are usually increment or decrement statements, for example,

$$a{+}{+} \text{ or } a{-}{-}$$

however, other updates like a = a+2, a *= 2 are also possible.

Example-5.1: Let's write a code involving for-loop. For this purpose, we first write the for-loop structure as in Code-5.1.

Code 5.1
```cpp
#include <iostream>
using namespace std;

int main() {

for ( ; ; ) {

}

}
```

Initialization is written as in Code-5.2.

Code 5.2
```cpp
#include <iostream>
using namespace std;

int main() {

for (int a = 0; ; ) {

}

}
```

Conditional expression is added in Code-5.3.

Code 5.3
```cpp
#include <iostream>
using namespace std;

int main() {

for (int a = 0; a < 3; ) {

}

}
```

Finally, update is written in Code-5.4.

Code 5.4
```cpp
#include <iostream>
using namespace std;

int main() {

for (int a = 0; a < 3; a++) {

}

}
```

Two cout statements are written in Code-5.5.

Code 5.5
```cpp
#include <iostream>
using namespace std;

int main() {
```

```
for (int a = 0; a < 3; a++) {

cout << "Inside for-loop ";
}

cout << "Outside for-loop ";
}
```

Example-5.2: We can write the update part of the for-loop in the body of the for-loop.

Code 5.6
```
#include <iostream>
using namespace std;

int main() {

for (int a = 0; a < 3; ) {
cout << "Inside for-loop, a = " << a << endl;
a++;
}

cout << "\nOutside for-loop";
}
```

Output(s):
```
Inside for-loop, a = 0
Inside for-loop, a = 1
Inside for-loop, a = 2
Outside for-loop
```
Example-5.3: Update can be decrement operation. In Code-5.7 decrement is used for update operation.

Code 5.7
```
#include <iostream>
using namespace std;

int main() {

for (int a = 2; a >= 0; a—) {
cout << "Inside for-loop, a = " << a << endl;
}

cout << "\nOutside for-loop";
}
```

Output(s):
```
Inside for-loop, a = 2
```

Inside for-loop, a = 1
Inside for-loop, a = 0
Outside for-loop

Example-5.4: The variable defined at the initialization part of the for-loop is not accessible outside the body of the for loop.

Code 5.8

```cpp
#include <iostream>
using namespace std;

int main() {

for (int a = 0; a < 3; a++) {
cout << "a = " << a << endl;
}

cout << "a = " << a; // a is not accessible, error
}
```

Output(s):
[Error] 'a' undeclared (first use in this function)

Example-5.5: A local variable outside the for-loop structure can be used for counting index as in Code-5.9.

Code 5.9

```cpp
#include <iostream>
using namespace std;

int main() {

int a;

for (a = 0; a < 3; a++) {

cout << "Inside for-loop, a = " << a << endl;
}

cout << "\nOutside for-loop, a = " << a << endl;
}
```

Output(s):
Inside for-loop, a = 0
Inside for-loop, a = 1
Inside for-loop, a = 2
Outside for-loop, a = 3

Example-5.6: Initialization part of the for-loop can be written outside the for-loop structure as in Code-5.10.

Code 5.10

```cpp
#include <iostream>
using namespace std;

int main() {

int a = 0;

for (; a < 3; a++) {
cout << "Inside for-loop, a = " << a << endl;
}

cout << "\nOutside for-loop";
}
```

Output(s):
Inside for-loop, a = 0
Inside for-loop, a = 1
Inside for-loop, a = 2
Outside for-loop, a = 3

Example-5.7: In Code-5.11, both initialization and update parts of the for-loop are written outside the for-loop header.

Code 5.11

```cpp
#include <iostream>
using namespace std;

int main() {

int a = 0;

for (; a < 3; ) {
cout << "Inside for-loop, a = " << a << endl;
a++;
}
cout << "\nOutside for-loop a = " << a << endl;
}
```

Output(s):
Inside for-loop, a = 0
Inside for-loop, a = 1
Inside for-loop, a = 2
Outside for-loop, a = 3

Example-5.8: More than one variable can be used at the header of the for-loop.

Code 5.12

```cpp
#include <iostream>
using namespace std;
```

```cpp
int main() {

for (int a = 0, b = 0; a < 3, b < 3; a++, b++) {

cout << "Inside for-loop, a = " << a;
cout << " b = " << b << endl;
}
cout << "\nOutside for-loop";
}
```

Output(s):
```
Inside for-loop, a = 0 b = 0
Inside for-loop, a = 1 b = 1
Inside for-loop, a = 2 b = 2
Outside for-loop
```
Example-5.9: Conditional part of the for-loop can contain multi-conditional expressions.

Code 5.13
```cpp
#include <iostream>
using namespace std;

int main() {

for (int a = 0, b = 0; a < 3 && b < 3; a++, b++) {

cout << "Inside for-loop, a = " << a;
cout << " b = " << b << endl;
}

cout << "\nOutside for-loop";
}
```

Output(s):
```
Inside for-loop, a = 0 b = 0
Inside for-loop, a = 1 b = 1
Inside for-loop, a = 2 b = 2
Outside for-loop
```
Example-5.10: The logical operator && produces false, if one of the operands evaluates to false.

Code 5.14
```cpp
#include <iostream>
using namespace std;
int main() {
for (int a = 0, b = 0; a < 3 && b < 785; a++, b = b + 2) {
cout << "Inside for-loop, a = " << a;
cout << " b = " << b << endl;
}
```

```
cout << "\nOutside for-loop";
}
```

Output(s):
Inside for-loop, a = 0 b = 0
Inside for-loop, a = 1 b = 2
Inside for-loop, a = 2 b = 4
Outside for-loop

Example-5.11: In this example, logical OR || is used at the conditional part of the for-loop.

Code 5.15

```
#include <iostream>
using namespace std;

int main() {

    for (int a = 0, b = 0; a < 3 || b < 4; a++, b ++) {

    cout << "Inside for-loop, a = " << a;
    cout << " b = " << b << endl;
    }

    cout << "\nOutside for-loop";
}
```

Output(s):
Inside for-loop, a = 0 b = 0
Inside for-loop, a = 1 b = 1
Inside for-loop, a = 2 b = 2
Inside for-loop, a = 3 b = 3
Outside for-loop

Example-5.12: Different updates can be used at the update part of the for-loop.

Code 5.16

```
#include <iostream>
using namespace std;
int main() {
for (int a = 0, b = 2; a < 3 || b < 4; a++, b = b + 5) {
cout << "Inside for-loop, a = " << a;
cout << " b = " << b << endl;
}
cout << "\nOutside for-loop";
}
```

Output(s):
Inside for-loop, a = 0 b = 2
Inside for-loop, a = 1 b = 7
Inside for-loop, a = 2 b = 12

Outside for-loop

Example-5.13: Floating point variables can be used at the header of the for-loop.

Code 5.17
```cpp
#include <iostream>
using namespace std;

int main() {

int a;
double b;

for (a = 0, b = 2.7; a*b < 25.6; a++, b++) {

cout << "Inside for-loop, a = " << a;
cout << " b = " << b << endl;
}

cout << "\nQuitted for-loop\n\n";
cout << "Outside for-loop, a = " << a;
cout << " b = " << b << endl;
}
```

Output(s):
Inside for-loop, a = 0 b = 2.7
Inside for-loop, a = 1 b = 3.7
Inside for-loop, a = 2 b = 4.7
Inside for-loop, a = 3 b = 5.7
Quitted for-loop
Outside for-loop, a = 4 b = 6.7

Example-5.14: In this example, it is shown that two for loops can employ the same parameter at their headers.

Code 5.18
```cpp
#include <iostream>
using namespace std;
int main() {
int a;
for (a = 0; a < 3; a++) {
cout << "Inside for-loop-1, a = " << a << "\n";
}
cout << "\nOutside for-loop-1, a = " << a << "\n\n";
for (a = 8; a < 11; a++) {
cout << "Inside for-loop-2, a = " << a << "\n";
}
cout << "\nOutside for-loop-2, a = " << a << "\n";
}
```

Output(s):

Inside for-loop-1, a = 0
Inside for-loop-1, a = 1
Inside for-loop-1, a = 2
Outside for-loop-1, a = 3
Inside for-loop-2, a = 8
Inside for-loop-2, a = 9
Inside for-loop-2, a = 10
Outside for-loop-2, a = 11

Example-5.15: Infinite loop can be created using the structure in Code-5.19.

Code 5.19
```cpp
#include <iostream>
using namespace std;

int main() {

for (; ; ) {
cout << "Infinite loop\n";
}
}
```

Output(s):
Infinite loop
Infinite loop
Infinite loop

.

.

Example-5.16: Another infinite loop is written in Code-5.20.

Code 5.20
```cpp
#include <iostream>
using namespace std;

int main() {

for (; 7.34 ; ) {
cout << "Another infinite loop\n";
}
}
```

Output(s):
Another infinite loop
Another infinite loop
Another infinite loop

.

.

Example-5.17: In Code-5.21, the for-loop header has only conditional part, and the condition becomes false when the value of 'b' equals 3.

Code 5.21

```cpp
#include <iostream>
using namespace std;
int main() {
bool a = true;
int b = 0;
for (; a ; ) {
cout << "Inside for-loop, b = " << b << endl;
b++;
if(b >= 3)
a = false;
}
cout << "\nOutside for-loop, b = " << b << endl;
}
```

Output(s):

```
Inside for-loop, b = 0
Inside for-loop, b = 1
Inside for-loop, b = 2
Outside for-loop, b = 3
```

5.1.1 Nested For Loop

For loops can be used in a nested manner. The structure of nested for loops is shown in Code-5.22.

Code 5.22
```
for(init1; condition1; update1) {

// outer loop statements1

for(init2; condition2; update2) {
// inner loop statements
}

// outer loop statements2
}
```

Example-5.18: Let's write a nested for loop. For this purpose, first let's place the first for-loop as in Code-5.23.
Code 5.23
```
##include <iostream>
using namespace std;




int main() {
    for(int indxN = 0; indxN < 3; indxN++) {




}
    }
```
We write a cout statement inside the first loop as in Code-5.24.
Code 5.24
```
#include <iostream>
using namespace std;
int main() {
for(int indxN = 0; indxN < 3; indxN++) {
cout <<"\n\nInside outer loop, indxN = " << indxN;
}
}
```
Inside the first for-loop, we place the structure of the second for-loop as in Code-5.25.
Code 5.25
```
#include <iostream>
using namespace std;
int main() {
for(int indxN = 0; indxN < 3; indxN++) {
cout <<"\n\nInside outer loop, indxN = " << indxN;
```

```
for(int indxM = 0; indxM < 3; indxM++) {
}
}
}
```

Two cout statements, one inside the second for-loop, and the other one outside both of for-loops, are written as in Code-5.26.

Code 5.26

```cpp
#include <iostream>
using namespace std;
int main() {
for(int indxN = 0; indxN < 3; indxN++) {
cout <<"\n\nInside outer loop, indxN = " << indxN;
for(int indxM = 0; indxM < 3; indxM++) {
cout << "\nInside inner loop, indxM = " << indxM;
}
}
cout << "\n\nOutside outer loop";
}
```

Output(s):

```
Inside outer loop, indxN = 0
Inside inner loop, indxM = 0
Inside inner loop, indxM = 1
Inside inner loop, indxM = 2
Inside outer loop, indxN = 1
Inside inner loop, indxM = 0
Inside inner loop, indxM = 1
Inside inner loop, indxM = 2
Inside outer loop, indxN = 2
Inside inner loop, indxM = 0
Inside inner loop, indxM = 1
Inside inner loop, indxM = 2
Outside outer loop
```

5.2 while-Loop

In while-loop, first initialization is performed, then loop condition is checked, and loop body is executed, updating can be performed inside loop body. The syntax of the while-loop is

// Initialization statements

while (condition) {

// Loop statements

}

The statements inside the while-loop parentheses are executed as long as the condition is true. The operation of the while-loop is illustrated in Figure-5.1.

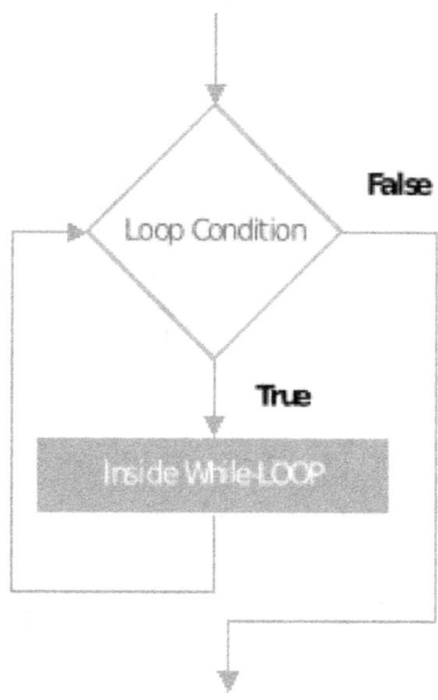

Figure-5.1 while-loop execution logic

Example-5.19: This example illustrates the use of while-loop.

Code 5.27

```cpp
#include <iostream>
using namespace std;
int main() {
int a = 2;
while(a < 9) {
cout << "Inside while-loop, a = " << a << endl;
a = a+2;
}
cout << "\nOutside while-loop, a = " << a;
}
```

Output(s):
Inside while-loop, a = 2
Inside while-loop, a = 4
Inside while-loop, a = 6
Inside while-loop, a = 8
Outside while-loop, a = 10

Example-5.20: Inside while-loop, we can use conditional statements as in Code5.28.

Code 5.28
```cpp
#include <iostream>
using namespace std;
int main() {
int a = 2;
while(a) {
cout << "Inside while-loop, a = " << a << endl;
if(a == 8) {
a = 0;
}
else {
a = a + 2;
}
}
cout << "\nOutside while-loop, a = " << a;
}
```

Output(s):
Inside while-loop, a = 2
Inside while-loop, a = 4
Inside while-loop, a = 6
Inside while-loop, a = 8
Outside while-loop, a = 0

Example-5.21: While-loop condition can contain logical expressions.

Code 5.29
```cpp
#include <iostream>
using namespace std;

int main() {

int a = 2;

while(a < 10) {

cout << "Inside while-loop, a = " << a << endl;
a = a + 2;
}
cout << "\nOutside while-loop, a = " << a;
```

```
}
```

Output(s):
```
Inside while-loop, a = 2
Inside while-loop, a = 4
Inside while-loop, a = 6
Inside while-loop, a = 8
Outside while-loop, a = 10
```

Example-5.22: It is possible to define an infinite while-loop as in Code-5.30.

Code 5.30
```cpp
#include <iostream>
using namespace std;

int main() {

int a = 2;

while(1) {

cout << " a = " << a << endl;

a = a + 2;
}
}
```

Output(s):
```
a = 2
a = 4
a = 6
.

.
```

Example-5.23: Multi-conditional expressions may appear inside the while-loop.
Code 5.31
```cpp
#include <iostream>
using namespace std;
int main() {
int a = 1;
while(a < 20) {
if(a % 7 == 0 || a % 9 == 0)
cout << "Inside while-loop, a = " << a << endl;
a++;
}
cout << "\nOutside while-loop, a = " << a << endl;
}
```
Output(s):

```
Inside while-loop, a = 7
Inside while-loop, a = 9
Inside while-loop, a = 14
Inside while-loop, a = 18
Outside while-loop, a = 20
```

5.2.1 Nested while-Loop

The structure of the nested while-loop is shown in Code-5.32.

Code 5.32
```cpp
while(condition1) {
// outer loop statements1

while(condition2) {
// inner loop statements
}

// outer loop statements2
}
```

Example-5.24: Let's form a nested while-loop. For this purpose, we write the first while-loop as in Code-5.33.

Code 5.33
```cpp
#include <iostream>
using namespace std;

int main() {

int indxN = 0;

while(indxN < 3) {

}

}
```

We add cout and update statements as in Code-5.34.
Code 5.34
```cpp
#include <iostream>
using namespace std;
int main() {
int indxN = 0, indxM = 0;
while(indxN < 3) {
cout << "\n\nInside outer loop, indxN = " << indxN;
indxN++;
}
}
```

The structure of the second while-loop is placed into the first while-loop as in Code-5.35.

Code 5.35

```cpp
#include <iostream>
using namespace std;
int main() {
int indxN = 0, indxM = 0;
while(indxN < 3) {
cout << "\n\nInside outer loop, indxN = " << indxN;
while(indxM < 3) {


}

    indxN++;
    }
    }
```

We add cout and parameter update expressions inside the second while-loop, and add one cout statement outside both loops as in Code-5.36.

Code 5.36

```cpp
#include <iostream>
using namespace std;
int main() {
int indxN = 0, indxM = 0;
while(indxN < 3) {
cout << "\n\nInside outer loop, indxN = " << indxN;
while(indxM < 3) {
cout << "\nInside inner loop, indxM = " << indxM;
indxM++;
}
indxN++;
indxM = 0;
}
cout << "\n\nOutside outer loop";
}
```

Output(s):

```
Inside outer loop, indxN = 0
Inside inner loop, indxM = 0
Inside inner loop, indxM = 1
Inside inner loop, indxM = 2
Inside outer loop, indxN = 1
Inside inner loop, indxM = 0
Inside inner loop, indxM = 1
Inside inner loop, indxM = 2
Inside outer loop, indxN = 2
Inside inner loop, indxM = 0
```

Inside inner loop, indxM = 1
Inside inner loop, indxM = 2
Outside outer loop

5.3 do-while Loop

The syntax of the do-while loop is as

```
// Initialization statements

do {

// Loop statements

} while (condition);
```

Loop statements are executes as long as the condition is true. Note that; do-while loop is executed at least once.

Example-5.25: Do-while loop is executed at least once.

Code 5.37

```cpp
#include <iostream>
using namespace std;
int main() {
int a = 0;
do {
cout << "do-while Loop is executed at least once.\n";
} while(a);
cout << "Outside do-while loop.";
}
```

Output(s):

```
do-while Loop is executed at least once.
Outside do-while loop.
```

Example-5.26: Loop condition can be a logical expression.

Code 5.38

```cpp
#include <iostream>
using namespace std;
int main() {
int a = 2;
do {
cout << "Inside do-while loop, a = " << a << endl;
a = a + 2;
} while(a < 9);
cout << "\nOutside do-while loop, a = " << a;
}
```

Output(s):

```
Inside do-while loop, a = 2
Inside do-while loop, a = 4
Inside do-while loop, a = 6
Inside do-while loop, a = 8
Outside do-while loop, a = 10
```

Example-5.27: In this example, we form a product table using do-while loop.

Code 5.39

```cpp
#include <iostream>
using namespace std;
int main() {
int a = 7, b = 1;
do {
cout << a << " x " << b << " = " << a * b << endl;
b++;
} while (b < 5);
}
```

Output(s):

```
7 x 1 = 7
7 x 2 = 14
7 x 3 = 21
7 x 4 = 28
```

5.4 Continue Statement

Continue statement is used to skip the rest of the statements when a condition is met, and program execution returns to the beginning of the loop.

The use of the continue statement in while-loop is illustrated in Figure-5.2.

```
while(condition1){
    // statements
    if(condition2){
        continue;
    }
    // statements
}
```

Figure-5.2 Behavior of continue statement in while-loop.

The use of the continue statement in for-loop is illustrated in Figure-5.3.

```
for(initialization; condition1; update){
    // statements
    if(condition2){
        continue;
    }
    // statements
}
```

Figure-5.3 Behavior of continue statement in for-loop.

The use of the continue statement in do-while loop is illustrated in Figure-5.4.

```
do {
    // statements
    if(condition1)
    {
        continue;
    }
    // statements
} while(condition2);
```

Figure-5.4 Behavior of continue statement in do-while loop.

Example-5.28: In this example, we use the continue statement in a for-loop.

Code 5.40
```
#include <iostream>
using namespace std;

int main() {
```

```cpp
for(int a = 0; a < 7; a++) {
if(a == 3)
continue;

cout << "a = " << a << " ";
}
}
```

When a == 3, the cout statement is not executed, program execution goes to the beginning of the loop.

Output(s):

a =0 a = 1 a = 2 a = 4 a = 5 a = 6

Example-5.29: In this example, we use the continue statement in a while-loop

Code 5.41

```cpp
#include <iostream>
using namespace std;
int main() {
int a = 0;
while(a < 5) {
a++;
cout << "while-loop upper part is executed, a = " << a << endl;
if(a == 3) {
cout << "\ncontinue statement is executed, a = "
<< a << endl;
cout << "while-loop lower part is skipped\n\n";
continue;
}
cout << "while-loop lower part is executed, since a = "
<< a << endl;
}
cout << "\nOutside while-loop";
}
```

When a==3, the rest of the code is not executed, program execution goes to the beginning of the loop.

Output(s):

while-loop upper part is executed, a = 1
while-loop lower part is executed, since a = 1
while-loop upper part is executed, a = 2
while-loop lower part is executed, since a = 2
while-loop upper part is executed, a = 3
continue statement is executed, a = 3
while-loop lower part is skipped
while-loop upper part is executed, a = 4
while-loop lower part is executed, since a = 4
while-loop upper part is executed, a = 5
while-loop lower part is executed, since a = 5

Outside while-loop

5.5 Break Statement

Break statement is used to quit the loop when a condition is met.

The use of the break statement in while-loop is illustrated in Figure-5.5.

```
while(condition1){
   // statements
   if(condition2){
      break;
   }
   // statements
}
```

Figure-5.5 Behavior of break statement in while-loop.

The use of the break statement in for-loop is illustrated in Figure-5.6.

```
for(initialization; condition1; update){
   // statements
   if(condition2){
      break;
   }
   // statements
}
```

Figure-5.6 Behavior of break statement in for-loop.

The use of the break statement inside the do-while loop is illustrated in Figure-5.7.

```
do{
   // statements
   if(condition1){
      break;
   }
   // statements
}while(condition2)
```

Figure-5.7 Behavior of break statement in do-while loop.

Example-5.30: Let's use the break statement for a for-loop. First let's form the structure of the for-loop as in Code-5.42.

Code 5.42

```
#include <iostream>
using namespace std;

int main() {
```

```
    int a;

    for(a = 0; a < 7; a++) {

    }

}
```

We add cout statement in Code-5.43.

Code 5.43

```cpp
#include <iostream>
using namespace std;

int main() {

int a;

for(a = 0; a < 7; a++) {

cout << "Inside for-loop, a = " << a << endl;
}

}
```

We add a condition part as in Code-5.44.

Code 5.44

```cpp
#include <iostream>
using namespace std;

int main() {

int a;

for(a = 0; a < 7; a++) {

if(a == 3) {

}

cout << "Inside for-loop, a = " << a << endl;
}

}
```

Inside condition part, we add cout and break statements, and add one more cout statement outside for-loop as in Code-5.45.

Code 5.45

```cpp
#include <iostream>
using namespace std;
int main() {
int a;
for(a = 0; a < 7; a++) {
if(a == 3) {
cout << "Quitting for-loop, a = " << a << endl;
break;
```

```cpp
}
cout << "Inside for-loop, a = " << a << endl;
}
cout << "\nOutside for-loop, a = " << a;
}
```

Output(s):

```
Inside for-loop, a=0
Inside for-loop, a=1
Inside for-loop, a=2
Quitting for-loop, a=3
Outside for-loop, a=3
```

Example-5.31: In this example, we use break statement inside a while-loop.

Code 5.46

```cpp
#include <iostream>
using namespace std;
int main() {
int a = 2;
while(1) {
cout << "Inside while-loop, a = " << a << endl;
a = a+2;
if (a > 8)
break;
}
cout << "\nOutside while-loop, a = " << a;
}
```

Output(s):

```
Inside while-loop, a = 2
Inside while-loop, a = 4
Inside while-loop, a = 6
Inside while-loop, a = 8
Outside while-loop, a = 10
```

Example-5.32: In this example, we use **bool** data type for the while-loop condition.

Code 5.47

```cpp
#include <iostream>
using namespace std;
int main() {
bool a = true;
double b = 0;
while(a) {
cout << "Inside while-loop, b = " << b << endl;
b = b + 2.6;
if(b > 10)
a = false;
}
```

```
cout << "\nOutside while-loop, b = " << b << endl;
}
```

Output(s):
Inside while-loop, b = 0.0
Inside while-loop, b = 2.6
Inside while-loop, b = 5.2
Inside while-loop, b = 7.8
Outside while-loop, b = 10.4

Example-5.33: In this example, we use break statement in an infinite do-while loop after an if statement. No curly parentheses are used for if statement.

Code 5.48

```
#include <iostream>
using namespace std;
int main() {
int a = 2;
do {
cout << "Inside do-while loop, a = " << a << endl;
a = a + 2;
if (a > 8)
break;
} while(1);
cout << "\nOutside do-while loop, a = " << a << endl;
}
```

Output(s):
Inside do-while loop, a = 2
Inside do-while loop, a = 4
Inside do-while loop, a = 6
Inside do-while loop, a = 8
Outside do-while loop, a = 10

Example-5.34: In this example, we use break statement inside parentheses of a conditional expression.

Code 5.49

```
#include <iostream>
using namespace std;
int main() {
int a;
do {
cout << "Please enter a negative number : ";
cin >> a;
cout << "Inside the do-while loop, you entered "
<< a << endl;
if (a > 0) {
cout << "\nYou entered a positive number. "
<< "Quitting the loop.";
break;
```

```
    }
} while(1);
cout << "\n\nOutside the do-while loop, you last entered "
<< a << endl;
}
```

Output(s):

```
Please enter a negative number : -2
Inside the do-while loop, you entered -2
Please enter a negative number : -3
Inside the do-while loop, you entered -3
Please enter a negative number : 1
Inside the do-while loop, you entered 1
You entered a positive number. Quitting the loop.
Outside the do-while loop, you last entered 1
```

Problems

1) What are the outputs of Code-5.50?

Code 5.50
```cpp
#include <iostream>
using namespace std;

int main() {

for (int a = 5; a > 0; a = a-2) {

cout << "Inside for-loop " << endl;
}

cout << "\nOutside for-loop";
}
```

2) Write a program which displays the first 10 even integers. Use for-loop in your code.

3) Write a C++ program which inputs an integer from the user and calculates the factorial of the entered number.

4) Write a program which calculates and display the sum of the series

$$1 + \frac{1}{3} + \left(\frac{1}{3}\right)^2 + \left(\frac{1}{3}\right)^3 + \ldots$$

5) Write three separate C++ programs which display the patterns in Figure-5.8.

```
*                    1
* *                  22
* * *                333
* * * *              4444
* * * * *            55555
* * * * * *          666666


         *
       *   *
     *   *   *
   *   *   *   *
 *   *   *   *   *
```

Figure-5.8 Patterns to be displayed.

6) Write a C++ program that inputs an integer from the user determines the number of digits in the entered number.

7) Write a C++ which converts a binary number to decimal.

Chapter-6

Functions and Lambda Expressions

Abstract: In this chapter we explain functions. Functions are program units written for performing specific tasks. A function may or may not return a value. In fact every C++ program contains at least one function, which is the main function. Once you have a main function, you can write other functions for performing specific calculations.

6.1 Introduction

A C++ function is a set of statements written for a specific task enclosed by curly braces. A function may return a value.

The syntax of a function is as

returned_data_type function_name(dataType1 var1, dataType1 var1, ...){

// statements

...

...

return value;

}

In Code-6.1, we show how to place the prototype and body of a function in a program.

Code 6.1

// function prototype

returned_data_type function_name (parmeter_list);

int **main**() {

// statements

}

// function implementation

returned_data_type function_name (parmeter_list) {

// function statements

}

The body of the function can be placed before the main function as shown in Code-6.2.

Code 6.2

// function implementation

returned_data_type function_name(parmeter_list) {

// function statements

}

int **main**() {

// statements

}

If a function is written after main function, its declaration must be written before the main function. The declaration of the function only contains the function header. Its variables names can be omitted, however, variable data types have to be written.

In Figure-6.1, structure of a function is explained.

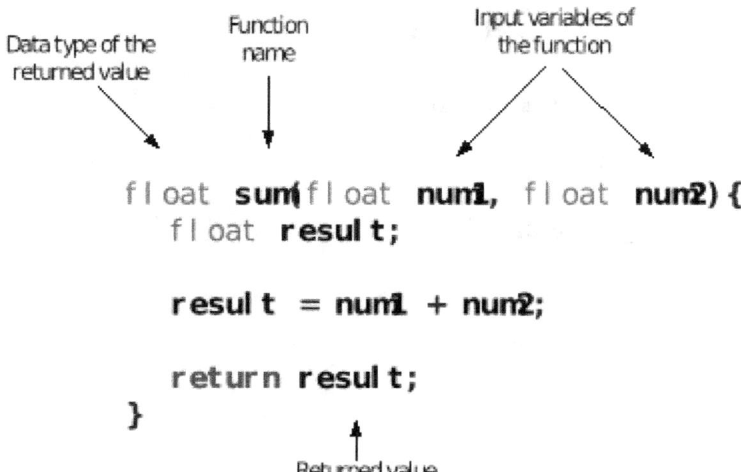

Figure-6.1 Explanation of a function parts.

The prototype, i.e., declaration of the function can be written either as

float **sum**(float **num1**, float **num2**);

or as

float **sum**(float, float);

Note that semicolon ';' is used at the end of the function declarations.

Example-6.1: Function definition can be written before the main part.

Code 6.3

```
#include <iostream>
using namespace std;

double mult(double a, double b) {

double result;

result = a * b; // double result = a * b;

return result;
}

int main() {

double r = mult(3.14, 8.97);

cout << "Result is: " << r;
}
```

Output(s): Result is: 28.17

Example-6.2: If function definition is written after main part, then the prototype of the function should be written before the main part.

Code 6.4

```cpp
#include <iostream>
using namespace std;
double mult(double a, double b); // function prototype
int main() {
double r = mult(3.14, 8.97);
cout << "Result is: " << r;
}
double mult(double a, double b) {
double result;
result = a * b; // double result = a * b;
return result;
}
```

Example-6.3: In function prototypes, variables names can be omitted.

Code 6.5

```cpp
#include <iostream>
using namespace std;

double mult(double, double); // function prototype

int main() {

double r = mult(3.14, 8.97);
cout << "Result is: " << r;
}
double mult(double a, double b) {
double a * b;
}
```

Example-6.4: In this example, we write a function which finds the greater of two integers. Integers are entered by the user.

Code 6.6

```cpp
#include <iostream>
using namespace std;

int myMax(int x, int y);

int main() {

int a, b, c;

cout << "Please enter two different integers : ";
```

```cpp
cin >> a >> b;

c = myMax(a, b);

if(c!=-1)
cout << "The maximum of " << a << " and "
<< b <<" is " << c << endl;
else
cout << "The numbers are equal to each other.";
}
int myMax(int x, int y) {

if(x > y)
return x;
else if(x < y)
return y;

return -1;
}
```

Output(s):
Please enter two different integers : 8 11
The maximum of 8 and 11 is 11

6.2 Types of Functions

We don't need to write every function. Some of the functions are already written and they are called library or built-in functions. These functions are part of the compiler and they can be used directly. Some of the library functions are

exp(), pow(), sqrt()

To be able to use these function we need no know their prototypes. The prototypes of the function can be found in the header file <math.h> and the prototypes are defined as

double **exp**(double **x**);

double **pow**(double **x**, double **y**);

double **sqrt**(double **x**);

and these function are used to calculate the mathematical expressions

$$e^x \qquad x^y \qquad \sqrt{x}$$

Example-6.5: In this example, we use built-in functions exp, pow and sqrt.

Code 6.7
```cpp
#include <iostream>
#include <cmath>

using namespace std;

int main() {

cout << exp(2.5) << " ";
cout << pow(2.5, 1.3) << " ";
cout << sqrt(2.5) << " ";
}
```

Output(s):
12.1825 3.29096 1.58114
The functions written by a developer are called user defined functions.

6.3 Passing Parameters to Functions

Function parameter values can be supplied with two methods. These are

Pass by value method

Pass by reference method

Example-6.6: Function call by pass by value is illustrated in this example.

Code 6.8

```cpp
#include <iostream>
using namespace std;

void myFunc(int a, int b); // function prototype

int main() {

int a = 10, b = 20;

cout << "Before function call \n";
cout << "a = " << a;
cout << " b = " << b;

myFunc(a, b);

cout << "\n\nAfter function call \n";
cout << "a = " << a;
cout << " b = " << b;
}

void myFunc(int a, int b) {
a = a + 15;
b = b + 15;
}
```

Output(s):

Before function call

a = 10 b = 20

After function call

a = 10 b = 20

Example-6.7: Function call by pass by reference is illustrated in this example.

Code 6.9
```cpp
#include <iostream>
using namespace std;

void myFunc(int* x, int* y); // function prototype

int main() {

int a = 10, b = 20;

cout << "Before function call \n";
cout << "a = " << a;
cout << " b = " << b;

myFunc(&a, &b);

cout << "\n\nAfter function call \n";
cout << "a = " << a;
cout << " b = " << b;
}

void myFunc(int* x, int* y) {

*x = *x + 15;
*y = *y + 15;
}
```

Output(s):
Before function call
a = 10 b = 20
After function call
a = 25 b = 35

Example-6.8: Swapping can be achieved by reference call.

Code 6.10
```cpp
#include <iostream>
using namespace std;

void swap(int *x, int *y);

int main() {

int a = 34, b = 45;

cout << "Before swap operation : a = " << a
<< " b = " << b << endl;
```

```cpp
swap(&a, &b); // swap a and b

cout << "After swap operation : a = " << a
<< " b = " << b << endl;
}

void swap(int* x, int* y) {

int t = *x;
*x = *y;
*y = t;
}
```

Output(s):
Before swap operation : a = 34 b = 45
After swap operation : a = 45 b = 34

6.4 Returning More than One Value

A function returns only a single value. However, two methods can be employed to return more than one value. In the first method, global variables can be used. In the second approach, we can use pointers to return more than one value.

Example-6.9: Global variables can be used inside a function to return more than one value.

Code 6.11
```cpp
#include <iostream>
using namespace std;

int a, b; // global variables

void myFunc(int x, int y);

int main() {

int x = 6, y = 7;

myFunc(x, y);

cout << "Squares of " << x << " and " << y
<< " are " << a << " and " << b;
}

void myFunc(int x, int y) {

a = x * x;
b = y * y;
}
```

Output(s): Square of 6 and 7 are : 36 and 49

Example-6.10: Pointers can be used in function arguments to return more than one value.

Code 6.12
```cpp
#include <iostream>
using namespace std;
void myFunc(int* x, int* y);
int main() {
int x = 6, y = 7;
cout << "Square of " << x << " and " << y << " are: ";
myFunc(&x, &y);
cout << x << " and " << y;
}
void myFunc(int* x, int* y) {
*x = (*x) * (*x);
*y = (*y) * (*y);
```

}
Output(s): Square of 6 and 7 are : 36 and 49

6.5 Recursive Functions

Recursive functions are self-calling function. In Code-6.13, the structure of a recursive function is shown.

Code 6.13
```
void myFunc() {
// ...

myFunc();

//..
}
```

Recursive functions can contain conditional expressions before self calling as in Code-6.14.

Code 6.14
```
void myFunc() {
// ...

if (condition)
myFunc();

//..
}
```

Example-6.11: Let's write a recursive function which displays the integers
```
a   a - 1   a - 2...0
```
We will use $a = 6$ to test the recursive function. First we write the Code-6.15.

Code 6.15
```
void countDown(int a) {

printf("%d ", a);
}
```

In the second step, we add the self calling and decrement statements as in Code-6.16.

Code 6.16
```
void countDown(int a) {

cout << a << " ";

a—;

countDown(a);
}
```

Conditional part for self calling is added as in Code-6.17.

Code 6.17

```cpp
void countDown(int a) {

cout << a << " ";
a—;

if (a >= 0)
countDown(a);
}
```

The recursive function can be tested inside a main function as in Code-6.18.

Code 6.18

```cpp
#include <iostream>
using namespace std;

void countDown(int a);

int main() {

countDown(6);
}

void countDown(int a) {

cout << a << " ";
a—;

if (a >= 0)
countDown(a);
}
```

Output(s): 6 5 4 3 2 1 0

Example-6.12: Factorial of integers can be calculated using a recursive function.

Code 6.19

```cpp
#include <iostream>
using namespace std;

int myFactorial(int a);

int main() {

int a;
```

```cpp
cout << "Enter a: ";

cin >> a;

int result = myFactorial(a);

cout << result;
}

int myFactorial(int a) {

int r;

if (a > 0) {
r = a * myFactorial(a - 1);
return r;
}
else if(a==0) {

return 1;
}
else {
cout << "You entered a negative number ";
exit(1);
}
}
```

Output(s):
Enter a: 4
24
The function myFactorial can be written in a compact form as in Code-6.20.
Code 6.20
```cpp
int myFactorial(int a) {
return ((a == 1 || a == 0) ? 1 : a * myFactorial(a - 1));
}
```

6.6 Lambda Expressions in C++

Lambda expressions can be considered as anonymous functions with some enhances properties. They can do the work of a classical function, besides; they can capture the variables from the code enclosing the lambda function.

The syntax of Lambda expression is

[capture] (parameters) mutable -> returnType {

// statements

}

capture

It can contain the variables that are defined before the Lambda expression. Besides, we can define new variables in the capture part and initialize them and use them in the body part.

parameters

They can be considered as function arguments passed to the function.

mutable

It is an optional keyword, and it enables us modify the values of the variables captured by the lambda expression.

Example-6.13: In this example we write a simple lambda expression, the keyword auto determines the return type automatically.

Code 6.21

```cpp
auto myFunc = []() { // lambda function

cout << "Hello World!";
};
```

Example-6.14: The lambda expression can be called as a function in main function.

Code 6.22

```cpp
void myFunc() {

// function body
}
```

The function in Code-6.22 can be written as in Code-6.23.

Code 6.23

```cpp
#include <iostream>
using namespace std;

int main() {

auto myFunc = []() { // lambda function

cout << "Hello World!";
};
```

```
myFunc(); // call lambda function
}
```

Output(s):
Hello World!

Example-6.15: If Code-6.24 is executed we get no output.

Code 6.24
```
#include <iostream>
using namespace std;

int main() {

[]() { // lambda function

cout << "Hello World!";
};
}
```

The lambda function can be run as in Code-6.25 by adding () parentheses to the end of the curly braces.

Code 6.25
```
#include <iostream>
using namespace std;

int main() {

[]() { // lambda function

cout << "Hello World!";
} ();
}
```

Output(s):
Hello World!

6.6.1 Lambda Expression with Input Parameters

Example-6.16:

Code 6.26

```cpp
#include <iostream>
using namespace std;

int main() {

auto mySum = [] (float x, float y) {
cout << "Sum = " << x + y;
};

mySum(5.8, 9.4);
}
```

Output(s):

```
Sum = 15.2
```

Code 6.27

```cpp
auto mySum = [] (int x, int y) {
cout << "Sum = " << x + y;
};

void mySum(int x, int y) {
cout << "Sum = " << x + y;
}
```

6.6.2 Lambda Expression with Explicit Return Type

Example-6.17:

Code 6.28

```cpp
#include<iostream>
using namespace std;

int main() {

float a = 1.6;
float b = 2.9;

// explicit return type 'float'
auto mySum = [] (float x, float y) -> float {

return x + y;
};

auto sm = mySum(a, b);

cout << "Sum = " << sm << endl;
}
```

Output(s):

```
Sum = 4.5
```

6.6.3 C++ Lambda Expression with Capture Clause

By default, lambda expressions cannot access variables defined in the main part. Lambda expression can access those variables using the capture clause.

Capture by Value

[ ](){} means that nothing is captured.

[=](){} means that all variables enclosing the lambda expression can be captured by value.

[&](){}means that all variables enclosing the lambda expression can be captured by reference.

Both [=] and [&] expressions can be used in one capture clause.

For example, [=, &var1, &var2] means that all variables are captured by value but variables var1 and var2 are captured by reference.

The expression, [&, var1, var2] means that all variables are captured by reference but variables var1 and var2 are captured by value.

Example-6.18: In this example, all the variables in the main() function are captured by value.

Code 6.29

```cpp
#include<iostream>
using namespace std;

int main() {

double a = 3.3;
double b = 6.7;

auto myFunc = [ = ] (double c) -> double {

return a * b + c;
};

cout << myFunc(2.5);
}
```

Output(s): 24.61

6.6.4 Lambda Expression with Explicit Return Value

Example-6.19: The lambda expression used in this example has **double** return type. All the variables are captured by value.

```
Code 6.30
#include<iostream>
using namespace std;

int main() {

double a = 3.3;
double b = 6.7;

auto myFunc = [ = ] (double c) -> double {

return a * b + c;
};

cout << myFunc(2.5);
}
```

Output(s): 24.61

Example-6.20: In this example, all the variables are captured by reference.

```
Code 6.31
#include<iostream>
using namespace std;

int main() {

double a = 3.3;
double b = 6.7;
double r;

auto myFunc = [ & ] (double c) -> double {

a += 5; b += 5;
return a * b + c;
};

cout << "Before lambda call " << endl;
cout << "a = " << a << endl;
cout << "b = " << b << endl;

r = myFunc(2.5);
```

```
cout << "After lambda call " << endl;
cout << "r = " << r << endl;
cout << "a = " << a << endl;
cout << "b = " << b << endl;
}
```

Output(s):

```
Before lambda call
a = 3.3
b = 6.7
After lambda call
r = 99.61
a = 8.3
b = 11.7
```

Example-6.21: Lambda expression can be written outside the main() function, and it can be called inside the main() function.

Code 6.32
```cpp
#include <iostream>
using namespace std;

auto myFunc = [](int a) {

int b = a + 6;

return b;
};

int main() {

auto r = myFunc(5);

cout << "r = " << r;
}
```

Output(s):
```
r = 11
```

Example-6.22: In this example, lambda expression does not have a name, and it is called automatically when it is defined.

Code 6.33
```cpp
#include <iostream>
using namespace std;

int main() {

float r;

r = [] (float x, float y) -> float {

return x + y;

}(7.7, 8.9);

cout << "r = " << r;
}
```

Output(s):
```
r = 16.6
```

Example-6.23:

Code 6.34
```cpp
#include <iostream>
```

```cpp
using namespace std;
int main(){
int a = 87;
int b = 53;
[] () { cout << a << " " << b; }(); // error
[a, b] () { cout << a << " " << b << endl; }(); // ok
[ = ] () { cout << a << " " << b << endl; }(); // ok
[ &a, &b ] () { cout << a << " " << b << endl; }(); // ok
[ & ] () { cout << a << " " << b << endl; }(); // ok
}
```

Mutable

Mutable keyword is necessary to assign a new value to the parameters in the capture clause.

Example-6.24: In this example, we do not use mutable keyword and error arises due to a new value assignment to the captured variable.

Code 6.35

```cpp
#include <iostream>
using namespace std;
int main() {



int a = 10;
    auto myFunc = [a] () {
a = 30; // error, assignment of read-only variable 'a'
cout << "a = " << endl;
};
myFunc();
}
```

Code-6.35 can be made error free if mutable keyword is used as in Code-6.36.

Code 6.36

```cpp
#include <iostream>
using namespace std;

int main() {

int a = 10;
auto myFunc = [a] () mutable {

a = 30; // ok
cout << "a = " << a << endl;
};
cout << "a = " << a << endl;
myFunc();
}
```

Output(s):
```
a = 10
a = 30
```

Example-6.25: In this example, we pass a lambda expression to the argument of a function, which has an integer and a function pointer in its arguments.

Code 6.37

```cpp
#include <iostream>
using namespace std;
void myFunc (int x, int (*ptr)(int)) {
int y = (*ptr)(6); // call Lambda expression
// a = 6
cout << "x = " << x << endl;
cout << "y = " << y << endl;
}
int main() {
myFunc(4, [](int a) {
int ret = a + 8;
return ret;
}
);
}
```

Output(s):
```
x = 4
y = 14
```

Problems

1) Write a C++ function which takes two integers and swaps their values.

2) Write a C++ function which finds the largest element of an array and returns it.

3) Write C++ function which determines whether an integer is a prime number or not.

4) What is the output of Code-6.38.

Code 6.38
```cpp
#include <iostream>
using namespace std;

void myFunc(int* x, int* y);

int main() {

int x = 13, y = 67;

myFunc(&x, &y);

cout << x << " and " << y;
}

void myFunc(int* x, int* y) {

*x = (*x) + (*x);
*y = (*x) + (*y) - 5;
}
```

5) Using pass by reference method, write a C++ function which takes three integer arguments and and replaces each number by its square.

6) Write a lambda expression which gets an integer N and calculates the N factorial.

7) Write lambda epressions for the problems 1, 2, and 3.

Chapter-7

Arrays

Abstract: In this chapter, we explain arrays in C++ programming. Arrays can be considered as a group of variables belonging to the same data type, and these variables are place in a sequential manner in memory. Arrays can be used to keep some records. For instance, midterm and final marks of students for a course kept in an array.

7.1 Syntax for Array Declaration

The syntax for array declaration is

    dataType arrayName[arraySize] = {val1, val2,...,valN};

7.2 Accessing Array Elements

We can access array elements using subscript operator [ ] and the index value of the element as in

arrayName[index]

The indexing in the array always starts with 0 and the index of the last element is N − 1, new values to the array elements are assigned using

array_name[i] = new_value;

Example-7.1: We can define **int**, **char**, **float** and **double** arrays as in Code-7.1.

Code 7.1

```cpp
int main() {

int a[6];
char b[5];

float c[4];
double d[7];
}
```

Example-7.2: Array elements can be initialized.

Code 7.2

```cpp
int main() {

int a[1]={1};

int b[2]={4, 6};
}
```

Example-7.3: Code-7.3 and Code-7.4 perform the same task.

Code 7.3

```cpp
int main() {
int a[3]={7, 13, 54};
}
```

Code 7.4

```cpp
int main() {
int a[3];
a[0] = 7;
a[1] = 13;
a[2] = 54;
}
```

Example-7.4: Initialization starts from the first element, non-initialized elements equal zero by default.

Code 7.5

```cpp
#include <iostream>

using namespace std;
```

```cpp
int main() {

int a[4] = {2, 7};

cout << "a[0] = " << a[0];
cout << ", a[1] = " << a[1];
cout << ", a[2] = " << a[2];
cout << ", a[3] = " << a[3] << endl;
}
```

Output(s):
a[0] = 2, a[1] = 7, a[2] = 0, a[3] = 0

Example-7.5: Array name shows an address in the memory. If we use an index value larger than the array size, we refer to a memory location which is not reserved for the array variable, and these locations may be inaccessible, or if they are accessible, they can contain values.

Code 7.6
```cpp
#include <iostream>

using namespace std;

int main() {

int a[2] = {3, 6};

cout << "a[0] = " << a[0];
cout << ", a[1] = " << a[1];
cout << ", a[7] = " << a[7];

cout << ", a[10] = " << a[10];
cout << ", a[100] = " << a[100];
}
```

Output(s):
a[0] = 3, a[1] = 6, a[7] = 32600, a[10] = -759483959, a[100] = -1906254005

7.3 Array Initialization without Size

We can define an array and initialize as in

dataType arrayName[] = {val1, val2,...,valN};

In this case, array size is determined by the compiler considering the number of initialization values.

Example-7.6: In Code-7.7 we define an array without size and initialize it when it is defined.

Code 7.7
```cpp
#include <iostream>

using namespace std;

int main() {

int a[]={3, 6, 8, 9};

cout << "a[0] = " << a[0];
cout << ", a[1] = " << a[1] << endl;
cout << "a[2] = " << a[2];
cout << ", a[3] = " << a[3];
}
```

Output(s):
```
a[0] = 3, a[1] = 6
a[2] = 8, a[3] = 9
```

Example-7.7: In Code-7.8, for the initialization of the array, 2 values are used, and array size is automatically decided as 2, and if indexes larger than array size are used to access the array elements, arbitrary values are displayed.

Code 7.8
```cpp
#include <iostream>

using namespace std;

int main() {

int a[] = {3, 6};

cout << "a[0] = " << a[0];
cout << ", a[1] = " << a[1];
cout << ", a[55] = " << a[55];

cout << ", a[10] = " << a[10];
cout << ", a[867] = " << a[867];
}
```

Output(s):

a[0] = 3, a[1] = 6, a[55] = 0, a[10] = -1836150327, a[867] = 0

Example-7.8: Size of an integer array equals $4 \times$ number of elements.

Code 7.9

```cpp
#include <iostream>

using namespace std;

int main() {

int a[] = {3, 6, 8, 9};

cout << "Size of a is " << sizeof(a);
}
```

Output(s): Size of a is 16

7.4 Array Initialization Using Loops

Arrays can be initialized using loops, usually for loops are used for the initialization of the arrays.

Example-7.9: In this example, we first initialize the array and then print the array elements.

Code 7.10

```cpp
#include <iostream>
using namespace std;
int main() {
float a[5];
for (int i = 0; i < 5; i++) {
a[i] = i*3.12;
}
for (int i = 0; i < 5; i++) {
cout << "a[" << i <<"]" << " = " << a[i] << ", ";
}
}
```

Output(s):

a[0] = 0, a[1] = 3.12, a[2] = 6.24, a[3] = 9.36, a[4] = 12.48

Example-7.10: Array elements can be initialized by the user entered values.

Code 7.11

```cpp
#include <iostream>
using namespace std;
int main() {
int a[3];
for (int i = 0; i < 3; i++) {
cout << "Please enter a[" << i << "]" << " = ";
cin >> a[i];
}
cout << "\nYou entered: \n\n";
for (int i = 0; i < 3; i++) {
cout << "a[" << i << "]" << " = " << a[i] << endl;
}
}
```

Output(s):

Please enter a[0] = 67
Please enter a[1] = 43
Please enter a[2] = 98
You entered:
a[0] = 67
a[1] = 43
a[2] = 98

Example-7.11: In this example, the maximum value of all the array elements is found.

Code 7.12

```cpp
#include <iostream>
```

```cpp
using namespace std;
int main() {
int numbers[5] = { 123, 45, 345, 67,78 };
int maxNum = numbers[0];
for (int i = 1; i < 5; i++) {
if (maxNum < numbers[i]) {
maxNum = numbers[i];
}
}
cout << "The maximum of the numbers in the array is "
<< maxNum;
}
```

Output(s):

The maximum of the numbers in the array is 345

Example-7.12: In Code-7.13, we use hexadecimal numbers to initialize array elements.

Code 7.13

```cpp
int main() {

int a[2];

a[0] = 0x12345678;
a[1] = 0xABCDEF94;
}
```

Each of the integers a[0] and a[1] are stored to 4 byte consecutive memory locations. The letter 'a' indicates the address of the first byte in the memory used to store the first integer a[0]. For the simplicity of explanation, let's assume that a=100 which is the address of the first byte of a[0] stored into memory. In Figure-7.1, the storage of the integer bytes in consecutive register locations is illustrated. We assumed that little-endian is used by the compiler.

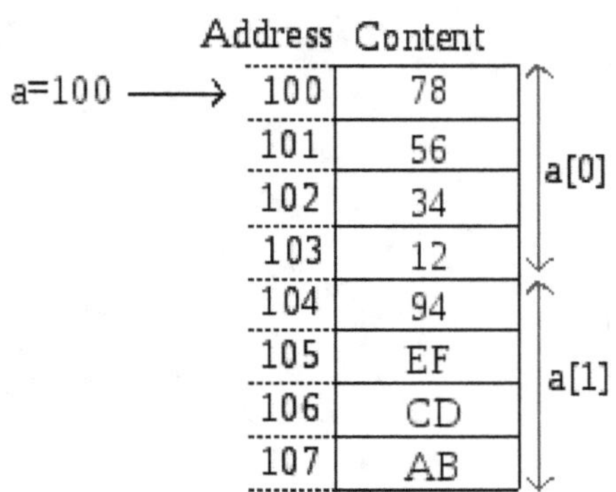

Figure-7.1 Typical memory map for Example-7.12.

Example-7.13: Array name indicates a register address which is the starting address of a block where array values are stored.

Code 7.14

```cpp
#include <iostream>
using namespace std;
```

```cpp
int main() {
int a[2];
a[0] = 0x12345678;
a[1] = 0xABCDEF94;
cout << "a[0] = " << hex << a[0] << endl;
cout << "a[1] = "<< hex << a[1] << endl;
cout << "Adress (a) is " << a << endl;
cout << "Address size is " << sizeof(a);
}
```

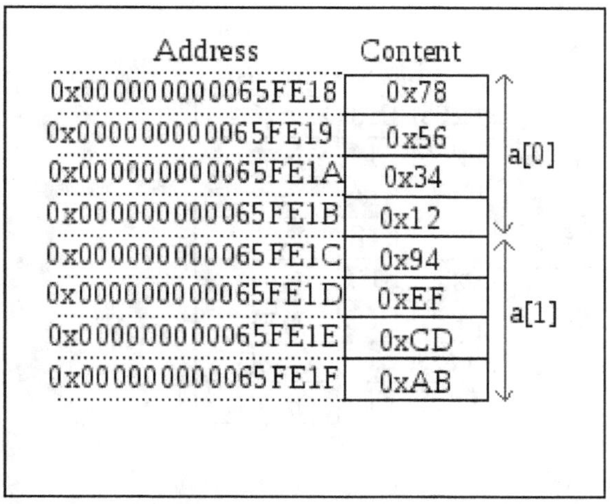

Address	Content	
0x000000000065FE18	0x78	a[0]
0x000000000065FE19	0x56	a[0]
0x000000000065FE1A	0x34	a[0]
0x000000000065FE1B	0x12	a[0]
0x000000000065FE1C	0x94	a[1]
0x000000000065FE1D	0xEF	a[1]
0x000000000065FE1E	0xCD	a[1]
0x000000000065FE1F	0xAB	a[1]

Output(s):

a[0] = 12345678
a[1] = abcdef94
Adress (a) is 0x000000000065fe18
Address size is 8

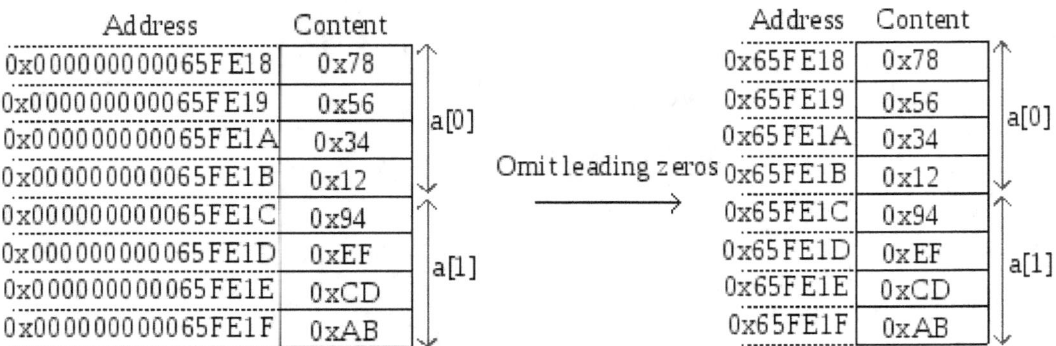

Example-7.14: In this example, we define a character array and display its elements. Array name is the address of storage block.

Code 7.15
```cpp
#include <iostream>

using namespace std;

int main() {

char a[3] = {'A','b','c'};

cout << "a[0] = " << a[0] << endl;

cout << "a[1] = " << a[1] << endl;
cout << "a[2] = " << a[2] << endl;

cout << "Address of (a) is " << &a;
}
```

Output(s):
```
a[0] = A
a[1] = b
a[2] = c
Address of (a) is 0x7ffc04e78a05
```

Example-7.15: Characters are also 8-bit numbers. In this example, we show hexadecimal values of array characters, and illustrate how they are stored in memory.

Code 7.16
```cpp
#include <iostream>

using namespace std;

int main() {
```

```cpp
char a[3] = {'A','b','c'};

cout << "a[0] = " << a[0] << endl;

cout << "a[1] = " << a[1] << endl;
cout << "a[2] = " << a[2] << endl;

cout << "Address of (a) is " << &a << endl;

cout << "a[0] = " << hex << (int) a[0] << endl;

cout << "a[1] = " << hex << (int) a[1] << endl;
cout << "a[2] = " << hex << (int) a[2] << endl;
}
```

Output(s):

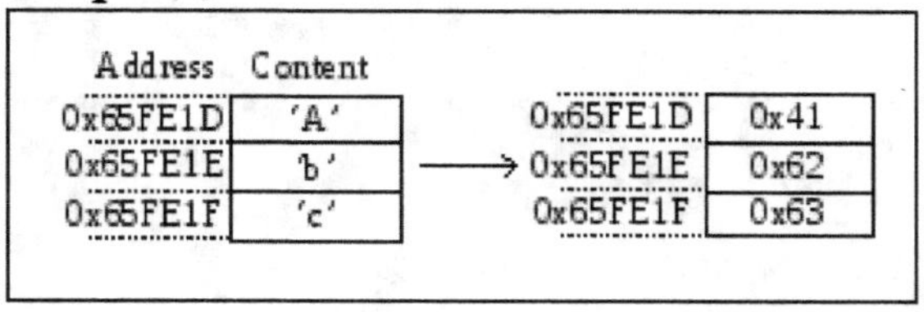

Address	Content
0x65FE1D	'A'
0x65FE1E	'b'
0x65FE1F	'c'

Address	
0x65FE1D	0x41
0x65FE1E	0x62
0x65FE1F	0x63

```
a[0] = A
a[1] = b
a[2] = c
Address of (a) is 000000000065fe1d
a[0] = 41
a[1] = 62
a[2] = 63
```

7.5 Strings as Array of Characters

The array of characters terminated by a NULL character is called a string. The array of characters terminated by a NULL can be printed using a for loop or using cout function.

Example-7.16: A string can be printed using a for-loop, or using a cout function.

Code 7.17

```cpp
#include <iostream>

using namespace std;

int main() {

char a[6] = { 'H', 'e', 'l', 'l', 'o', '\0' };

for(int i = 0; i < 6; i++) {

cout << a[i] << " ";
}

cout << a;
}
```

Output(s):
H e l l o Hello
If the array of characters is NOT terminated by a NULL, then it may not be printed properly.
Example-7.17:

Code 7.18

```cpp
#include <iostream>

using namespace std;

int main() {

char a[5] = { 'H', 'e', 'l', 'l', 'o' };

for(int i = 0; i < 5; i++) {

cout << a[i] << " ";
}

cout << a;
}
```

Output(s):
H e l l o Hello♣

The array of characters and the array of NULL terminated characters are two different concepts. The latter one is the strings, and for string manipulations, a number of built-in library functions are available, and these functions do not work properly for the array of characters which are not NULL terminated.

Example-7.18: In this example, we define a string in two different ways.

Code 7.19

```cpp
#include <iostream>

using namespace std;

int main() {

char a[6] = { 'H', 'e', 'l', 'l', 'o', '\0' };

char b[6] = "Hello"; // a equals to b

for(int i = 0; i < 6; i++) {
cout << b[i];
}

cout << " " << a;
cout << " " << b;
}
```

Output(s):
Hello Hello Hello

7.6 Multidimensional Arrays

A Two-Dimensional array is defined as

$$dataType\ arrayName[size1][size2];$$

and this array can be considered as a single dimensional array having size1 elements each of which is an array having size2 elements of dataType.

$$arrayName[index1][index2];$$

Example-7.19: A multidimensional array can be initialized in two different methods.

Code 7.20
```cpp
int main() {

int a[2][3] = { 10, 20, 30, 40, 50, 60 };

int b[2][3] = {
{10, 20, 30},
{40, 50, 60}
};
}
```

In this example, both initialization methods assign the same values to the same index locations.

Example-7.20: Nested for loops can be used to initialize a multidimensional array.

Code 7.21
```cpp
int main() {

int M = 4, N=4;

int a[M][N];

for (int i = 0; i < M; i++) {

for (int j = 0; j < N; j++) {

a[i][j] = 0;
}

}
}
```

Example-7.21: The multidimensional array elements can be displayed using nested for loops.

Code 7.22
```cpp
#include <iostream>

using namespace std;
```

```cpp
int main() {

int a[2][3] = { 67, 20, 87, 34, 50, 70 };

int b[2][3] = {
{67, 20, 87},
{34, 50, 70}
};

for (int i = 0; i < 2; i++) {

for (int j = 0; j < 3; j++) {

cout << " " << a[i][j];
}
cout << "\n";
}

cout << "\n";

for (int i = 0; i < 2; i++) {

for (int j = 0; j < 3; j++) {
cout << " " << b[i][j];
}
cout << "\n";
}

}
```

Output(s):
```
67 20 87
34 50 70
67 20 87
34 50 70
```

Example-7.22: The first dimension of a multidimensional array can be omitted. In this case, the value of the first dimension is determined considering the initialization data.

Code 7.23
```cpp
int main() {
int a[][2] = {
{1,2},
{3,4},
{5,6}
};

// int b[][2] = { {1,2}, {3,4}, {5,6} };
```

```
        }
```

Example-7.23: Only the first dimension of a multidimensional array can be omitted, all the other dimensions must be written.

Code 7.24

```
int main() {
int a[][2] = { {1,2}, {3,4}, {5,6} };
int b[][][2] = { { {1,2}, {3,4}, {5,6} },
{ {7,8}, {9,10}, {11,12} } };
// error: declaration of 'b' as multidimensional array must have bounds
// for all dimensions except the first
}
```

Example-7.24: Only the first dimension of a multidimensional array can be omitted, all the other dimensions must be written.

Code 7.25

```cpp
int main() {
int a[][2] = { {1,2}, {3,4}, {5,6} };
int b[][3][2] = { { {1,2}, {3,4}, {5,6} },
{ {7,8}, {9,10}, {11,12} } }; // ok
}
```

7.7 Passing an Array to a Function in C

Arrays can be used in function arguments. Function arguments contain array definition without the first dimension. Array names are solely used in function calls.

Example-7.25:

Code 7.26

```cpp
#include <iostream>
using namespace std;
void dispArray(double a[]);
int main() {
double a[4] = {2.3, 5.6, 3.1, 12.35};
cout << "Number of elements is "
<< sizeof(a)/sizeof(double) << endl;
dispArray(a); // only array name is passed to the function call
}
void dispArray(double a[]) {
for (int i = 0; i < 4; i++) {
cout << "a[" << i << "]" << " = " << a[i] << " ";
}
}
```

Output(s):

Number of elements is 4

a[0] = 2.30 a[1] = 5.60 a[2] = 3.10 a[3] = 12.35

If we use N dimensional arrays at the inputs of the functions, except for the first array dimension all the other dimensions must be specified at the declaration of functions.

Example-7.26: The first dimension of the array is not written in function arguments,

Code 7.27

```cpp
#include <iostream>
using namespace std;
void dispArray(int a[][3], int n) {// first dimension is not used
for (int i = 0; i < n; i++) {
for (int j = 0; j < 3; j++) {
cout << a[i][j] << " ";
}
}
}
int main() {
int a[][3] = {{7, 8, 3}, {9, 2, 1}, {4, 0, 5}};
dispArray(a, 2);
}
```

Output(s): 7 8 3 9 2 1

Example-7.27: Dimensions of an array can be written separately in function arguments.

Code 7.28

```cpp
#include <iostream>
using namespace std;
const int M = 3, N = 3;
void dispArray(int a[][N]) {
for (int i = 0; i < M; i++) {
for (int j = 0; j < N; j++) {
cout << a[i][j] << " ";
}
}
}
int main() {
int a[][3] = {{7, 8, 3}, {9, 2, 1}, {4, 0, 5}};
dispArray(a);
}
```

Output(s): 7 8 3 9 2 1 4 0 5

Problems

1) Input 5 integers from the user, store them in an array and print them.

2) Write a program in C++ which inputs 6 integers from user, stores them in an array and prints them.

3) Write a C++ program which calculates the sum of all elements of an integer array.

4) Write a C++ program which finds the maximum number of a float array.

5) Write a C++ program which calculates the frequency of each element of an array.

6) Write a C++ program to sort the elements of the array in ascending order.

7) Write C++ program to find equal elements of an integer array.

8) Initialize the array in Code-7.29, and print its elements.

Code 7.29

```cpp
#include <iostream>

using namespace std;

int main() {

float a[10];

// initialize the array using for-loop
// and print the array elements
}
```

9) Write a function which takes an array as its argument, reverses the elements of the array and returns it.

Chapter-8

Complex Numbers in Modern C++ Programming

Abstract: In this chapter, we explain complex number data type used in C++ programming. Complex numbers are frequently used in electrical and computer engineering applications. Complex number header file is available in C++ language. The C++ language provides powerful tools for the calculation of operations involving complex numbers. For instance, trigonometric operations involving complex numbers, such as sine of a complex number, can be easily done using built-in functions in C++ libraries.

8.1 How to Define a Complex Number

To define complex numbers and to perform operations on complex numbers we need to include the header file <complex> in our program.

The complex variable is defined as

    complex<dataType> varName(real_value, imaginary_value);

The complex variables with default zero real and imaginary parts can be defined as

    complex<int> varName;

    complex<float> varName;

    complex<double> varName;

    complex<long double> varName;

Example-8.1: In Code-8.1, we define some complex numbers which have zero default values for real and imaginary parts.

Code 8.1
```
#include <complex>
#include <iostream>

using namespace std;

int main() {

complex<int> c1;
complex<float> c2;
complex<double> c3;
complex<long double> c4;

cout << c1 << c2 << c3 << c4;
}
```

Output(s): (0,0)(0,0)(0,0)(0,0)

Example-8.2: In Code-8.2, we define some complex numbers having non-default values.

Code 8.2
```
#include <complex>
#include <iostream>

using namespace std;

int main() {
```

```
complex<int> c1(2,3);
complex<float> c2(3.4, 5.6);
complex<double> c3(9.1, 2.7);
complex<long double> c4(0.51, 1.9);

cout << c1 <<endl;
cout << c2 <<endl;
cout << c3 <<endl;
cout << c4 <<endl;
}
```

Output(s):
```
(2,3)
(3.4,5.6)
(9.1,2.7)
(0.51,1.9)
```

Example-8.3:

Code 8.3
```
#include <complex>
#include <iostream>

using namespace std;

int main() {

cout << complex<double>(9.1, 2.7) << endl;
cout << complex<int>(3, 4) << endl;
}
```

Output(s):
```
(9.1,2.7)
(3,4)
```
Example-8.4:

Code 8.4
```
#include <complex>
#include <iostream>

using namespace std;

int main() {

cout << complex<double>(9.1, 2.7) << endl;
cout << complex<int>(3, 4) << endl;
}
```

Output(s):
(9.1,2.7)
(3,4)

8.2 Real and Imaginary Part of a Complex Number

Real and imaginary part of a complex number can be extracted using the functions
real() and imag()

Example-8.5: In Code-8.5, we define a complex number whose real and imaginary parts are of double data type, and print the real and imaginary parts of the complex number using the function real() and imag().

Code 8.5

```cpp
#include <complex>
#include <iostream>

using namespace std;

int main() {

complex<double> a(9.1, 2.7);

cout << "real part is " << a.real() << endl;
cout << "imaginary part is " << a.imag() << endl;

cout << "real part is " << real(a) << endl;
cout << "imaginary part is " << imag(a) << endl;
}
```

Output(s):
real part is 9.1
imaginary part is 2.7
real part is 9.1
imaginary part is 2.7

8.3 Phase and Magnitude of a Complex Number

The absolute value and angle, i.e., argument of a complex number can be obtained using the functions

abs() and arg()

Example-8.6: In Code-8.6, we define a complex number and print its absolute value and argument.

Code 8.6

```cpp
#include <complex>
#include <iostream>

using namespace std;

int main() {

complex<double> a(3, 4);

cout << "Absolute value is " << abs(a) << endl;
cout << "Argument is " << arg(a) << endl;
}
```

Output(s):
Absolute value is 5
Argument is 0.927295

Example-8.7: In Code-8.7, we define a complex number and print its norm value.

Code 8.7

```cpp
#include <complex>
#include <iostream>

using namespace std;

int main() {

complex<int> a(3, 4);

cout << "Norm value is " << norm(a) << endl;
}
```

Output(s): Norm value is 25
The conjugate of a complex number can be obtained using the function

conj()

Example-8.8:

Code 8.8

```cpp
#include <complex>
```

```cpp
#include <iostream>
using namespace std;
int main() {
complex<double> a(3, 4);
cout << "a = " << a << endl;
cout << "conj(a) = " << conj(a) << endl;
cout << "a * conj(a) = " << a *conj(a) << endl;
}
```

Output(s):

```
a = (3,4)
conj(a) = (3,-4)
a * conj(a) = (25,0)
```

8.4 Complex Operations

Standard arithmetic operators +, -, *, / can be used with real, complex types in any combination.

Example-8.9: In Code-8.9, we show that two complex numbers can be summed, and a constant can and a complex number can be summed as well.

Code 8.9
```cpp
#include <complex>
#include <iostream>

using namespace std;

int main() {

complex<int> a(3, 4);
complex<int> b(5, 6);

complex<int> c = a + 15;
complex<int> d = a + b;
cout << "a = " << a << endl;
cout << "b = " << b << endl;
cout << "c = " << c << endl;
cout << "d = " << d << endl;
}
```

Output(s):
```
a = (3,4)
b = (5,6)
c = (18,4)
d = (8,10)
```

Example-8.10: We can multiply two complex numbers as in Code-8.10.

Code 8.10
```cpp
#include <complex>
#include <iostream>

using namespace std;

int main() {

complex<int> a(3, 4);
complex<int> b(5, 6);

complex<int> c = a * b;
complex<int> d(a * b);
```

```
    cout << "a = " << a << endl;
    cout << "b = " << b << endl;
    cout << "c = " << c << endl;
    cout << "d = " << d << endl;
    }
```

Output(s):
a = (3,4)
b = (5,6)
c = (-9,38)
d = (-9,38)

Example-8.11 We can divide two complex numbers as in Code-8.11.

Code 8.11
```
#include <complex>
#include <iostream>

using namespace std;

int main() {

complex<double> a(3, 4);
complex<double> b(5, 6);

complex<double> c = a / b;
complex<double> d(a / b);

cout << "c = " << c << endl;
cout << "d = " << d << endl;
}
```

The output of the Code-8.11 is
c = (0.639344,0.0327869)
d = (0.639344,0.0327869)

If we use integer data types as in Code-8.12

Code 8.12
```
#include <complex>
#include <iostream>

using namespace std;

int main() {

complex<int> a(3, 4);
complex<int> b(5, 6);
```

```
complex<int> c = a / b;
complex<int> d(a / b);

cout << "c = " << c << endl;
cout << "d = " << d << endl;
}
```

the output becomes as in

 c = (0,0)

 d = (0,0)

For this reason, we suggest the reader to use **double** data type while defining the complex numbers; otherwise some unexpected results may be obtained.

8.5 Polar form of a Complex Number

We can form a complex number using the polar() function which takes magnitude and angle of a complex number and returns the complex number in Cartesian coordinates. The prototype of the function is as

complex<T> polar(const T&, const T&);

Example-8.12: In this example, show how to use the polar() function to form a complex number.

```cpp
Code 8.13
#include <complex>
#include <iostream>

using namespace std;

int main() {

double mag = 5;
double theta = atan(4.0/3.0);

complex<double> a = polar(mag, theta);

cout << "a = " << a;
}
```

Output(s): a = (3,4)

polar(r, theta) is equivalent to any of the following expressions:

r * exp(theta * i)

r * (cos(theta) + sin(theta) * i)

complex(r * cos(theta), r * sin(theta))

Example-8.13: In this example, we express a complex number using

mag * exp(theta * i)


```cpp
Code 8.14
#include <complex>
#include <iostream>

using namespace std;

int main() {

double mag = 5;
```

```
double theta = atan(4.0/3.0);

complex<double> i(0, 1);

complex<double> a = mag * exp(theta * i);

cout << "a = " << a;
}
```

Output(s): a = (3,4)

Example-8.14: In this example, we express a complex number using

```
complex(mag * cos(theta), mag * sin(theta))
```

Code 8.15
```
#include <complex>
#include <iostream>
using namespace std;
int main() {
double mag = 5;
double theta = atan(4.0/3.0);
complex<double> a = complex<double>(mag * cos(theta), mag * sin(theta));
cout << "a = " << a;
}
```
Output(s): a = (3,4)

8.6 Calculation of Complex Exponentials

For complex number

$$z = a + ib$$

the exponential term

$$e^z$$

is calculated as

$$e^z = e^{a+ib} \rightarrow e^z = e^a(\cos b + i\sin b)$$

Example-8.15:

Code 8.16

```cpp
#include <complex>
#include <iostream>
using namespace std;
int main() {
double myPi = acos(-1.0);
complex<double> i(0.0, 1.0);
complex<double> a(1, sqrt(3));
cout << fixed << "exp(i * pi ) = " << exp(i * myPi) << endl;
cout << fixed << "exp(0.5 + i*sqrt(3)) = " << exp(a) << endl;
}
```

Output(s):

```
exp(i * pi ) = (-1.000000,0.000000)
exp(0.5 + i*sqrt(3)) = (-0.436438,2.683017)
```

8.7 Logarithm of a Complex Number

Complex natural logarithm of complex float, complex double and complex long long double numbers can be calculated using log() function whose prototype is

```
complex<T> log( const complex<T>& );
```

The complex logarithm with bas-10 is calculate using the function

```
complex<T> log10( const complex<T>& );
```

Example-8.16: In this example, natural logarithm of a complex number is calculated and displayed.

Code 8.17
```cpp
#include <complex>
#include <iostream>

using namespace std;

int main() {

complex<double> a(1, 2);

cout << "a = " << a << endl;
cout << fixed << "ln(a) = " << log(a) << endl;
}
```

Output(s):
```
a = (1,2)
ln(a) = (0.804719,1.107149)
```

Example-8.17: In this example, log10 of a complex number is calculated and displayed.

Code 8.18
```cpp
#include <complex>
#include <iostream>
using namespace std;
int main() {
complex<double> a(2, -3);
cout << "a = " << a << endl;
cout << fixed << "log10(a) = " << log10(a) << endl;
}
```

Output(s):
```
a = (2,-3)
log10(a) = (0.556972,-0.426822)
```

8.8 Complex Power Calculation

The expression x^y can be calculated using the functions

```
complex<T> pow( const complex<T>& x, int y );
```

```
complex<T> pow( const complex<T>& x, const complex<T>& y );
```

```
complex<T> pow( const complex<T>& x, const T& y );
```

```
complex<T> pow( const T& x, const complex<T>& y );
```

Example-8.18: In this example, complex power calculation is illustrated.

Code 8.19

```cpp
#include <complex>
#include <iostream>

using namespace std;

int main() {

    complex<double> a(2, -3);
    complex<double> b(2.5, 4);

    complex<double> r1 = pow(a, 3);
    complex<double> r2 = pow(a, b);
    complex<double> r3 = pow(a, 2.4);
    complex<double> r4 = pow(3.2, a);

    cout << "r1 = " << r1 << endl;
    cout << "r2 = " << r2 << endl;
    cout << "r3 = " << r3 << endl;
    cout << "r4 = " << r4 << endl;
}
```

Output(s):
```
r1 = (-46,-9)
r2 = (-1122.44,568.295)
r3 = (-15.3923,-15.3152)
r4 = (-9.62667,3.49068)
```

8.9 Square root of a complex number

The square root of a complex number can be calculated using the function

```
complex<T> sqrt( const complex<T>& z );
```

Example-8.19: In this example, square root of a complex number is calculated and the result is printed.

Code 8.20

```cpp
#include <complex>
#include <iostream>

using namespace std;

int main() {

complex<double> a(-2, 4);
complex<double> r = sqrt(a)
cout << "a = " << a << endl;
cout << "sqrt(a) = " << r << endl;
}
```

Output(s):
```
a = (-2,4)
sqrt(a) = (1.11179,1.79891)
```

8.10 Complex Trigonometric Functions

The sine, cosine, tangent, arcsine, arccosine, arctangent of complex numbers can be calculated using the fucntions

```cpp
complex<T> sin( const complex<T>& z );
complex<T> cos( const complex<T>& z );
complex<T> tan( const complex<T>& z );
complex<T> asin( const complex<T>& z );
complex<T> acos( const complex<T>& z );
complex<T> atan( const complex<T>& z );
```

Example-8.20: In this example, complex sine, cosine and tangent of a complex number are calculated and the results are printed.

Code 8.21

```cpp
#include <complex>
#include <iostream>

using namespace std;

int main() {

complex<double> a(-2, 4);

complex<double> r1 = sin(a);
complex<double> r2 = cos(a);
complex<double> r3 = tan(a);

cout << "a = " << a << endl;
cout << "sin(a) = " << r1 << endl;
cout << "cos(a) = " << r2 << endl;
cout << "tan(a) = " << r3 << endl;
}
```

Output(s):
a = (-2,4)
sin(a) = (-24.8313,-11.3566)
cos(a) = (-11.3642,24.8147)
tan(a) = (0.000507981,1.00044)

Example-8.21: In this example, complex arcsine, arccosine and arctangent of a complex number are calculated and the results are printed.

Code 8.22

```cpp
#include <complex>
#include <iostream>

using namespace std;

int main() {

complex<double> a(-2, 4);

complex<double> r1 = asin(a);
complex<double> r2 = acos(a);
complex<double> r3 = atan(a);

cout << "a = " << a << endl;
cout << "asin(a) = " << r1 << endl;
cout << "acos(a) = " << r2 << endl;
cout << "atan(a) = " << r3 << endl;
}
```

Output(s):
a = (-2,4)
asin(a) = (-0.45387,2.19857)
acos(a) = (2.02467,-2.19857)
atan(a) = (-1.46705,0.200587)

8.11 Hyperbolic functions

Hyperbolic functions of complex numbers can be calculated using built-in hyperbolic complex function. The hyperbolic sine, hyperbolic cosine, hyperbolic tangent, hyperbolic arcsine, hyperbolic arccosine, hyperbolic arctangent of complex numbers can be calculated using the functions

```
complex<T> sinh( const complex<T>& z );
complex<T> cosh( const complex<T>& z );
complex<T> tanh( const complex<T>& z );
complex<T> asinh( const complex<T>& z );
complex<T> acosh( const complex<T>& z );
complex<T> atanh( const complex<T>& z );
```

Example-8.22: In this example, complex hyperbolic sine, hyperbolic cosine and hyperbolic tangent of a complex number are calculated and the results are printed.

Code 8.23
```
#include <complex>
#include <iostream>

using namespace std;

int main() {

complex<double> a(-2, 4);

complex<double> r1 = sinh(a);
complex<double> r2 = cosh(a);
complex<double> r3 = tanh(a);

cout << "a = " << a << endl;
cout << "sinh(a) = " << r1 << endl;
cout << "cosh(a) = " << r2 << endl;
cout << "tanh(a) = " << r3 << endl;
}
```

Output(s):
```
a = (-2,4)
sinh(a) = (2.37067,-2.84724)
cosh(a) = (-2.45914,2.74482)
tanh(a) = (-1.00468,0.0364234)
```

Example-8.23: In this example, complex hyperbolic arcsine, hyperbolic arccosine and hyperbolic arctangent of a complex number are calculated and the results are printed.

Code 8.24
```
#include <complex>
```

```cpp
#include <iostream>

using namespace std;

int main() {

complex<double> a(-2, 4);

complex<double> r1 = asinh(a);
complex<double> r2 = acosh(a);
complex<double> r3 = atanh(a);

cout << "a = " << a << endl;
cout << "asinh(a) = " << r1 << endl;
cout << "acosh(a) = " << r2 << endl;
cout << "atanh(a) = " << r3 << endl;
}
```

Output(s):
```
a = (-2,4)
asinh(a) = (-2.18359,1.09692)
acosh(a) = (2.19857,2.02467)
atanh(a) = (-0.0964156,1.37154)
```

Problems

1) Which header file should we include in the source code to be able to define the complex numbers?

2) Define a complex number and initialize it to $3 + 4i$, and print it.

3) Fill the inside of cout operator to print the real and imaginary part of the complex number a in Code-8.25.

Code 8.25
```cpp
#include <complex>
#include <iostream>

using namespace std;

int main() {

complex<double> a(-2, 4);

cout << ... ;
}
```

4) Write a program that inputs the real and imaginary parts of a complex number from the user, and calculates its magnitude and displays it.

5) Write a C++ program that calculates, and prints the magnitude and phase of $-7 + 4i$. Phase is printed both in radian and degree units.

6) Write a C++ program that calculates, and prints the sine, cosine, Ln of the complex number $2 - \sqrt{3}\,i$

Chapter-9

Pointers and Dynamic Memory Allocation

Abstract: In this chapter we explain pointers in C++ programming. Pointer is one of the most powerful features in C++. It is the heart and soul of the C++ programming language. Many of the C++ language features and libraries are built using pointers. Pointer variable holds the memory address. Through the pointer, the dereference operator * can be used to access the actual value at a specific memory location.

9.1 Definition

Pointer variables, simply called pointers, are declared to hold memory addresses as their values. Normally, a variable contains a data value—e.g., an integer, a floating-point value, and a character. However, a pointer contains the memory address of a variable that in turn contains a data value.

Pointers are data types which are used to keep the address of memory locations where values of other variables are stored. A pointer variable is defined as

dataType* ptr;

where datatype can be any built-in data types available in C++, such as int, float, double, struct, etc.

9.2 Address of a Variable

The address of a variable can be obtained using the & operator. For instance, the address of variable a in

$$\textbf{int } a = 10;$$

is obtained using &a, and the contend of the address is obtained using the dereferencing operator *, i.e.,

$$\textbf{*address} = \text{content of the address};$$

For instance, if

$$\textbf{int } a = 10;$$

then

$$*(\&a) \text{ equals } 10$$

Example-9.1: In this example, address and dereferencing operators are used together.

Code 9.1
```cpp
#include <iostream>
using namespace std;

int main() {

int a = 10;

cout << "a = " << a << endl;

cout << "&a = " << &a << endl;
}
```

Output(s):
```
a = 10
&a = 0x7ffe4f370914
```

Example-9.2: Integers are 4 byte numbers. In this example, the storage address of an integer is displayed. Little-endian storage type is assumed.

Code 9.2
```cpp
#include <iostream>
using namespace std;
int main() {
int a = 0x1245A78F; // 4-byte integer value
int* ptr = &a;
cout << "a = " << showbase << hex << a << endl;
cout << "&a = " << hex << &a << endl;
cout << "ptr = " << ptr << endl;
}
```

Output(s):
```
a = 0x1245a78f
&a = 0x7ffe405072cc
ptr = 0x7ffe405072cc
```

	Address	Content	
ptr=&a=	0x00007FFE405072CC	0x8F	
	0x00007FFE405072CD	0xA7	a
	0x00007FFE405072CE	0x45	
	0x00007FFE405072CF	0x12	

Figure-9.1 Address and content relations for Example-9.2.

It is seen from the above memory map that address of a or pointer value is the value of memory address where the least significant byte (little-endian) of the integer a is stored.

Example-9.3: Pointer is a data type, its size can be calculated using the sizeof operator.

Code 9.3

```cpp
#include <iostream>
using namespace std;
int main() {
int a = 0x1245A78F;
int* ptr = &a;
cout << "Pointer value: " << ptr << endl;
cout << "Sizeof pointer variable: " << sizeof(ptr) << endl;
}
```

Output(s):

```
Pointer value: 0x7ffd3d8b7cfc
Sizeof pointer variable: 8
```

Example-9.4: Pointed address has content, and the content can be read by dereferencing operator.

Code 9.4

```cpp
#include <iostream>
using namespace std;
int main() {
int a = 0x1245A78F;
int* ptr = &a;
cout << "Address value, ptr = " << ptr << endl;
cout << "Value at adress, *ptr = " << hex << showbase << *ptr;
}
```

Output(s):

```
Address value, ptr = 0x7ffd95831f9c
Value at adress, *ptr = 0x1245a78f
```

	Address	Content	
ptr=	0x00007FFD95831F9C	0x8F	
	0x00007FFD95831F9D	0xA7	a = *ptr
	0x00007FFD95831F9E	0x45	
	0x00007FFD95831F9F	0x12	

Figure-9.2 Address and content relations for Example-9.4.

Example-9.5: Pointer data type is used for addresses, i.e., pointers hold addresses, and these address values are stored in registers which have addresses as well.

Code 9.5

```cpp
#include <iostream>
using namespace std;
int main() {
int a = 0x1245A78F;
int* ptr1 = &a;
int** ptr2 = &ptr1;
cout << "ptr1 = " << ptr1 << endl;
cout << "*ptr1 = " << hex << showbase << *ptr1 << endl << endl;
cout << "ptr2 = " << ptr2 << endl;
cout << "*ptr2 = " << *ptr2 << endl;
}
```

Output(s):

```
ptr1 = 0x7ffdfa15a694
*ptr1 = 0x1245a78f
ptr2 = 0x7ffdfa15a698
*ptr2 = 0x7ffdfa15a694
```

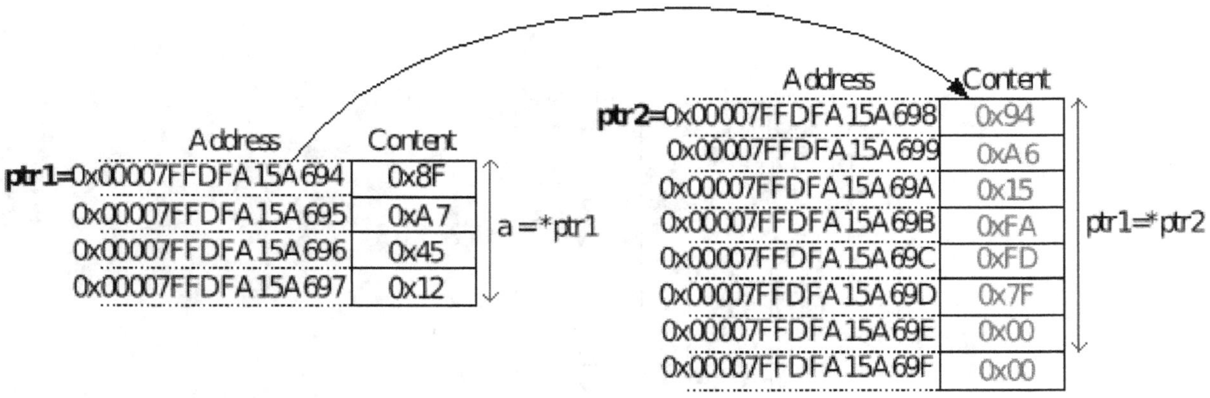

Address	Content
ptr1=0x00007FFDFA15A694	0x8F
0x00007FFDFA15A695	0xA7
0x00007FFDFA15A696	0x45
0x00007FFDFA15A697	0x12

a = *ptr1

Address	Content
ptr2=0x00007FFDFA15A698	0x94
0x00007FFDFA15A699	0xA6
0x00007FFDFA15A69A	0x15
0x00007FFDFA15A69B	0xFA
0x00007FFDFA15A69C	0xFD
0x00007FFDFA15A69D	0x7F
0x00007FFDFA15A69E	0x00
0x00007FFDFA15A69F	0x00

ptr1=*ptr2

Figure-9.3 Visual illustration for Example-9.5.

Example-9.6: A pointer can point to the address of another pointer.

Code 9.6

```cpp
#include <iostream>
using namespace std;

int main() {

int a = 0x1245A78F;

int* ptr1 = &a;
int** ptr2 = &ptr1;
int*** ptr3 = &ptr2;

cout << "ptr1 = " << ptr1 << endl;
```

```cpp
    cout << "ptr2 = " << ptr2 << endl;
    cout << "ptr3 = " << ptr3 << endl;
}
```

Output(s):

ptr1 = 0x7ffdfa15a694

ptr2 = 0x7ffdfa15a698

ptr3 = 0x7ffdfa15a69C

Pointed addresses and stored values are shown in Figure-9.4.

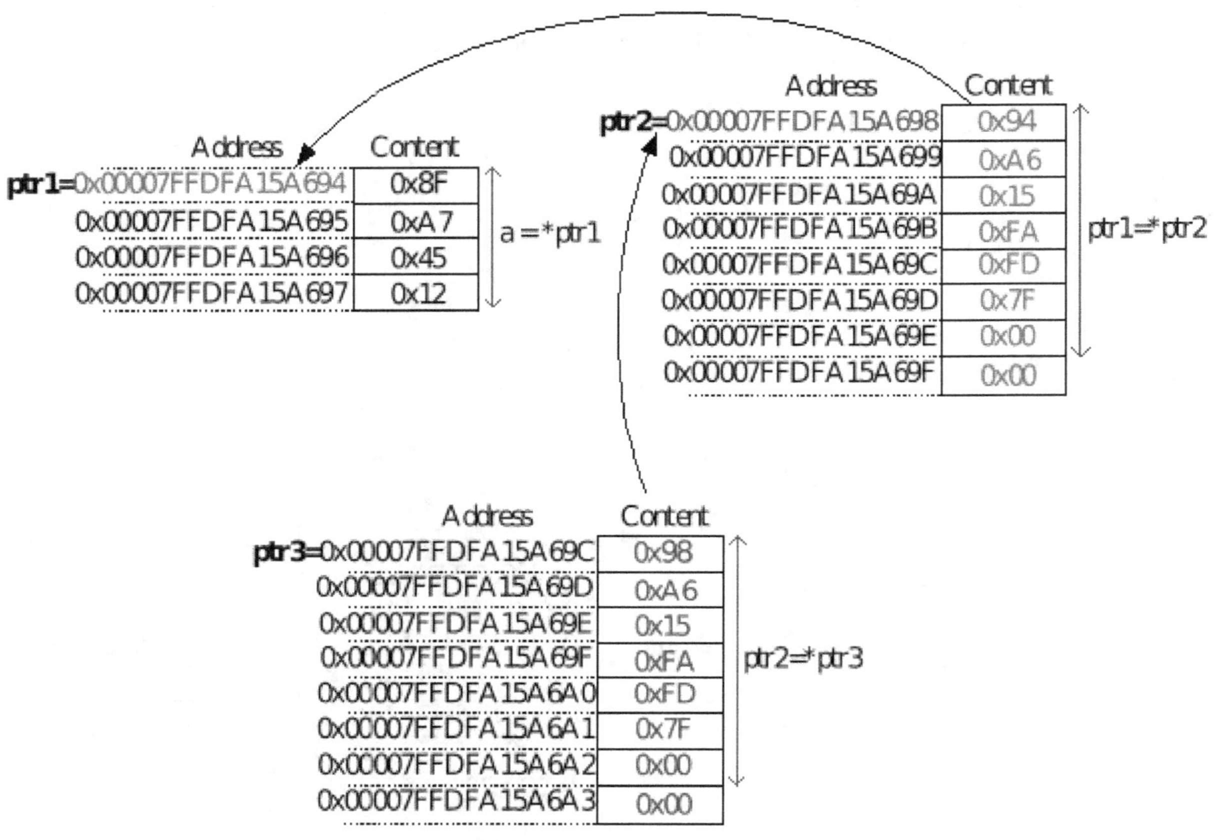

Figure-9.4 Visual illustration for Example-9.6.

Example-9.7: A pointer can point to the address of another pointer.

Code 9.7

```cpp
#include <iostream>
using namespace std;

int main() {

int a = 0x1245A78F;

int* ptr1 = &a;
int** ptr2 = &ptr1;

cout << "Pointer value ptr1 = " << ptr1 << endl;
cout << "Pointer value ptr2 = " << ptr2 << endl;
```

```cpp
cout << "*ptr2 = " << hex << *ptr2 << endl;
}
```

Output(s):

```
Pointer value ptr1 = 0x7ffe81142ea4
Pointer value ptr2 = 0x7ffe81142ea8
*ptr2 = 0x7ffe81142ea4
```

Example-9.8: A pointer can point to the address of another pointer.

Code 9.8

```cpp
#include <iostream>
using namespace std;
int main() {
int a = 0x1245A78F;
int* ptr1 = &a;
long long* ptr2 = (long long*) &ptr1;
cout << "Pointer value ptr1 = " << ptr1 <<endl;
cout << "Pointer value ptr2 = " << ptr2 <<endl;
cout << "*ptr2 = " << hex << showbase << *ptr2 << endl;
}
```

Output(s):

```
Pointer value ptr1 = 0x7ffed514c134
Pointer value ptr2 = 0x7ffed514c138
*ptr2 = 0x7ffed514c134
```

Property

Let

dataType a;

dataType* p=&a

If the value of p is v, then the value of p+1 is

v+sizeof(**dataType**)

Example-9.9: If ptr is a pointer pointing an integer variable, the value of ptr+1 is 4 more than value of ptr.

Code 9.9

```cpp
#include <iostream>
using namespace std;
int main() {
int a = 0x1245A78F;
int* ptr = &a;
cout << "Pointer value ptr = " << ptr <<endl;
cout << "Pointer value ptr+1 = " << ptr+1 <<endl;
}
```

Output(s):

```
Pointer value ptr = 0x7fffd967533c
Pointer value ptr+1 = 0x7fffd9675340
```

Example-9.10: If ptr is a pointer pointing a long long integer variable, the value of ptr+1 is 8 more than value of ptr.

Code 9.10

```cpp
#include <iostream>
using namespace std;
int main() {
long long int a = 0x1245A78F1245A78F;
long long int* ptr = &a;
cout << "Pointer value ptr = " << ptr << endl;
// ptr+1 is 8 more than ptr
cout << "Pointer value ptr+1 = " << ptr+1 << endl;
}
```

Output(s):

Pointer value ptr = 0x7ffd7db581e8

Pointer value ptr+1 = 0x7ffd7db581f0

Example-9.11: If ptr is a pointer pointing a char variable, the value of ptr+1 is 8 more than value of ptr.

Code 9.11

```cpp
#include <iostream>
using namespace std;
int main() {
char a = 'A';
char* ptr = &a;
cout << "Pointer value ptr = " << showbase
<< hex << (long int) ptr << endl;
cout << "Pointer value ptr+1 = " << (long int) ptr+1 << endl;
cout << "Value of *ptr is = " << *ptr << endl;
}
```

Output(s):

Pointer value ptr = 0x7ffcf14f663f

Pointer value ptr+1 = 0x7ffcf14f6640

Value of *ptr is = A

Example-9.12: We can use pointers to change the value of a variable.

Code 9.12

```cpp
#include <iostream>
using namespace std;

int main() {

float a = 4.8;
float* ptr = &a;

*ptr = (*ptr) * 3.8 + 4.7;

cout << "a = " << a << endl;
}
```

Output(s):

a = 22.94

9.3 NULL Pointer

A pointer having no address value is called a NUL pointer. NULL pointers can be obtained assigning NULL value to the pointer. If a pointer is not initialized to NULL value, and it may have an arbitrary value, and it may be dangerous to assign a value to pointer arbitrarily.

Example-9.13: It is better convention to initialize the pointers.

Code 9.13

```cpp
#include <iostream>
using namespace std;
int main() {
int* ptr1;
int* ptr2 = NULL;
cout << "Pointer value ptr1 = " << ptr1 << endl;
cout << "Pointer value ptr2 = " << ptr2 << endl;
}
```

Output(s):

```
Pointer value ptr1 = 0x28ff78
Pointer value ptr2 = 0
```

9.4 Void Pointer

Void pointer is also called generic pointer. Its pointer data type can be changed.

Example-9.14: Size of void pointer can be obtained using the sizeof operator.

Code 9.14

```cpp
#include <iostream>
using namespace std;
int main() {
void* vp = 0; // or void* ip = NULL;
cout <<"sizeof (void*) is " << sizeof(vp) <<endl;
cout <<"vp = " << vp;
}
```

Output(s):

```
sizeof (void*) is 8
vp = 0
```

Example-9.15: Void pointers can point to any variable.

Code 9.15

```cpp
#include <iostream>
using namespace std;
int main() {
int a = 0x12345678;
void* vp = NULL;
cout << "Before assignment\n";
cout << "sizeof (void*) is " << sizeof(vp) <<endl;
cout << "vp = " << vp << endl << endl;
vp = &a;
cout << "After assignment" << endl;
cout << "vp = " << vp << endl;
cout << "sizeof (void*) is " << sizeof(vp);
}
```

Output(s):

```
Before assignment
sizeof (void*) is 8
vp = 0
After assignment
vp = 0x7ffd88eb5e1c
sizeof (void*) is 8
```

Example-9.16: Void pointers can point to any data type, but casting must be used to print the value of the pointed data.

Code 9.16

```cpp
#include <iostream>
using namespace std;
int main() {
int a = 0x12345678;
```

```
void* vp = NULL;
cout << "Before assignment" << endl;
cout << "sizeof (void*) is " << sizeof(vp) << endl;
cout << "vp = " << vp << endl << endl;
vp = &a;
cout << "After assignment" << endl;
cout << "vp = " << vp << endl;
cout << "sizeof (void*) is " << sizeof(vp) << endl << endl;
//cout <<"a = %x", *vp); // gives error
cout << "If casting is used" << endl;
cout << "sizeof (int*) is " << sizeof((int*)vp) << endl;
cout << "vp = " << (int*)vp << endl;
cout << "a = *vp = " << *(int*)vp << endl;
}
```

Output(s):

```
Before assignment
sizeof (void*) is 8
vp = 0
After assignment
vp = 0x7ffc3a154ecc
sizeof (void*) is 8
If casting is used
sizeof (int*) is 8
vp = 0x7ffc3a154ecc
a = *vp = 305419896
```

Example-9.17: The address pointed by void pointer can be changed. Explicit type conversion should be done to print the value of pointed variable.

Code 9.17

```
#include <iostream>
using namespace std;
int main() {
int a = 0x12345678;
char b ='k';
void* vp = NULL;
vp = &a;
cout << "a = *vp = " << hex << showbase << *(int*)vp << endl;
vp = &b;
cout << "b = *vp = " << *(char*)vp << endl;
}
```

Output(s):

```
a = *vp = 0x12345678
b = *vp = k
```

Example-9.18: The default increment amount for void pointer is one, however, when void pointer is converted to any other pointer type, increment amount changes depending on the pointed data type.

Code 9.18

```cpp
#include <iostream>
using namespace std;

int main() {

    int a = 0x12345678;
    void* vp = NULL;
    vp = &a;

    cout << "No casting:" << endl;
    cout << "vp = " << vp << endl;
    cout << "vp+1 = " << vp+1 << endl << endl;

    cout << "If (int*) casting is used:" << endl;
    cout << "vp = " << (int*)vp << endl;
    cout << "vp+1 = " << (int*)vp+1;
}
```

Output(s):

```
No casting:
vp = 0x7ffd7235390c
vp+1 = 0x7ffd7235390d
If (int*) casting is used:
vp = 0x7ffd7235390c
vp+1 = 0x7ffd72353910
```

Example-9.19: Void pointer can be converted to any other pointer type by explicit conversion.

Code 9.19

```cpp
#include <iostream>
using namespace std;
int main() {
int a = 0x12345678;
long long int b = 34.5;
double d = 45.67;
void* vp = NULL;
vp = &a;
cout << "Integer is pointed, No casting:" << endl;
cout << "vp = " << vp << endl;
cout << "vp+1 = " << vp+1 << endl << endl;
cout << "If (int*) casting is used:" << endl;
cout << "vp = " << (int*)vp << endl;
cout << "vp+1 = " << (int*)vp+1 << endl << endl;
vp = &b;
cout << "Long long integer is pointed, No casting:" << endl;
cout << "vp = " << vp << endl;
```

```cpp
cout << "vp+1 = " << vp+1 << endl << endl;
cout << "If (long long int*) casting is used:" << endl;
cout << "vp = " << (long long int*)vp << endl;
cout << "vp+1 = " << (long long int*)vp+1 << endl << endl;
vp = &d;
cout << "Double is pointed, No casting:" << endl;
cout << "vp = " << vp << endl;
cout << "vp+1 = " << vp+1 << endl << endl;
cout << "If (double*) casting is used:" << endl;
cout << "vp = " << (double*)vp << endl;
cout << "vp+1 = " << (double*)vp+1 << endl << endl;
cout << "Sizeof double is " << sizeof(double);
}
```

Output(s):

```
Integer is pointed, No casting:
vp = 0x7ffd6aed3e4c
vp+1 = 0x7ffd6aed3e4d
If (int*) casting is used:
vp = 0x7ffd6aed3e4c
vp+1 = 0x7ffd6aed3e50
Long long integer is pointed, No casting:
vp = 0x7ffd6aed3e50
vp+1 = 0x7ffd6aed3e51
If (long long int*) casting is used:
vp = 0x7ffd6aed3e50
vp+1 = 0x7ffd6aed3e58
Double is pointed, No casting:
vp = 0x7ffd6aed3e58
vp+1 = 0x7ffd6aed3e59
If (double*) casting is used:
vp = 0x7ffd6aed3e58
vp+1 = 0x7ffd6aed3e60
Sizeof double is 8
```

Example-9.20: Using void pointer it is possible to get read value at any memory location.

Code 9.20

```cpp
#include <iostream>
using namespace std;
int main() {
int a = 0x12345678;
void* vp = NULL;
vp = &a;
cout << "Integer is pointed, No casting:" << endl;
cout << "vp = " << vp << endl;
char* cp =(char*)(vp+2);
```

```
cout << "cp = vp+2 = " << hex
<< showbase << (long) cp << endl;
cout << "The value at position vp+2 is ";
cout << "*cp = " << int (*((char*) vp+2)) << endl;
}
```

Output(s):

Integer is pointed, No casting:
vp = 0x000000000065fe0c
cp = vp+2 = 0x000000000065fe0e
The value at position vp+2 is *cp = 0x34

	Address	Content	
vp=&a=	0x000000000065FE0C	0x**78**	
	0x000000000065FE0D	0x56	a
cp=vp+2=	0x000000000065FE0E	0x34	*cp
	0x000000000065FE0F	0x12	

Figure-9.5 Visual illustration for Example-9.19.

9.5 Types of Pointers

9.5.1 Pointer to a Constant Value

A pointer to a constant value is defined as

const dataType* ptr;

The data pointed by the pointer is a constant and its value cannot be changed. The pointer can change the pointed variable, i.e., the pointed address may be changed but the content of the address cannot be changed.

Example-9.21: If address content is constant, it cannot be changed.

Code 9.21

```
int main() {
int a = 45;
int b = 67;
const int* ip = &a; // ok, point to the address of a
*ip = 40; // error, address content cannot be changed
// it is constant
ip = &b; // ok, pointed address can be changed
*ip = 67; // error, address content cannot be changed
}
```

Pointers to constant values are usually employed in function arguments to prevent the accident change of the values used in function calls.

Example-9.22: Function arguments can contain pointers to constant values.

Code 9.22

```
#include <iostream>
using namespace std;

int myFunc(const int* ip) {

int b = *ip+2; // ok

*ip = *ip+2; // error

return b;
}

int main() {

int a = 10, d;

d = myFunc(&a);
}
```

9.5.2 Pointer to a Constant Address (Constant pointer)

The pointer points to a constant memory address, and the value at that address can be changed because it is a variable, but the pointer can only point to the same address and the pointed address cannot be changed. The syntax of the constant pointer is as

dataType* **const** ptr = &varName

Note that initialization has to be performed when constant pointer is declared.

Example-9.23: For constant address pointers, the pointed variable cannot be changed.

Code 9.23

```cpp
#include <iostream>
using namespace std;
int main() {
int a = 45;
int b = 67;
int* const ip = &a; // ok, point to the address of a
*ip = 40; // ok, content can be changed
ip = &b; // error, address is constant, it cannot be changed
}
```

Example-9.24: For constant address pointers, initialization must be done when pointer is defined.

Code 9.24

```cpp
#include <iostream>
using namespace std;
int main() {
int a = 45;
int* const ip; // initialization must be done here
ip = &a; // error, initialization
// should be done in the previous line
}
```

9.5.3 Constant Pointer to a Constant Value

A constant pointer to a constant value is defined as

const dataType* **const** ptr = &varName

Example-9.25: For constant address, constant value pointers, neither pointed address nor content of the address can be changed.

Code 9.25

```cpp
#include <iostream>
using namespace std;
int main() {
int a = 45, b = 67;
const int* const ip = &a; // initialization must be done here
*ip = 98; // error, content can not be changed
ip = &b; // error, address can not be changed
}
```

9.6 Function Pointers

Variables are stored in memory locations and each variable has a memory address, similarly instructions of a function are stored in memory and each function has an address.

The name of an array is a pointer to the head of the memory address where array values are stored. The name of a function is a pointer to the memory address where function instructions are stored.

Example-9.26: Function and array names are also pointers.

Code 9.26

```cpp
#include <iostream>
using namespace std;
void myFnc() {
cout << "Inside function " << endl;
}
int main() {
int a = 34;
int b[3] = {3, 5, 6};
cout << "Address of a: " << &a << endl;
cout << "Address of array b: " << b << endl;
cout << "Address of the myFnc(): " << (void*) myFnc << endl;
cout << "Address of the myFnc(): "
<< (void*) &myFnc << endl; // second method
}
```

Output(s):

```
Address of a: 0x7fff4ab64ed8
Address of array b: 0x7fff4ab64edc
Address of the myFnc(): 0x55a5b30351e9
Address of the myFnc(): 0x55a5b30351e9
```

9.6.1 Syntax of Function Pointer in C

The syntax of the function pointer is

returnedDataType (*PointerName)(argument1, argument2, ...);

For example, for the function declaration

int myFunc(**int, int**);

a function pointer in C can be defined as

float (*fncPointer)(**int, int**);

and function address is assigned to the pointer using either as

fncPointer= myFunc

or as

fncPointer=&myFunc

and the function is called using the function pointer using either as

fncPointer(**intVal1, intVal2**);

or as

(*fncPointer)(**intVal1, intVal2**);

Example-9.27: This example illustrates the use of the function pointers.

Code 9.27

```cpp
#include <iostream>
using namespace std;
int mySum(int a, int b) {
return a+b;
}
int main() {
int a = 34, b = 65, sm;
int (*fp)(int, int); // define a function pointer
fp = mySum; // assign function address to the function pointer,
// alternative assignment is fp=&mySum
sm = fp(a, b); // or use sm = (*fp)(a, b);
cout << "Sum of the integers " << a
<< " and " << b << " is " << sm;
}
```

Output(s):

Sum of the integers 34 and 65 is 99

Example-9.28: Explain the prototype

void* (*func_ptr)(**int ***, **int ***);

We should inspect such statements inside out. Here,

(*func_ptr)(**int ***, **int ***)

is a function pointer taking two inputs which are integer pointers, and the return expression

void*

is a void pointer

Example-9.29: It is possible to define an array of function pointers.

Code 9.28

```cpp
#include <iostream>
using namespace std;
int mySum(int a, int b) { return a+b; }
int mySubt(int a, int b) { return a-b; }
int myMult(int a, int b) { return a*b; }
int main() {
int a = 34, b = 65, sm, df, ml;
int (*fp[3])(int, int); // define an array of function pointers
fp[0] = mySum; //assign mySum address to the function pointer
fp[1] = mySubt; //assign mySubt address to the function pointer
fp[2] = myMult; //assign myMult address to the function pointer
sm = fp[0](a, b);
df = fp[1](a, b);
ml = fp[2](a, b);
cout << "a = " << a << " b = " << b
<< ", a + b = " << sm << endl;
cout << "a = " << a << " b = " << b
<< ", a - b = " << df << endl;
cout << "a = " << a << " b = " << b
<< ", a * b = " << ml << endl;
}
```

Output(s):

```
a = 34 b = 65, a + b = 99
a = 34 b = 65, a - b = - 31
a = 34 b = 65, a * b = 2210
```

Example-9.30: Functions can have function pointers in their arguments, and function names can be passed for function pointers.

Code 9.29

```cpp
#include <iostream>
using namespace std;

void myFunc1() {

cout << "Inside function-1"
<< endl;
}
void myFunc2() {

cout << "Inside function-2"
<< endl;
}

void callFunc(void (*fp)()) {
fp();
```

```cpp
}
int main() {

callFunc(myFunc1);
callFunc(myFunc2);
}
```

Output(s):
Inside function-1
Inside function-2

Example-9.31: In this example we define a function pointer in main function and pass it to a function whose arguments involve a function pointer.

Code 9.30
```cpp
#include <iostream>
using namespace std;

int squaredSum(int a, int b, int (*fp)(int, int)) {

int sqSum;
sqSum = fp(a*a, b*b);

return sqSum;
}

int mySum(int a, int b) {

return a+b;
}

int main() {

int a = 5, b = 4, sm;

int (*fp)(int, int); // define a function pointer

// assign function address to the function pointer,
fp = mySum;

// call the function squaredSum
int res = squaredSum(a, b, mySum);

cout << "Squared sum of the integers "
<< a << " and " << b << " is " << res;
}
```

Output(s):

Squared sum of the integers 5 and 4 is 41.

9.6.1 Functions Returning Pointers

Pointer is a data type, its size is 8. Function can return pointers as returned values.

Example-9.32: Pointer values are addresses, and a function can return an address of a global variable.

Code 9.31

```cpp
#include <iostream>
using namespace std;
int a = 18; // global variable
int* myFunc() {
return (&a);
}
int main() {
int* ptr;
ptr = myFunc();
cout << "Pointed address is " << ptr << endl;
cout << "Value at address is " << *ptr;
}
```

Output(s):

```
Pointed address is 0000000000403010
Value at address is 18
```

Example-9.33: Local variables inside a function are destroyed when function is terminated. Returning local variable addresses creates a problem.

Code 9.32

```cpp
#include <iostream>
using namespace std;
int* myFunc() {
int a = 18; // local variable
return (&a);
// local variables are destroyed, when function is quitted
}
int main() {
int* ptr;
ptr = myFunc();
cout << "Pointed address is " << ptr; // wrong output
cout << "Value at address is " << *ptr; // no output
}
```

Output(s):

```
Pointed address is 0000000000000000
warning: function returns address of local variable [-Wreturn-local-addr]
```

Example-9.34: Functions can be called by pass by value method. In this case, the values in the function arguments can be considered as local variables inside function.

Code 9.33

```cpp
#include <iostream>
using namespace std;
```

```cpp
float* findLarger(float*, float*);
int main() {
float a = 24.6, b = 56.8;
float* larger_num;
larger_num = findLarger(&a, &b);
cout << "Larger of " << a << " and "
<< b << " is " << *larger_num;
}
float* findLarger(float* c, float* d) {
// pass by value is used here
// c and d can be considered as local variables
if (*c > *d) {
return c;
}
else
return d;
}
```

Output(s): Larger of 24.6 and 56.8 is 56.8

9.7 Pointers and Arrays

Pointer and arrays are closely related to each other. Array names can be considered as constant pointers pointing to the first element of the array.

Example-9.35: A string itself indicates a constant address in memory.

Code 9.34
```cpp
#include <iostream>
using namespace std;

int main() {

char* a = "Hello";

cout << "a is " << a << endl;
cout << "&a is " << &a << endl;

cout << "&Constant address is " << &"Hello";
}
```

Output(s):
a is Hello
&a is 0x7ffd859526c0
&Constant address is 0x561ace3da005

In the expression char* a, the letter a indicates an address, and the assigned value should be an address, thus the string "Hello" on the right hand side of char* a="Hello"; is also an address.

The constant on the right hand side of char* a="Hello"; is stored on the code memory.

On the other hand, the pointer variable 'a' is stored on the stack memory.

Example-9.36:

Code 9.35
```cpp
#include <iostream>
using namespace std;
int main() {
char* a = "Hello";
char b[6] = "Hello";
cout << "Size of a is " << sizeof(a) << endl;
cout << "Size of b is " << sizeof(b) << endl;
}
```

Output(s):
warning: ISO C++ forbids converting a string constant to 'char*' [-Wwrite-strings]
Size of a is 8
Size of b is 6

In this example, 'a' is a pointer, its size is 8, and 'b' is an array variable, its size is 6, i.e., it is an array of 6 characters.

Example-9.37:

Code 9.36

```cpp
#include <iostream>
using namespace std;

int main() {

char* a = "Hello";

char b[6] = "Hello";

cout << "Size of a is " << sizeof(a) << endl;
cout << "Size of b is " << sizeof(b) << endl;

cout << "b is " << b << endl;
cout << "&b is " << &b << endl;
cout << "Size of &b is " << sizeof(&b) << endl;
}
```

Output(s):
warning: ISO C++ forbids converting a string constant to 'char*' [-Wwrite-strings]
Size of a is 8
Size of b is 6
b is Hello
&b is 0x7ffef0effc52
Size of &b is 8

In this example, we see the strange sides of C compilers. Although size of b is 6, it can be displayed as pointer. b and &b have the same values. Size of &b is 8.

Example-9.38: Array name is a constant pointer, its value is constant, and it cannot be modified.

Code 9.37

```cpp
#include <iostream>
using namespace std;

int main() {

char* a = "Hello";

char b[6] = "Hello";

cout << "a is " << a << endl; // ok
cout << "++a is " << ++a << endl; // ok

cout << "++b is " << ++b << endl; // error
}
```

Example-9.39: A string can be considered as an address. It cannot be assigned to an array name. Since array name is a constant address, it cannot be changed.

Code 9.38

```cpp
#include <iostream>
using namespace std;

int main() {

char* a = "Hello";
char b[6] = "Hello";

a = "World"; // ok
b = "World"; // error
}
```

Example-9.40: In this example, we explain the differences between a character array and a character pointer initialized with a string.

Code 9.39

```cpp
#include <iostream>
using namespace std;

int main() {

char* a = "Hello";
const char* a1 = "Hello";

char b[6] = "Hello";
char c[6] = {'H','e','l','l','o','\0'};

cout << a <<" " << b << " " << c << endl;

// a[1] = 'A'; // Does not work
b[1] = 'A'; // ok
c[1] = 'A'; // ok

cout << a <<" " << b << " " << c << endl;
}
```

Output(s):
Hello Hello Hello
Hello HAllo HAllo
Differences between **char** a="Hello" and **char** b[]="Hello"

char b[]="Hello";	**char*** a="Hello";
b is a variable name for an array	a is a pointer
sizeof(b) is 6	pointer size is 8
b and &b are the same	a and &a are different
"Hello" is stored in the stack	a is at the stack memory but "Hello" is stored at the code section of memory
b="Hallo" is not valid	a="Hallo" is valid also an address
b is an address and string constant is also an address	a++ is valid
b++ is invalid	a[1]='A' is invalid, code section is read-only memory
b[1]="A" is valid	

Example-9.41: Array names are constant pointers. They can be assigned to non-constant pointers.

```
Code 9.40
#include <iostream>
using namespace std;

int main() {

int a[] = {41, 25, 38, 47, 58} ;
int* ptr = a;

cout << ptr[2] << ", " << *( ptr + 2) ;
}
```

Output(s): 38, 38

Example-9.42: We can use pointers to access array elements.

```
Code 9.41
#include <iostream>
using namespace std;

int main() {

int a[3] = {1, 2, 3};
int* b;
b = a;

cout << "b[0] = " << b[0] << " b[1] = " << b[1]
<< " b[2] = " << b[2];
}
```

Output(s): b[0] = 1 b[1] = 2 b[1] = 3

Example-9.43: Although array name behaves as a pointer, its size depends on the number and types of its elements.

```
Code 9.42
#include <iostream>
using namespace std;

int main() {

int a[] = {3, 4, 5};
int* ip = a;

cout << "Size of a[] is " << sizeof(a) << endl;
cout << "Size of ip is " << sizeof(ip);
}
```

Output(s):
Size of a[] is 12
Size of ip is 8
Example-9.44: Array names behave as constant pointers.

Code 9.43
```cpp
#include <iostream>
using namespace std;

int main() {

int a[] = {3, 4, 5}, b = 23;
int* ip = &b; // ok

a = &b; // error
a = ip; // error
}
```

If **a** is an array name, ptr is a pointer, and ptr=a, array elements can be accessed using one of
$$a[i] \;*(a+i)\; ptr[i] \;*(ptr+i)$$
where i is the index value.

Example-9.45: Array elements can be accessed in different ways.
Code 9.44
```cpp
#include <iostream>
using namespace std;
int main() {
int a[] = {3, 4, 5};
int* ip = a; // ok
cout << "Array elements are " << endl;
cout << "a[0] = " << a[0] << " a[1] = " << a[1]
<< " a[2] = " << a[2] << endl;
cout << "a[0] = " << *a << " a[1] = " << *(a+1)
<< " a[2] = " << *(a+2) << endl;
cout << "a[0] = " << ip[0] << " a[1] = " << ip[1]
<< " a[2] = " << ip[2] << endl;
cout << "a[0] = " << *ip << " a[1] = " << *(ip+1)
<< " a[2] = " << *(ip+2) << endl;
}
```

Output(s):
Array elements are
a[0] = 3 a[1] = 4 a[2] = 5
a[0] = 3 a[1] = 4 a[2] = 5
a[0] = 3 a[1] = 4 a[2] = 5
a[0] = 3 a[1] = 4 a[2] = 5

9.8 Multiple Pointers

It is possible to define a pointer which points to another pointer.

Example-9.46: In this example, we explain the use of multiple pointers.

Code 9.45

```cpp
#include <iostream>
using namespace std;
int main() {
int a = 0xABCD;
int* ip1, ** ip2, *** ip3;
/* int* ip1;
int** ip2;
int*** ip3; */
ip1 = &a;
ip2 = &ip1;
ip3 = &ip2;
cout << "Pointer value ip1 = " << ip1 << endl;
cout << "Pointer value ip2 = " << ip2 << endl;
cout << "Pointer value ip3 = " << ip3 << endl << endl;
cout << "*ip3 = " << *ip3 << endl;
cout << "**ip3 = " << **ip3 << endl;
cout << "***ip3 = " << hex << ***ip3 << endl;
}
```

Output(s):

```
Pointer value ip1 = 000000000065fe14
Pointer value ip2 = 000000000065fe08
Pointer value ip3 = 000000000065fe00
*ip3 = 000000000065fe08
**ip3 = 000000000065fe14
***ip3 = abcd
```

The relationships between addresses are explained in Figure-9.6. For better illustration we used capital letters in Figure-9.6.

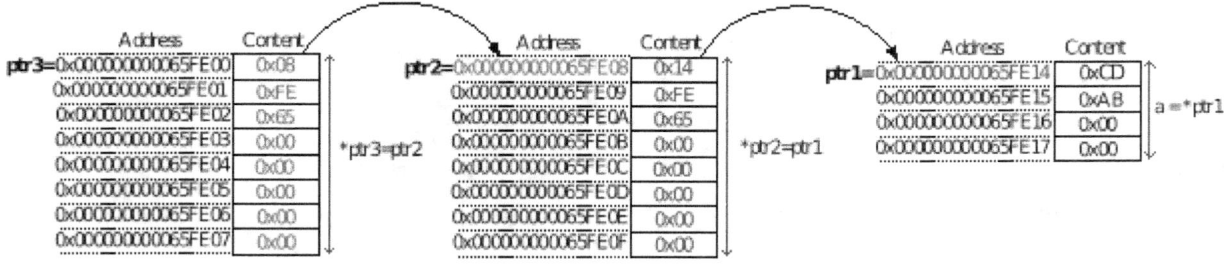

Figure-9.6 Visual illustration Example-9.46

Example-9.47: A pointer pointing to another pointer holds the address of another pointer.

Code 9.46

```cpp
#include <iostream>
```

```cpp
using namespace std;
int main() {
int a = 36;
int* ip1, ** ip2, *** ip3;
ip1 = &a;
ip2 = &ip1;
ip3 = &ip2;
cout << "Pointer value ip1 = " << ip1 << endl;
cout << "Pointer value ip2 = " << ip2 << endl;
cout << "Pointer value ip3 = " << ip3 << endl;
unsigned char* ucp = (unsigned char*) ip3;
cout << showbase;
cout << "ucp = " << hex << (unsigned long) ucp << endl;
cout << "*ucp = " << hex << (unsigned long) *ucp << endl;
ucp++;
cout << "ucp++ = " << hex << (unsigned long) ucp << endl;
cout << "*ucp = " << hex << (unsigned long) *ucp << endl;
ucp++;
cout << "ucp++ = " << hex << (unsigned long) ucp << endl;
cout << "*ucp++ = " << hex << (unsigned long) *ucp << endl;
}
```

Output(s):

```
Pointer value ip1 = 0x7ffc34c67c14
Pointer value ip2 = 0x7ffc34c67c18
Pointer value ip3 = 0x7ffc34c67c20
ucp = 0x7ffc34c67c20
*ucp = 0x18
ucp++ = 0x7ffc34c67c21
*ucp = 0x7c
ucp++ = 0x7ffc34c67c22
*ucp++ = 0xc6
```

Exercise: Draw the memory maps for this example, and show the relationships between pointers.

9.9 Heap Stack and Code Memories

The variables, functions, instruction codes, and dynamically created variables are stored at different parts of the memory. In Figure-9.7, different parts of the memory and their relations to code parameters are explained.

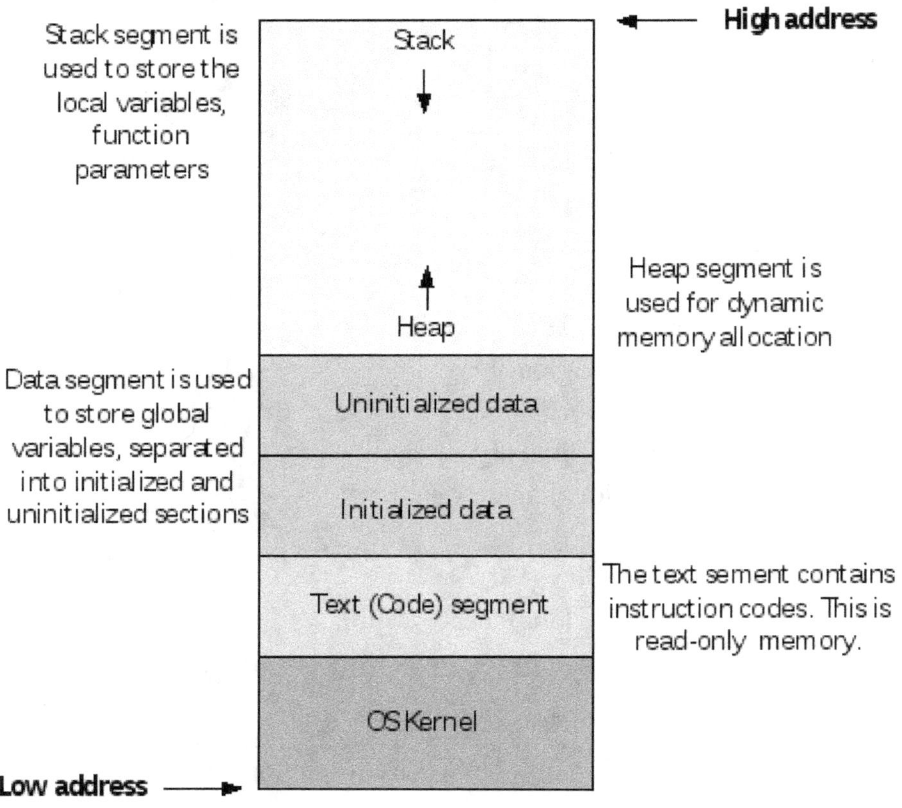

Figure-9.7 Heap stack and code memories.

In the sample code in Figure-9.8, it is illustrated that dynamic allocation is performed in the heap section of the program memory.

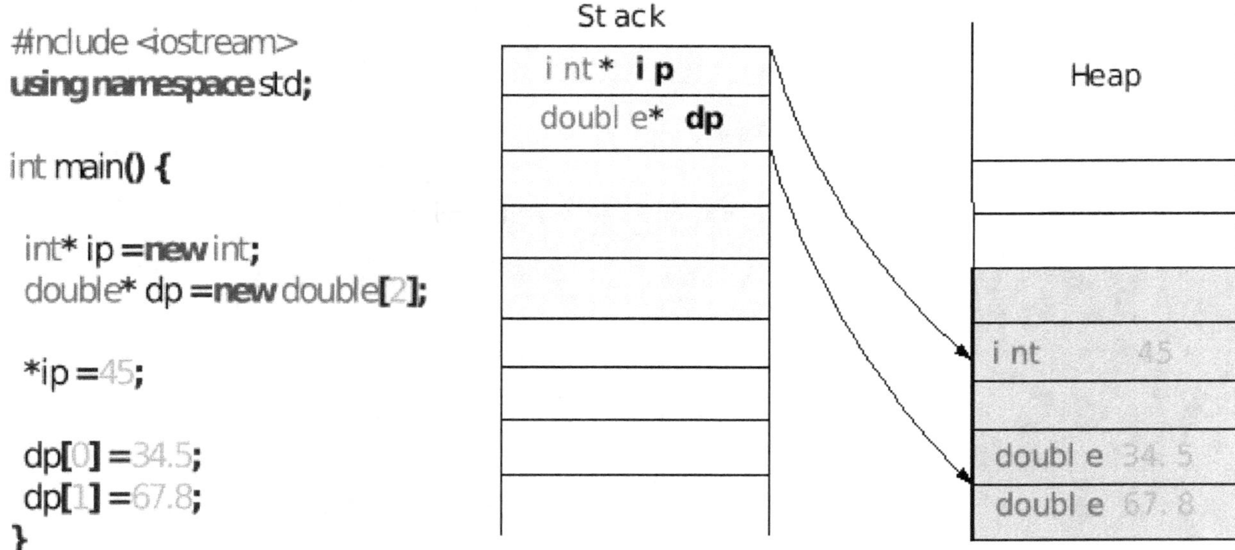

Figure-9.8 Dynamic memory allocation.

Example-9.48: In Code-9.47, all these variables are stored on stack

```
Code 9.47
int main() {

int a;
int b[6];
int c = 34;
double d = 4.5;
float e;
int* p;
}
```

Example-9.49: In Code-9.48, memory allocation is performed for 5 double numbers on the heap.

```
Code 9.48
int main() {
  double* dp = new double[5];
}
```

9.10 Dynamic Memory Allocation in C++

New operator is used to dynamically allocate memory, and the starting address of the allocated memory is assigned to a pointer. To delete the allocated memory we use the delete operator. The new operator is used for single memory location as

```
ptr = new dataType; // not initialized
ptr = new dataType(value); //initialized
```

and it is used for array allocation as

```
ptr = new dataType[N]; // not initialized
ptr = new dataType[N] {val1, val2,..., valN}; //initialized
```

The allocated memory is be freed using the delete operator, and the delete operato is used as

```
delete ptr;
delete [] ptr;
```

Example-9.50: Pointers can be assigned to NULL before they are used for new operator.

Code 9.49
```
#include <iostream>
using namespace std;

int main() {
int* ptr = NULL;
ptr = new int; // ptr = new int()
// ptr = new int{}
*ptr = 5;
cout << ptr[0] << ", ";
cout << *ptr;
}
```

Output(s): 5, 5
Example-9.51:

Code 9.50
```
#include <iostream>
using namespace std;

int main() {

int* ptr1 = new int; // ptr = new int{}
int* ptr2 = new int (5); // initialize to 5
int* ptr3 = new int {6}; // dinitialize to 5
```

```cpp
cout << ptr1[0] << ", ";
cout << ptr2[0] << ", ";
cout << *ptr3;
}
```

Output(s): 0, 5, 6

Example-9.52:

Code 9.51
```cpp
#include <iostream>
using namespace std;

int main() {

int* ptr = new int [4] {7, 8};

cout << ptr[0] << ", " << ptr[1] << ", "
<< ptr[2] << ", " << ptr[3] << endl;
}
```

Output(s): 7, 8, 0, 0

Example-9.53:

Code 9.52
```cpp
#include <iostream>
using namespace std;

int main() {

int* ptr = new int [4];

ptr[0] = 7;
ptr[1] = 8;

cout << ptr[0] << ", " << ptr[1] << ", "
<< ptr[2] << ", " << ptr[3] << endl;
}
```

Output(s): 7, 8, 0, 0

9.11 Nothrow Statement

If sufficient memory is not available in the heap memory to allocate, bad_alloc exception is thrown. To prevent the exception thrown, nothrow keyword can be used with new operator. In this case, NULL is returned if sufficient memory is not available.

Example-9.54:

Code 9.53

```cpp
#include <iostream>
using namespace std;
int main() {
int* ptr = new(nothrow) int [4] {7, 8};
if (!ptr) { // ptr == nullptr
cout << "There is no sufficient memory to allocate";
} else {
cout << "Memory allocation is sufficient";
}
}
```

Output(s): Memory allocation is sufficient

9.12 Delete Operator

The allocated memory is can be deleted using the delete operator. If a single memory location is deleted, the delete operator is used as

$$\textbf{delete } ptr;$$

to delete a block of memory location we use the delete operator as

$$\textbf{delete } [] \text{ } ptr;$$

Example-9.55:

Code 9.54
```cpp
#include <iostream>
using namespace std;

int main() {

int* ptr1 = new int {3};
int* ptr2 = new int[4] {7, 8};

delete ptr1;
delete [] ptr2;
}
```

Example-9.56:

Code 9.55
```cpp
#include <iostream>
using namespace std;
int main() {
int* ptr = new int {3};
cout << "Before deallocation " << "*ptr = " << *ptr << endl;
delete ptr;
cout << "After deallocation " << "*ptr = " << *ptr;
}
```
Output(s):
```
Before deallocation *ptr = 3
After deallocation *ptr = 1486295505
```
Example-9.57:

Code 9.56
```cpp
#include <iostream>
using namespace std;

int main() {

int size = 4;
// cin >> size;
int* list = new int[size];
```

```cpp
    list[0] = 4;
    list[1] = 5;
    list[2] = 13;
    list[3] = 34;

    cout << list[0] << endl;

    delete[] list; // cancel reservation

    cout << list[0] << endl;
  }
```

Output(s):

4
1672236518

Example-9.58:

Code 9.57
```cpp
  #include <iostream>
  using namespace std;

  int main() {

  int size = 4;
  // cin >> size;
  int* a = new int[size];

    a[0] = 4;
    a[1] = 5;
    a[2] = 13;
    a[3] = 34;

    a[12] = 12; // ?? Can it be
    a[194] = 16; // ?? Can it be

    cout << a[0] << ", ";
    cout << a[9] << ", ";
    cout << a[12] << ", ";
    cout << a[33] << ", ";
    cout << a[7] << ", ";
    cout << a[194] << endl;
  }
```

Output(s):

4, 0, 12, 0, 0, 16
4, 0, 12, 6881476, 6881476, 16

Example-9.59:

Code 9.58

```cpp
#include <iostream>
using namespace std;

int main() {

int* list = new int[4];

list[0] = 4; list[1] = 5;
list[2] = 6; list[3] = 7;

cout << list[0] << endl;
delete[] list; // cancel reservation

cout << list[0] << endl;
list[0] = 45;
cout << list[0] << endl;
}
```

Output(s):

```
4
1661530792
45
```

Example-9.60:

Code 9.59

```cpp
#include <iostream>
using namespace std;
int main() {
int* a = new int(56); // reserve memory
cout << "Address is: " << a << endl;
cout << "Number is: " << *a << endl;
*a = 234;
cout << "Address is: " << a << endl;
cout << "Number is: " << *a << endl << endl;
delete a; // cancel reservation
cout << "After deletion, address is: " << a << endl;
cout << "After deletion, number is: " << *a << endl;
*a = 87;
cout << "After deletion, address is: " << a << endl;
cout << "After deletion, number is: " << *a << endl;
}
```

Output(s):

Address is: 0x55baaad3ceb0
Number is: 56
Address is: 0x55baaad3ceb0
Number is: 234
After deletion, address is: 0x55baaad3ceb0
After deletion, number is: 1537912124
After deletion, address is: 0x55baaad3ceb0
After deletion, number is: 87

9.13 Creating and Accessing Dynamic Objects

To create an object dynamically, we invoke the constructor for the object using the syntax

new className(arguments);

We can also create objects dynamically on the heap using the syntax

className* ptr = **new** className(); **or**

className* ptr = **new** className;

where default constructor is called. To create an object using the no-arg constructor and assigns the object address to the pointer we use the syntax

className* ptr = **new** className(arguments); **or**

className* ptr = **new** className{arguments};

Example-9.61:

Code 9.60

```cpp
#include <iostream>
using namespace std;

class A {

public:
float x, y;

A(float a = 0, float b = 0) { x = a; y = b;}

void disp() {
cout << "x is " << x << endl;
cout << "y is " << y << endl;
}
};
int main() {

A* ptr1 = new A; // A* ptr1 = new A{};
// default constructor is called

A* ptr2 = new A(2); // A* ptr3 = new A{2};
A* ptr3 = new A[3];

A* ptr4 = new A[2] { A(9, 6), A(7, 8) };
ptr4[1].disp();

delete ptr1;
delete ptr2;
delete [] ptr3;
delete [] ptr4;
}
```

Output(s):

x is 7

y is 8

Example-9.62: In this example, we allocate memory location for two integers and explain the allocated regions.

Code 9.61

```cpp
#include <iostream>
#include <iostream>
using namespace std;

int main() {

int* ip;

ip = new int [2];

if (ip == NULL) {

cout << "Memory allocation failed.";
exit(0);
}
else {
cout << "Memory allocation is successful.";
}

}
```

Output(s):

Memory allocation is successful.

ip = 00000000001E1400

Figure-9.9 Visual illustration for Example-9.50.

When memory allocation is performed using malloc() function, a number of consecutive memory locations are reserved for storage.

This can be considered as reserving a number of tables in a restaurant. However, this does not mean that non-reserved tables can be used. If they are free they can be used. However, there is no guarantee that free tables are available.

9.14 Swallow and Deep Copy

In this section we explain swallow and deep copy in C++. Swallow copy occurs when default copy constructor is used, and swallow copy can created programming bugs. Deep copy can be achieved if copy constructor is manually written by the programmer.

Example-9.63: This example illustrates the swallow copy issue.

Code 9.62

```cpp
#include <iostream>
using namespace std;
class A {
public:
double* d;
A() : d ( new double(10) ) {}
~A() { delete d; }
void setX(double a) { *d = a; }
void dispData() { cout << " Data is: " << *d << endl; }
};
int main() {
A obj1;
A obj2(obj1);
// Default Copy constructor works here
// obj2.d=obj1.d pointers point to the same address
obj2.setX(23);
obj1.setX(65);
obj2.dispData(); // Displays 65, since both object pointers
// points to the same address
}
```

Example-9.64: We prevent the bug in the previous example writing the copy constructor manually, and in this way we achieve deep copy operation.

Code 9.63

```cpp
#include <iostream>
using namespace std;
class A {
public:
double* d;
A() : d ( new double(10) ) { }
A(const A& obj) : d( new double(*obj.d)) { }
~A() { delete d; }
void setX(double a) { *d = a; }
void dispData() { cout << " Data is: " << *d << endl; }
};
int main() {
A obj1;
A obj2(obj1); // copy constructor
obj2.setX(23);
obj1.setX(65);
obj2.dispData(); // Displays 23, since both object pointers
// points to the different addresses
}
```

Example-9.65: In this example, memory allocation is performed for two integers. The **new** function returns a pointer to the head of the allocated block.

Code 9.64

```cpp
#include <iostream>
using namespace std;
int main() {
int* ptr;
ptr = new int[2];
if (ptr == NULL) {
cout << "Memory allocation failed.";
exit(0);
}
else {
cout << "Memory allocation is successful." << endl;
cout << "ptr = " << ptr << endl;
cout << "ptr[0] = " << ptr[0] << endl; // reserved
// may have arbitrary value
cout << "ptr[1] = " << ptr[1] << endl; // reserved
// may have arbitrary value
cout << "ptr[2] = " << ptr[2] << endl;
cout << "ptr[3] = " << ptr[3] << endl;
cout << "ptr[4] = " << ptr[4] << endl;
cout << "ptr[5] = " << ptr[5] << endl;
}
```

```
}
```

Output(s):

Memory allocation is successful.

ptr = 0x55f6ab1b5eb0

ptr[0] = 0

ptr[1] = 0

ptr[2] = 0

ptr[3] = 0

ptr[4] = 0

ptr[5] = 0

In this example, 'ip' holds the address of the head of the allocated block, and, ip+3, ip+4 are the addresses of the consecutive locations, but they are not reserved, however, these locations may also be accessible. They hold arbitrary values.

Output(s):

Memory allocation is successful.

ip = 0000000000A21400

ip[0] = A261F0

ip[1] = 0

ip[2] = A20150

ip[3] = 0

ip[4] = 454B5F49

ip[5] = 6F6E3D59

Example-9.66: In this example, we dynamically allocate memory and write values to allocated addresses. Besides, we also try to write values for non-allocated addresses.

Code 9.65

```cpp
#include <iostream>
using namespace std;
int main() {
int* ptr;
ptr = new int[2];
if (ptr == NULL) {
cout << "Memory allocation failed.";
exit(0);
}
else {
cout << "Memory allocation is successful." << endl;
cout << "ptr = " << ptr << endl;
ptr[0] = 0x34; // ok, reseved location
ptr[1] = 0x23456789; // ok, reseved location
ptr[2] = 0xABCD3456; // may give error, non-reseved location
ptr[3] = 0x6783DEFA; // may give error, non-reseved location
cout << "ptr[0] = " << hex << ptr[0] << endl;
cout << "ptr[1] = " << hex << ptr[1] << endl;
cout << "ptr[2] = " << hex << ptr[2] << endl;
cout << "ptr[3] = " << hex << ptr[3] << endl;
}
}
```

Output(s):

```
Memory allocation is successful.
ptr = 0x55a6fa6e0eb0
ptr[0] = 34
ptr[1] = 23456789
ptr[2] = abcd3456
ptr[3] = 6783defa
```

9.15 Smart Pointers

In this section, we explain smart pointers which are introduced in C++11 standard. There are three smart pointer types and these are unique, shared and weak pointers.

9.15.1 unique_ptr

A unique_ptr cannot be copied to another unique_ptr and it can be passed by value to a function. A unique_ptr can only be moved. Moving a unique_ptr means that the ownership of the memory resource is transferred to another unique_ptr and the original unique_ptr no longer owns it.

The unique_ptr can be defined in different ways. Let's explain these methods.

Method-1:

First define a classical pointer as in

$$\text{int* ptr} = \textbf{new}\ \text{int } \{5\};$$

then replace int* by unique_ptr<int> and do casting in front of new operator, i.e.,

$$\text{unique\_ptr<int> ptr} = (\text{unique\_ptr<int>})\ \textbf{new}\ \text{int } \{5\};$$

Method-2:

In second method, we use the syntax

$$\text{unique\_ptr<className> objectName } (\textbf{new}\ \text{className(...)});$$

to define the pointer, and methods of the class are accessed as

$$\text{objectName -> methodName()};$$

Example-9.67:

$$\text{unique\_ptr<int> ptr } (\ \textbf{new}\ \text{int } \{5\}\ );\ //\ \textbf{ok}$$

We get error, if we define the pointer with = sign as in

$$\text{unique\_ptr<int> ptr} = \textbf{new}\ \text{int } \{5\}\ ;\ //\ \textbf{error}$$

Example-9.68: Assume that A is a class with a constructor A(int, int), then we can define a unique pointer to this class as

$$\text{unique\_ptr<A> ptr } (\ \textbf{new}\ \text{A } (4, 5)\ );$$

Example-9.69:

Code 9.66

```cpp
#include <iostream>
#include <memory>
using namespace std;
int main() {
int* ptr1 = new int {5}; // (5) also ok
int* ptr2 = ptr1; // ok
int* ptr3 = new int {8};
unique_ptr<int> ptr4 = (unique_ptr<int>) new int {11};
cout << "*ptr4 = " << *ptr4 << endl;
unique_ptr<int> ptr5 = ptr4; // error
unique_ptr<int> ptr6 ( new int {14} );
cout << "*ptr6 = " << *ptr6 << endl;
unique_ptr<int> ptr7 = ( new int {5} ); // error
unique_ptr<int> ptr8 = new int {5}; // error
unique_ptr<int> ptr9 = make_unique<int> (17); // ok
unique_ptr<int> ptr9 = make_unique<int> {17} // error
// { } is not allowed
cout << "*ptr9 = " << *ptr9 << endl;
}
```

9.15.2 Moving Unique Pointer

It is possible to use the move() function with unique pointers. Using move() function we can copy the address of pointer to another pointer.

Example-9.70:

Code 9.67
```cpp
#include <iostream>
#include <memory>
using namespace std;

int main() {

int* ptr1 = new int {5};
int* ptr2 = nullptr;

cout << "Before move, ptr1 = " << ptr1 <<", "
<< "ptr2 = " << ptr2 << endl;

ptr2 = move(ptr1); // ok

cout << "After move, ptr1 = " << ptr1 <<", "
<< "ptr2 = " << ptr2 << endl
<< "*ptr2 = " << *ptr2 << endl;
}
```

Output(s):
Before move, ptr1 = 0x560d9eaf7eb0, ptr2 = 0
After move, ptr1 = 0x560d9eaf7eb0, ptr2 = 0x560d9eaf7eb0

Code 9.68
```cpp
#include <iostream>
#include <memory>
using namespace std;

int main() {

unique_ptr<int> ptr1(new int {5});
unique_ptr<int> ptr2(nullptr);

cout << "Before move, ptr1 = " << ptr1 <<", "
<< "ptr2 = " << ptr2 << endl;

ptr2 = move(ptr1); // ok

cout << "After move, ptr1 = " << ptr1 <<", "
<< "ptr2 = " << ptr2 << endl;
}
```

Output(s):

Before move, ptr1 = 0x558e39c9ceb0, ptr2 = 0
After move, ptr1 = 0, ptr2 = 0x558e39c9ceb0

9.15.3 Unique Pointer with Deleter

Deleter, which can be function object or lvalue reference to function or to function object, is called from the destructor.

Example-9.71:

Code 9.69

```cpp
#include <iostream>
#include <memory>
using namespace std;
void myDeleter(int* p) {
cout << "Inside myDeleter \n";
delete p;
}
int main() {
unique_ptr<int, decltype(&myDeleter)> ptr(new int(3), myDeleter);
ptr.reset();
cout << "Raw pointer size: " << sizeof (int*) << endl;
cout << "unique_ptr with deleter size: " << sizeof (ptr) << endl;
cout << "Unique pointer address after reset: " << ptr << endl;
}
```

Output(s):

```
Inside myDeleter
Raw pointer size: 8
unique_ptr with deleter size: 16
Unique pointer address after reset: 0
```

Example-9.72: We can use the keyword **auto** for delete functions.

Code 9.70

```cpp
#include <iostream>
#include <memory>
using namespace std;
auto myDeleter = [](int* ptr){
cout << "Inside myDeleter \n";
delete ptr;
};
int main() {
unique_ptr<int, decltype(myDeleter)> ptr (new int{5}, myDeleter);
ptr.reset();
}
```

Output(s):

```
Inside myDeleter
```

9.15.4 Release

Release function is used to leaver the ownership of the address and give it to another pointer.

Example-9.73:

Code 9.71

```cpp
#include <iostream>

using namespace std;

int main() {

unique_ptr<int> ptr1(new int {5});
int* ptr2;

cout << "Before release, ptr1 = " << ptr1 <<", "
<< "ptr2 = " << ptr2 << endl;

ptr2 = ptr1.release();

cout << "After release, ptr1 = " << ptr1 <<", "
<< "ptr2 = " << ptr2 << endl;
}
```

Output(s):
Before release, ptr1 = 0x55c5b7ce8eb0, ptr2 = 0
After release, ptr1 = 0, ptr2 = 0x55c5b7ce8eb0

9.15.5 Unique Pointer with Class Objects

Unique pointers can be used with class objects.

Example-9.74: This example illustrates the use of the unique pointer with a class object.

Code 9.72

```cpp
#include<iostream>
#include<memory>
using namespace std;
class A {
public:
int x;
A(int a = 0) : x(a) {
cout << "Inside Constructor-A, x = " << x << endl;
}
~A() {
cout << "Inside Destructor-A, x = " << x << endl;
}
};
int main() {
{
A* obj1 = new A(4);
}
{
// unique_ptr<A> obj2 = make_unique<A>(5);
unique_ptr<A> obj2(new A(5));
}
}
```

Output(s):

```
Inside Constructor-A, x = 4
Inside Constructor-A, x = 5
Inside Destructor-A, x = 5
```

Example-9.75:

Code 9.73

```cpp
#include<iostream>
#include<memory>
using namespace std;
class A {
public:
A() {
cout << "Inside default-constructor-A " << endl;
}
A(const A&) { cout << "Inside copy-constructor-A"; }
~A() {
cout << "Inside Destructor-A " << endl;
}
};
class D { // deleter
public:
D() {
cout << "Inside default-constructor-D" << endl;
}
D(const D&) {
cout << "Inside copy-constructor-D" << endl;
}
void operator()(A* ptr) const {
cout << "Deleter is deleting a A " << endl;
delete ptr;
};
};
int main() {
D d;
unique_ptr<A, D> ptr(new A, d);
}
```

Output(s):

```
Inside default-constructor-D
Inside default-constructor-A
Inside copy-constructor-D
Deleter is deleting a A
Inside Destructor-A
```

If we remove the delete statement in the delete function, i.e., if the delete function is written as in

```
void operator()(A* ptr) const {
cout << "Deleter is deleting a A " << endl;
};
```

then the output becomes as

```
Inside default-constructor-D
Inside default-constructor-A
Inside copy-constructor-D
Deleter is deleting a A
```

That is, destructor of the class A is not called.

9.15.6 Member Functions

Unique pointer objects have **reset** and **swap** member functions. In this section, we explain the use of these functions by examples.

Reset Function

The prototype of the reset function is as

$$\text{void reset(pointer ptr = pointer()) noexcept;}$$

Using reset function we can change the ownership of the pointer or cancel it totally.

Example-9.76:

Code 9.74

```cpp
#include <iostream>
#include <memory>
using namespace std;
class A {
public:
int x;
A(int a = 0 ) : x(a) {
cout << "Inside constructor-A, x = " << x << endl;
}
~A() {
cout << "Inside destructor-A, x = " << x << endl;
}
};
class D {
public:
int y;
D(int b = 0) : y(b) {}
void operator() (A* p) {
cout << "Inside deleter-A, x = " << p -> x;
cout << ", y = " << y << endl;
delete p;
}
};
int main() {
unique_ptr<A, D> obj(new A(1), D(1));
obj.reset(new A(2)); // Replace old object
// with a new object of A
// calls deleter for the old object
obj.reset(nullptr); // Release the current object and delete it
}
```

Output(s):

Inside constructor-A, x = 1

Inside constructor-A, x = 2

```
Inside deleter-A, x = 1, y = 1
Inside destructor-A, x = 1
Inside deleter-A, x = 2, y = 1
Inside destructor-A, x = 2
```

Swap Function

The prototype of the swap function is as

$$\text{void swap(unique\_ptr\& other) noexcept;}$$

This function swaps the objects and their deleters.

Example-9.77:

Code 9.75

```cpp
#include <iostream>
#include <memory>
using namespace std;
class A {
public:
int x;
A(int a = 0 ) : x(a) {
cout << "Inside constructor-A, x = " << x << endl;
}
A(const A&) { cout << "Inside copy-constructor-A"; }
~A() {
cout << "Inside destructor-A, x = " << x << endl;
}
};
class D {
public:
int y;
D(int b = 0) : y(b) {}
void operator() (A* p) {
cout << "Inside deleter-A, x = " << p -> x;
cout << ", y = " << y << endl;
delete p;
}
};
int main() {
unique_ptr<A, D> ptr1(new A(1), D(2));
unique_ptr<A, D> ptr2(new A(3), D(4));
cout << "Before swap " << endl;
cout << "ptr1 -> x = " << ptr1 -> x << endl;
cout << "ptr2 -> x = " << ptr2 -> x << endl << endl;
swap(ptr1, ptr2);
cout << "After swap " << endl;
cout << "ptr1 -> x = " << ptr1 -> x << endl;
cout << "ptr2 -> x = " << ptr2 -> x << endl << endl;
```

```
ptr1.reset();
ptr2.reset();
}
```

Output(s):

```
Inside constructor-A, x = 1
Inside constructor-A, x = 3
Before swap
ptr1 -> x = 1
ptr2 -> x = 3
After swap
ptr1 -> x = 3
ptr2 -> x = 1
Inside deleter-A, x = 3, y = 4
Inside destructor-A, x = 3
Inside deleter-A, x = 1, y = 2
Inside destructor-A, x = 1
```

9.15.7 Logical Comparison with Unique Pointers

Logical operators can be used with unique pointers.

Example-9.78:

Code 9.76

```cpp
#include <iostream>
#include <memory>
using namespace std;
class A {
public:
A( ){ }
~A(){ }
};
class D { // deleter
public:
void operator() (A* p) {
delete p;
}
};
int main() {
unique_ptr<A, D> ptr1(new A(), D());
unique_ptr<A, D> ptr2(new A(), D());
// ptr1 and ptr2 point to different memory locations,
// so ptr1 != ptr2
cout << "(ptr1 == ptr1) : " << (ptr1 == ptr1) << endl;
cout << "(ptr1 == ptr2) : " << (ptr1 == ptr2) << endl;
cout << "(ptr1 < ptr2) : " << (ptr1 < ptr2) << endl;
cout << "(ptr1 > ptr2) : " << (ptr1 > ptr2) << endl;
}
```

Output(s):

```
(ptr1 == ptr1) : 1
(ptr1 == ptr2) : 0
(ptr1 < ptr2) : 1
(ptr1 > ptr2) : 0
```

9.16 Three-way Comparison Operator in C++ 20

The three-way comparison operator "<=>" is called a spaceship operator. The spaceship operator determines for two objects A and B whether A < B, A = B, or A > B.

The prototype of the operator is as

operator<=>(const unique_ptr<T1, D1>& x, const unique_ptr<T2, D2>& y);

Traditionally, strcmp() is such a function. Given two strings it will return an integer where,

< 0 means the first string is less

== 0 if both are equal

> 0 if the first string is greater.

(A <=> B) < 0 is true if A < B

(A <=> B) > 0 is true if A > B

(A <=> B) == 0 is true if A and B are equal/equivalent.

Example-9.79:

Code 9.77

```cpp
#include <compare>
#include <iostream>
using namespace std;

int main() {
int x = 10;
int y = 20;

// 3 way comparison operator
auto r = x <=> y;

if (r < 0)
cout << "x < y";
else if (r > 0)
cout << "x > y";
else if (r == 0)
cout << "x == y";
else
cout << "Not comparable";
}
```

Output(s): x < y

The three-way comparison operator can also be used for objects.

9.17 Shared Pointer

The shared pointer keeps a counter which is incremented when another shared pointer points to the same object, and when the counter value is equal to zero, the object is destroyed.

Example-9.80:

Code 9.78

```cpp
#include <iostream>
#include <memory>
using namespace std;
class A {
private:
int x;
public:
A(int a = 0) : x(a) {}
void disp() {
cout << "Inside disp(), x = " << x << endl;
}
};
int main() {
shared_ptr<A> ptr1(new A(3));
cout << ptr1 << endl;
ptr1->disp();
shared_ptr<A> ptr2 = ptr1; // or use ptr2(ptr1)
ptr2->disp();
cout << ptr1 << endl;
cout << ptr2 << endl;
cout << "ptr1.use_count: " << ptr1.use_count() << endl;
cout << "ptr2.use_count: " << ptr2.use_count() << endl;
ptr1.reset(); // number of objects pointing to the same address
// is decremented
cout << "ptr1: " << ptr1 << endl;
cout << "ptr2.use_count: " << ptr2.use_count() << endl;
cout << "ptr2: " << ptr2 << endl;
}
```

Output(s):

```
0x559713fdeeb0
Inside disp(), x = 3
Inside disp(), x = 3
0x559713fdeeb0
0x559713fdeeb0
ptr1.use_count: 2
ptr2.use_count: 2
ptr1: 0
```

ptr2.use_count: 1
ptr2: 0x559713fdeeb0

9.18 Weak Pointer

A weak pointer has non-owning reference to an object managed by a shared pointer. Unlike a shared pointer, when a weak pointer points to shared address, the reference count is not incremented, that is it does not affect the lifetime of the object. A weak pointer can access the managed object of a shared pointer without extending its lifetime. A weak pointer can be used to check if the object still exists before attempting to access it.

The lock method of a weak pointer returns a shared pointer to the managed object if it still exists; otherwise it returns an empty shared pointer. The expired method of the weak pointer can be used to check whether the managed object is deleted or not.

Example-9.81:

Code 9.79

```cpp
#include <iostream>
#include <memory>
using namespace std;
int main(){
auto s_ptr {make_shared<int>(19)};
weak_ptr<int> w_ptr{s_ptr};
cout << "Count: " << s_ptr.use_count() << endl;
cout << "Count: " << w_ptr.use_count() << endl;
w_ptr.reset();
cout << "Count: " << s_ptr.use_count() << endl;
cout << "Count: " << w_ptr.use_count() << endl;
}
```

Output(s):

```
Count: 1
Count: 1
Count: 1
Count: 0
```

Example-9.82:

Code 9.80

```cpp
#include <iostream>
#include <memory>
using namespace std;
int main() {
shared_ptr<int> s_ptr1(new int(19));
weak_ptr<int> w_ptr(s_ptr1);
cout << "Count : " << w_ptr.use_count() << endl;
shared_ptr<int> s_ptr2(s_ptr1);
cout << "Count : " << w_ptr.use_count() << endl;
shared_ptr<int> s_ptr3(s_ptr1);
cout << "Count : " << w_ptr.use_count() << endl;
```

```cpp
w_ptr.reset();
cout << "Count : " << w_ptr.use_count() << endl;
cout << "Count : " << s_ptr1.use_count() << endl;
}
```

Output(s):

Count : 1

Count : 2

Count : 3

Count : 0

Count : 3

Problems

1) An integer variable is defined as

$$\text{int } a = 56;$$

Print the address value of this variable.

2) What is the output of Code-9.81?

Code 9.81
```cpp
#include <iostream>

using namespace std;

int main() {

int a = 56;

cout << "a = " << *(&a);
}
```

3) What is the output of Code-9.82?

Code 9.82
```cpp
#include <iostream>

using namespace std;

void myFunc(float*);

int main() {

float a = 4.8;
myFunc(&a);

cout <<"a = " << a;
}

void myFunc(float* fp) {
*fp = 7.9;
}
```

4) What is the output of Code-9.83?

Code 9.83
```cpp
#include <iostream>

using namespace std;

int main() {
```

```cpp
float a = 3.4;
float* fp = &a;

*fp += 2.3;

cout <<"a = " << a << endl;
cout <<"*fp = " << *fp;
}
```

5) Run the code in Code-9.84, and by drawing on a paper show how integer value is stored in memory.

Code 9.84
```cpp
#include <iostream>

using namespace std;

int main() {

int a = 0xACDEF9D4; // 4-byte integer value

int* ptr = &a;

cout << "Value of a is = " << a << endl;

cout << "Address of a is = " << &a << endl;;

cout << "Pointer value is = " << ptr << endl;
}
```

6) Assume that you have a pointer ptr pointing to an integer variable. If the value of pointer ptr is 0, then what is the value of ptr+1?

7) What is the size of a pointer variable?

8) What is the output of Code-9.85?

Code 9.85
```cpp
#include <iostream>
using namespace std;
int main() {
int myArray[] = {1, 2, 3, 4, 5, 6, 7, 8};
int *ptr1 = myArray;
int *ptr2 = myArray + 3;
cout << "Number of integers between two adresses are: "
<< ptr2 - ptr1 << endl;
cout << "Number of bytes between two adresses are: "
<< (char*)ptr2 - (char*) ptr1 << endl;
}
```

9) What is the output of Code-9.86?

Code 9.86

```cpp
#include <iostream>

using namespace std;

int main() {

int a;

char* cp;

cp = (char*) &a;

a = 0xAAAABBBB;

cp[0] = 0xDD;

cp[1] = 0xEE;

cout << hex << a;
}
```

10) Find the error in Code-9.87.

Code 9.87

```cpp
int main() {

int a = 67;

int b = 89;

const int* ip=&a;

*ip = 40;

ip = &b;

*ip = 67;
}
```

10) Find the error in Code-9.88.

Code 9.88

```cpp
void myFunc(const int* ip){

*ip = *ip+2;
}

int main() {
```

```cpp
int a = 10;

myFunc(&a);
}
```

11) Find the error in Code-9.89.

Code 9.89
```cpp
int main() {

int a = 45;

int* const ip;

ip = &a;
}
```

12) Find the error in Code-9.90.

Code 9.90
```cpp
#include <iostream>
using namespace std;
int main() {
float myArray[5] = {16.5, 70.6, 56.5, 36.4, 56.5};
float* fp = myArray;
fp = fp +2;
cout << "*fp = " << *fp;
}
```

13) What is the difference between heap and stack memory?

14) What is the output of Code-9.91?

Code 9.91
```cpp
#include <iostream>

using namespace std;

void myFunc(int** ptr) {
**ptr = 35;
}

int main() {

int a = 10, *ptr1, **ptr2;

ptr1 = &a;

ptr2 = &ptr1;
```

```
    myFunc(ptr2);

    cout << "a = " << a;
    }
```

Chapter-10

Directives and Macros in C++

Abstract: In this chapter we explain the use of directives and macros in C++ programming. Directives and macros are preprocessed units of C++ programs. They are expanded in C++ program to form the final version of the C++ program before compilation operation. Both built-in macros served from compiler's library and the ones written by code developer can be used inside the C++ program.

10.1 Introduction

The program lines that start with has symbol, #, are called directives, and directives are processed with a built-in program called preprocessor, where the prefix -pre- implies that preprocessors process codes before compilation. A directive has syntax

$$\#...$$

When the symbol # is met inside the code, the preprocessor replaces the corresponding directive with a code, and we get a code without # symbol, then the compiler compiles the code. The operation of directives is illustrated in Figure-10.1.

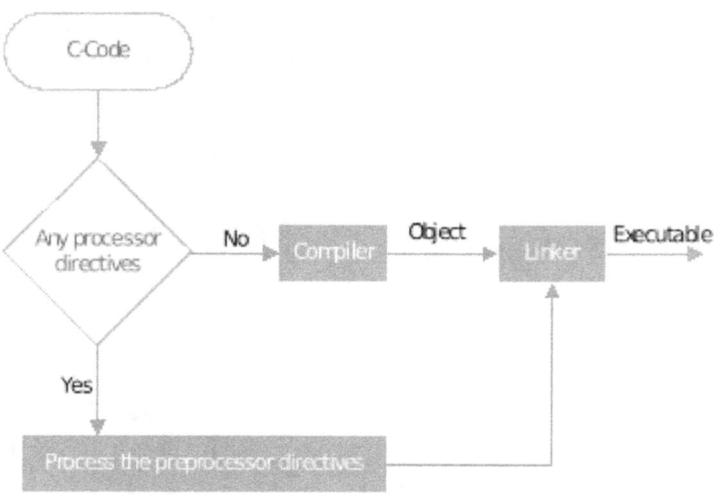

Figure-10.1 Macros are preprocessed.

We use preprocessor directives for

> writing macros
> for file Inclusion
> for conditional compilation

10.2 Preprocessor Directives as Macros

A macro is defined using the syntax

#define macroName macroValue

and after preprocessing, the macroName will be replaced by macroValue in the program whenever it is met.

Example-10.1: We define to macros called myInteger and myFloat.

Code 10.1
```cpp
#include <iostream>
using namespace std;

#define myInteger 12
#define myFloat 45.8

int main() {

cout << "myInteger = " << myInteger << endl;

double r = myInteger + myFloat;

cout << "r = " << r << endl;
}
```

Output(s):
```
myInteger = 12
r = 57.8
```

Example-10.2: The mathematical number π can be defined as macro and it can be used to calculate the area of a circle.

Code 10.2
```cpp
#include <iostream>
using namespace std;
#define PI 3.14
int main() {
int r;
cout << "Please enter radius of the circle: ";
cin >> r;
float a = PI * (r*r); // area of a circle
cout << "Circle are is " << a;
}
```

Output(s):
```
Please enter radius of the circle :4
Circle are is 50.24
```

10.3 Macros as Functions

Although a macro can perform a similar task to a function, they are completely different things. Macros are pre-processed before all the program is compiled. On the other hand, functions are compiled, they are NOT pre-processed.

Example-10.3: In Code-10.3 we define a macro which acts as a function.

```cpp
Code 10.3
#include <iostream>
using namespace std;

#define macFnc(a, b) (a < b ? a+b : a-b )

int main() {

int a = 6, b = 8;

cout << "result = " << macFnc(a, b);
}
```

Output(s): result = 14

Example-10.4: In this example, we calculate the discriminant of a second order mathematical equation using macro.

```cpp
Code 10.4
#include <iostream>
using namespace std;
#define macFnc(a, b, c) ((b)*(b)-4*(a)*(c)) /(2*(a))
int main() {
int a = 1, b = -5, c = 4;
cout << "result = " << macFnc(a, b, c);
}
```

Output(s): result = 4

Example-10.5: In this example, the area of a circle is calculated using a macro.

```cpp
Code 10.5
#include <iostream>
using namespace std;

#define PI 3.1415
#define circleArea(r) (PI*r*r)

int main() {

float r, a;

cout << "Please enter radius of the circle: ";
```

```cpp
cin >> r;

a = circleArea(r);

cout << "Circle are is " << a;
}
```

Output(s):

Please enter radius of the circle: 4
Circle are is 50.26

10.4 Multiline Macros

We can write multiline macros by placing "\" to the end of each line.

Example-10.6: In multiline macros, at the end of each line there is "\n".

Code 10.6

```cpp
#include <iostream>
using namespace std;
#define DISP(start, N)\
for(int indx = start; indx < N; indx++) \
{\
cout << "Hello World!\n";\
}
int main() {
DISP(0, 3);
}
```

Output(s):

```
Hello World!
Hello World!
Hello World!
```

Example-10.7: In the previous example, macro is called by some inputs. In this example, macro is called by just its name.

Code 10.7

```cpp
#include <iostream>
using namespace std;

#define disp {\
cout << "Hello World!\n";\
cout << "Hello World!";\
cout << "\n";\
}

int main() {

disp;
}
```

Output(s):

```
Hello World!
Hello World!
```

Example-10.8: Macro is expanded into code before compilation.

Code 10.8

```cpp
#include <iostream>
using namespace std;
```

```cpp
#define disp {\
cout << "Hello World!\n";\
cout << "Hello World!";\
cout << "\n";\
}

int main() {

if (1)
disp;
else
cout << "Macro is not called";
}
```

When this program is run, we get error: 'else' without a previous 'if'

Note that preprocessor expands the macros into the code, and then Code-10.8 happens to be as in Code-10.9 which is an erroneous code.

Code 10.9

```cpp
#include <iostream>
using namespace std;

int main() {
if (1)
cout << "Hello World!\n";
cout << "Hello World!";
cout << "\n";
else
cout << "Macro is not called";
}
```

To overcome this bottle neck, we can use curly parenthesis in if-else statement as in Code-10.10.

Code 10.10

```cpp
#include <iostream>
using namespace std;

#define disp {\
cout << "Hello World!\n";\
cout << "Hello World!";\
cout << "\n";\
}
int main() {

if (1) { // <—-
```

```
disp;

} // <—-
else
cout << "Macro is not called \n";
}
```

When the macro is expanded we get the error free Code-10.11.

Code 10.11
```
#include <iostream>
using namespace std;

int main() {

if (1) {

cout << "Hello World!\n";
cout << Hello World!";
cout << "\n";
}
else
cout << "Macro is not called \n";
}
```

Expansion of macro is illustrated in Figure-10.2.

```
#include <iostream>
using namespace std;

#define disp {\
            cout << "Hello World!\n";\
            cout << "Hello World!";\
            cout << "\n";\
        }

int main() {

  if (1) {
    disp;
  }
  else
    cout << "Macro is not called";
}
```

```
#include <iostream>
using namespace std;

int main() {

  if (1) {

    cout << "Hello World!\n";
    cout << Hello World!";
    cout << "\n";
  }
  else
    cout << "Macro is not called \n";
}
```

Figure-10.2 Macro is expanded into the code before compilation.

Identifiers are simple macros which do not contain programming statements.

10.5 Directives Used for File Inclusion

The preprocessor directive **#include** is used to include the header files. To include the header files in compiler's library we use the directive

#include <fileName.h>

and to include the user developed header files we use the directive

#include "fileName.h"

where we assume that the header file stays in the same folder as the source file, otherwise we should write the path of the header file, i.e., we use the directive as

#include "C:/.../ .../fileName.h"

Example-10.9: We have a header file with name myFile.h

```
// "myFile.h"

// content of myFile.h

#define PI 3.1415
#define circleArea(r) (PI*r*r)

#include <stdio.h>
#include "myFile.h"
```

and we include this header file in our course code

Code 10.12
```cpp
#include <iostream>
#include "myFile.h"

using namespace std;

int main() {

float r, a;

cout << "Please enter radius of the circle: ";

cin >> r;

a = circleArea(r);

cout << "Circle area is: " << a;
}
```

Output(s):
Please enter radius of the circle :4
Circle are is 50.26

10.6 Predefined Macros

Compilers have some predefined macros available in their libraries. These macros can be used directly in a C++ program. Let's see some of these macros.

__LINE__

This is a predefined macro that expands to the current line number in the C++ program as an integer. __LINE__ is used for log statements, for clarifying the error location of in a code, and for debugging code.

Example-10.10: In this example, the use of the predefined macro __LINE__ is illustrated.

Code 10.13
```
1 #include <iostream>
2
3 using namespace std;
4
5 int main() {
6
7 cout << "Line number is " << __LINE__;
8 }
```
Output(s): Line number is: 7

Code 10.14
```
1 #include <iostream>
2
3 using namespace std;
4
5 int main() {
6
7 //
8 //
9 cout << "Line number is " << __LINE__;
10 }
```

Output(s): Line number is 9

__FILE__

It expands to the file name of the current program running.

Example-10.11: In this example, the use of the predefined macro __FILE__ is illustrated.

Code 10.15
```
#include <iostream>

using namespace std;

int main() {
```

```
cout << "File name is " << __FILE__;
}
```

Output(s): File name is main.cpp

__DATE__

It is expanded to the compilation date of the program, and the date is in the format "month dd yyyy".

Example-10.12: In this example, the use of the predefined macro __DATE__ is illustrated.

Code 10.16
```
#include <iostream>

using namespace std;

int main() {

cout << "Compilation date is " << __DATE__;
}
```

Output(s): Compilation date is Nov 30 2023

__TIME__

It is expanded to the compilation time of the program, and the time is in the format hour:minute:second.

Example-10.13: In this example, the use of the predefined macro __TIME__ is illustrated.

Code 10.17
```
#include <iostream>

using namespace std;

int main() {

cout << "Compilation time is " << __TIME__;
}
```

Output(s): Compilation time is 18:25:11

Identifiers are simple macros which do not contain programming statements.

__func__

If this predefined identifier is inside a function, it is replaced by the name of the function, otherwise if it is inside the main function; it is replaced by the word "main".

Example-10.14: In this example, the use of the predefined macro __func__ is illustrated.

Code 10.18
```
#include <iostream>

using namespace std;

void myFunc() {

cout << __func__;
```

```
  }

int main() {

cout << __func__ << " ";
myFunc();
  }
```

Output(s): main myFunc

__cplusplus__

This directive can be used to identify whether the current compiler is a cpp compiler or not.

Example-10.15: In this example, the use of the predefined macro __cplusplus__ is illustrated.

Code 10.19
```
#include <iostream>

using namespace std;

int main() {

#ifdef __cplusplus
cout << "CPP is supported";
#else
cout << "CPP is NOT supported";
#endif
  }
```

Output(s): CPP is supported

10.7 Conditional Compilation

Conditional compilation directives are used to compile a specific part of the program and skip the rest. Conditional compilation is achieved using the directives

    #if conditionalExpression

    #ifdef identifier

    #ifndef identifier

    #elif conditionalExpression

    #elifdef identifier

    #elifndef identifier

    #else

    #endif

The syntax of #ifdef...#endif pair for conditional compilation is given in Code-10.20.

Code 10.20
```
#ifdef identifier
// statements
// to be compiled
#endif
```

If identifier is defined, then the code inside is compiled.

In a similar manner, we can use of #ifndef...#endif pair for conditional compilation, its syntax is shown in Code-10.21.

Code 10.21
```
#ifndef identifier
// statements
// to be compiled
#endif
```

In this case, If identifier is **NOT** defined, then the code inside is compiled.
Example-10.16: In this example, we define the macro P1 directly.

Code 10.22
```
#include <iostream>

using namespace std;
```

#define P1

int main() {

```
#ifdef P1
cout << "P1 is defined" << endl;
cout << "P1 has no value";
#else
cout << "P1 is NOT defined" << endl;
#endif
}
```

Output(s):
P1 is defined
P1 has no value

Example-10.17: In this example, we define the macro P1 inside a conditional expression.

Code 10.23

```cpp
#include <iostream>

using namespace std;

#ifndef P1
#define P1
#endif

int main() {

#ifdef P1
cout << "P1 is defined" << endl;
cout << "P1 has no value";
#else
cout << "P1 is NOT defined" << endl;
#endif
}
```

Output(s):
P1 is defined
P1 has no value

Example-10.18: The Code-10.22 can also be written as Code-10.24.

Code 10.24

```cpp
#include <iostream>

using namespace std;

#define P1

int main() {

#if defined P1
cout << "P1 is defined " << endl;
cout << "P1 has no value";
#else
cout << "P1 is NOT defined";
#endif
}
```

Output(s):
P1 is defined
P1 has no value

Example-10.19: A value different than 0 is accepted as true.

Code 10.25
```cpp
#include <iostream>

using namespace std;

#define P1 45.8

int main() {

#ifdef P1
cout << "P1 is defined" << endl;
cout << "P1 = " << P1;
#else
cout << "P1 is NOT defined";
#endif
}
```

Output(s):
P1 is defined
P1 = 45.8

Example-10.20: A macro previously defined can be undefined.

Code 10.26
```cpp
#include <iostream>

using namespace std;

#define P1 45.8
#undef P1

int main() {

#ifdef P1
cout << "P1 is defined" << endl;
cout << "P1 = " << P1;
#else
cout << "P1 is NOT defined";
#endif
}
```

Output(s): P1 is NOT defined

Example-10.21: In this example, the use of macros in a conditional ladder structure is illustrated.

Code 10.27

```cpp
#include <iostream>

using namespace std;

#define P1
#define P2

int main() {

#ifdef P1
#define VAL_A 16
cout << "P1 is defined" << endl;
cout << "VAL_A is now defined";
#elif defined P2
#define VAL_B 34
cout << "P2 is defined" << endl;
cout << "VAL_B is now defined";
#else
#define VAL_C 34
cout << "P1, P2 are NOT defined" << endl;
cout << "VAL_C is defined";
#endif
}
```

Output(s):

```
P1 is defined.
VAL_A is now defined.
```

Example-10.22: We use #undef macro in this example.

Code 10.28

```cpp
#include <iostream>

using namespace std;

#define P1
#define P2
#undef P1

int main() {

#ifdef P1
#define VAL_A 16
cout << "P1 is defined" << endl;
cout << "VAL_A is now defined";
#elif defined P2
```

```cpp
#define VAL_B 34
cout << "P2 is defined" << endl;
cout << "VAL_B is now defined";
#else
#define VAL_C 34
cout << "P1, P2 are NOT defined" << endl;
cout << "VAL_C is defined";
#endif
}
```

Output(s):
P2 is defined
VAL_B is now defined.

10.8 Concatenation Operator

The operator ## is used to concatenate macro arguments. It is also called either token pasting operator, or merging operator.

Syntax: #define macroName(p1, p2) p1##p2

Example-10.23: In this example, we concatenated two integers 12 and 96 using a macro.

Code 10.29

```cpp
#include <iostream>

using namespace std;

#define myConcat(a, b) a##b

int main() {

int a = myConcat(12, 96);

cout << "a = " << a;
}
```

output(s): a = 1296

Problems

1) In C++ programming, if a macro, which is not previously defined, appears inside an expression its value is accepted as zero. However, it is still undefined Considering this fact what the output of Code-10.30.

```cpp
Code 10.30
#include <iostream>
using namespace std;
#if M1 == 0
#define M2 6
#else
#define M2 8
#endif


int main() {
    cout << "M1 = " << M2;
    //cout << "M1 = " << M1; // gives error, it is still undefined
}
```

2) While Code-10.31 is ok, Code-10.32 gives error. Explain the reasoning behind this error.

```cpp
Code 10.31
#include <iostream>
using namespace std;

#define X \
cout << "Hello World";

int main() {
X;
}
```

```cpp
Code 10.32
#include <iostream>
using namespace std;

#define X 5

#if X \
cout << "Hello World";
#endif

int main(){
X;
}
```

3) What is the output of Code-10.33?

Code 10.33

```cpp
#include <iostream>
using namespace std;

#define cube(a) (a)*(a)*(a)

int main() {

float b = 64.0 / (cube(8));

cout << b;
}
```

4) There is a big difference between

$$\text{\#define cube(a) (a)*(a)*(a)}$$

and

$$\text{\#define cube(a) a*a*a}$$

Give an example which shows this difference.

5) Convert the function in Code-10.34 to a Macro.

Code 10.34

```cpp
void disp() {

cout << Hello World!" << endl;
}
```

Chapter-11

Type Qualifiers, Enumerations, and Storage Classes in C++

Abstract: In this chapter we explain type qualifiers, enumerations and storage classes in C++ programming. The primary type qualifiers are **const, restrict** and **volatile**. Storage classes are **auto, extern, static** and **register**. The keywords **restrict, volatile** and **register** are especially important for hardware programmers, whereas the keywords **const, auto** and **extern** are of equal importance for every C++ programmer.

11.1 Type Qualifiers in C

The type qualifiers used in C programming are

const restrict volatile

11.1.1 const

A type qualifier is used to add additional attributes to a variable. For instance, in the definition

double num;

num is the variable name, the data type used by the variable is a double data. If we use **const** qualifier for the variable num, we get

const double num;

and in this case the data type used by the variable is still a double data but its value cannot be changed, i.e., the variable has an additional property.

The type qualifier **const** can be used with pointers. In this case, the one to the right of **const** has constant value and cannot be changed.

Example-11.1:

```
float num = 3.4;

const float* fp = &num;
```

in the pointer expression, to the right of **const** there is data type **float**, this shows that data value is constant.

Example-11.2:

```
float num = 3.4;

float* const fp = &num;
```

in the pointer expression, to the right of **const** there is pointer variable **fp**, this shows that pointer value is constant. It means the pointer cannot point to another variable, i.e., the pointer address cannot be changed.

Example-11.3: Constant data pointed by a pointer cannot be changed.

Code 11.1
```cpp
#include <iostream>
using namespace std;

int main() {

int a = 13;

const int* ptr = &a;

*ptr = 54; // error, value cannot be changed
}
```

Output(s): error: assignment of read-only location '*ptr'

Example-11.4: The address of a constant pointer cannot be changed.

Code 11.2

```cpp
#include <iostream>
using namespace std;
int main() {
int a = 23, b = 49;
int *const ptr = &a;
ptr = &b; //error, pointer address cannot be changed
}
```

Output(s): error: assignment of read-only variable 'ptr'

11.1.2 restrict

This keyword is useful for engineers working on embedded systems. This qualifier is used to optimize the performance of the compiler for memory access. The value pointed by restrict pointer is held in a register, i.e., catched, and during intermediate operations catched value is used.

A pointer having restrict qualifier indicates that a particular region of memory should be accessed by one pointer and never another. If a pointer is defined to be restrict and it points to a variable and then accesses to the variable happens by another pointer, then undefined behavior may happen.

Example-11.5:

Code 11.3

```
void myFnc(int* ptra, int* ptrb, int* ptrc) {
*ptra += *ptrc;
// *ptrc is read from memory, and *ptra += *ptrc is performed
*ptrb += *ptrc;
// *ptrc is read from memory, and *ptrb += *ptrc is performed
}
```

In Code-11.3, four instructions are performed. Let's use the restrict keyword for the pointers as in Code-11.4.

Code 11.4

```
void myFnc(int* ptra, int* ptrb, int* restrict ptrc) {
*ptra += *ptrc;
// *ptrc is read from memory, and *ptra += *ptrc is performed
*ptrb += *ptrc;
// *ptrb += *ptrc is performed
}
```

Due to the use of restrict keyword in Code-11.4, three instructions are performed. One less instruction is needed compared to Code-11.3.

11.1.3 volatile

This qualifier is useful especially for embedded software engineers or hardware programming engineers. The volatile keyword is used to take attention of the compiler to the variables whose values can change instantly, and the compiler avoids optimization techniques which can cause the miss of detection of instant changes of variables.

For instance, a global variable representing a data port can receive a value whenever an interrupt occurs, and in this case the global variable which is used for the data port should be declared as volatile in order to catch the latest data available at the port. Electronic devices utilizing touch sensors should process every input immediately.

If the variable is not qualified as volatile, the compiler applies optimization methods to speed up the program execution, and when the port is read, it is placed into a catch, i.e., register, and the catched, value is used for some time as port value, the port is not read every time, and when the catch time expires the port value is updated with the new input if there is. Besides, in multi-thread applications shared global variables should be qualified as volatile due to a similar reasoning as in the case of hardware interrupts.

In summary, if a variable is qualified as volatile, then compiler does not do optimization for that variable.

```
volatile int a;
```

11.2 Storage Classes in C++

The keywords used to classify storage method in C are

auto extern static register mutable

11.2.1 Auto

Auto is used for default storage, and most time, it is not explicitly used.

Example-11.6:

auto int a;

is the same as

int a;

11.2.2 Extern

To understand the role of keyword **extern**, let's explain what declaration and definition mean.

Declaration

Declaration of a variable or function is nothing but making compiler aware of the existence of a variable or a function. That means giving pre-information to the compiler about a variable or a function. Function declaration involves function name, input arguments and returned data type. Memory is not allocated for variable or function. It is similar to calling a restaurant and making them aware of you for a potential customer, but a reservation is not made for you. To declare a variable, we use the keyword **extern**.

Definition

When a variable or function is defined memory is automatically allocated for variable or function. It is similar to calling a restaurant and reserving a table for your dinner.

Example-11.7: A declaration is made in

```
extern float a;
```

Example-11.8: A function declaration is made in

```
float myFunc(float, double);
```

or

```
float myFunc(float a, double d);
```

Example-11.9: A definition is made in

```
float a;
```

Example-11.10: A function definition is made in

```
float myFunc(float a, float b) {

return a*b;

}
```

Example-11.11: A declaration and a definition is made in

```
extern float a =20.45;
```

Here, we inform the compiler that the variable a can be used in another file.

Example-11.12: Declaration is made for variable 'a' in Code-11.5, and 'a' is defined in Code-11.6

Code 11.5

```cpp
// file name is : main.cpp

#include <iostream>
using namespace std;

extern float a;

int main() {
```

```
cout << "a = " << a;
}
```

Code 11.6
```
// file name is variables.cpp

float a = 23.56;
```

When these two files are compiled in a project, we get the output a = 23.56

Example-11.13: If we write a header file, variables.h, and include it in our code, then it is not necessary to declare the variable using the keyword extern.

Code 11.7
```
// file name is : main.cpp

#include <iostream>
#include "variables.h"

using namespace std;

// no need for extern declaration
// extern float a;

 int main() {

 cout << "a = " << a;
 }
```

Code 11.8
```
// file name is variables.h

float a = 23.56;
```

Example-11.14: In this example, we have three separate files. The file main.cpp contains two extern declarations.

Code 11.9
```
// main.cpp
 #include <iostream>
 using namespace std;

 extern float a;
 extern void myFunc();

 int main() {

 cout << "Inside main, a = " << a << endl;

 myFunc();
 }
```

The file variables.cpp contains definition for the variable **a**.

Code 11.10
```
// variables.cpp

float a = 23.56;
```

The file functions.cpp contains the declaration n for the variable **a**.

Code 11.11
```
// functions.cpp

#include <iostream>
using namespace std;

extern float a;

void myFunc() {

cout << "Inside function, a = " << a << endl;
}
```

When these three files are compiled in a project, we get the output
Inside main, a = 23.56
Inside function, a = 23.56
Let's remove the extern declaration from functions.cpp as in Code-11.12.

Code 11.12
```
// functions.cpp
#include <iostream>
using namespace std;
void myFunc() {
cout << "Inside function, a = " << a << endl;
}
```
When we now compile three files, we get the output
functions.cpp:10:38: error: 'a' was not declared in this scope
That is, we get an error.

11.2.3 Static

Static variables preserve their last values until the main program terminates. A static value needs to be initialized at its declaration. A static variable is defined as

$$static\ dataType\ variable\_name = value;$$

Example-11.15: The last value of a static variable is kept, and this property is very useful in function calls.

Code 11.13

```cpp
#include <iostream>
using namespace std;

void myFunc() {

static int a = 10;

a++;

cout << "Inside function, a = " << a << endl;
}

int main() {

myFunc();
myFunc();
myFunc();
}
```

Output(s):
Inside function, a = 11
Inside function, a = 12
Inside function, a = 13

11.2.4 register

The most frequently used variables can be attributed with register keyword. When a variable is defined as register variable the compiler tries to store the variable in special registers and these registers are accessed in a fast manner compared to stack memory. We can define a register variable as

$$\text{register float } a = 4.7;$$

The register variables are stored in the memory by the compiler if there are no free registers available.

The address of a register variable in C cannot be read, since the registers do not have an address. However, this restriction is removed in C++, the register keyword was deprecated in the C++11 standard. The keyword is unused and reserved. It remains reserved for future use by the standard since C++17.

Mutable

If an object of a class is defined as a constant object using the **const** qualifier, then the accessible elements of the objects cannot be modified. However, if some accessible elements are defined as mutable elements, then these elements can be modified even when the object is defined as a constant object.

Example-11.16: In Code-11.14, we declare a class and define a constant object for this class. The public members of the class cannot be modified due to constant declaration.

Code 11.14
```cpp
#include <iostream>

using namespace std;

class A {

public:

int x = 4;
int y = 9;
};

int main() {

const A obj; // constant object

obj.x = 17; // error

obj.y = 17; // error
}
```

However, if we use the mutable keyword for the variable x as in Code-11.15, its value can be modified.

Code 11.15
```cpp
#include <iostream>

using namespace std;

class A {

public:

mutable int x = 4;
int y = 9;
};

int main() {
```

```cpp
    const A obj;

    obj.x = 17; // ok

    obj.y = 17; // error
}
```

Problems

1) Is there any difference between the definitions

$$\text{int volatile } \mathbf{a};$$

and

$$\text{volatile int } \mathbf{a};$$

?

2) Explain the differences in the pointer definitions in the expressions

```
float volatile* fp;
volatile float* fp
float* volatile fp;
float (*volatile fp);
volatile float* volatile fp;
float volatile* volatile fp;
```

3) Why do we use **restrict** qualifier in C++ programming? Should every code use it? Which engineering field needs this qualifier the most?

4) What are the outputs of Code-11.16?

Code 11.16
```cpp
#include <iostream>

using namespace std;

void myFunc() {

static float a = 2.2;

a = a + 3.2;

cout << "Inside function, a = " << a << endl;
}

int main() {
myFunc();
myFunc();
myFunc();
}
```

Chapter-12

Signals in C++

Abstract: In this chapter we explain signals topic in C++ programming. Signals are used when normal flow of the program is to be paused and a special function is to be executed when a specific event occurs. Signals can be generated manually, for instance pressing Ctrl+C key, or they can be generated by hardware inputs, for instance receiving an input from a port of the computer, or they can be generated when a specific event occurs, for instance 0/0 division is performed in a mathematical calculation, or we can define a special event, for instance when 1.23 is obtained, and all upon the occurrence of all these events, normal flow of the program is halted and a special function either written by the user or a built-in one is called.

12.1 Introduction

Signals are generated when an interrupt is received. Signals can also be called as interrupt signals. Interrupts are abnormal cases and upon their occurrences, some signals are generated, and when these signals are detected some actions are performed.

The interrupts are can be divided into two main categories:

- Hardware interrupts
- Software interrupts.

When a signal is received either some default actions are performed or a user defined function is executed. For instance when Ctrl + C is pressed, a software interrupt is generated. The default action is to terminate the current process. However, a function, which is executed when Ctrl + C interrupt is received, can be written. Signals can also be generated from OS kernel directly when a hardware fault such as a bus error occurs or an illegal instruction is performed.

The default actions of signals are:

the signal is discarded after it is received,

the current process is terminated when the signal is received,

a core file is written, and the process is stopped,

the current process is stopped when the signal is received.

The signals can artificially be generated as well. For this purpose, C provides the raise() function.

$$\text{int } \mathbf{raise}(\text{int } \mathbf{sig})$$

where **sig** is the signal is an integer which defines the signal type and they are defined as macros in header file **<csignal >**

Some of these macros are

```
#define SIGHUP 1 /* hangup */
#define SIGINT 2 /* interactive interrupt */
#define SIGQUIT 3 /* quit (ASCII FS) */
#define SIGILL 4 /* illegal instruction (not reset when caught) */
#define SIGABRT 6 /* used by abort, replace SIGIOT in the future */
#define SIGKILL 9 /* kill (cannot be caught or ignored) */
#define SIGBUS 10 /* bus error */
#define SIGALRM 14 /* alarm clock */
#define SIGTERM 15 /* software termination signal from kill */
```

12.2 Signal Handling

When an interrupt occurs a signal is generated, and the generated signal can be caught by the built-in function called signal handler. The signal handler

- may let the default action to happen
- can block the signal, however, this may not be possible for every signal
- a function can be called by the signal handler

The built-in signal handler is defined as

$$\text{int } (*\textbf{signal}(\text{int } \textbf{sig}, \text{void } (*\textbf{func})()))();$$

which can be used as

$$\textbf{signal}(\textbf{signalMacroName}, \textbf{pointerName})$$

if default action is to be performed, or it can be used as

$$\textbf{signal}(\textbf{signalMacroName}, \textbf{functionName})$$

if a function with name **functionName** is to be called.

12.3 SIGINT

This signal macro is used to capture interactive attention signal. It can be considered as interrupt signal generated by user. For instance, this signal is generated when the user presses Ctrl + C from the keyboard.

If default action is to be considered when

signal(signalMacroName, pointerName)

is executed, the pointer name can be **SIG_DFL** which is a pointer to a system default function **SID_DFL()**, and the process is terminated upon the reception of interrupt signal.

If the pointer name is **SIG_IGN** which is a pointer to system ignore function **SIG_IGN()**, the signal action is ignored.

Example-12.1: Let's write a program involving signals. For this purpose, let's first write an infinite loop as in Code-12.1.

Code 12.1

```cpp
#include <iostream>

// for sleep() function
#ifdef _WIN32
#include <windows.h>
#else
#include <unistd.h>
#endif

using namespace std;

int main() {

while (1) {
cout << "Infinite Loop \n";
sleep(1); // sleep for 1 sec
}
}
```

Signal handler for SIGINT is added as in Code-12.2.

Code 12.2

```cpp
#include <iostream>
#include <csignal> // for signal functions

using namespace std;

int main() {

signal(SIGINT, myFunc);

while (1) {
```

```
cout << "Infinite Loop \n";
sleep(1); // sleep for 1 sec
}
}
```

We add the definition of signal handler function myFunc as in Code-12.3.

Code 12.3
```
#include <iostream>
#include <csignal>
using namespace std;
void myFunc(int sig) {
cout << "Interrupt signal is received: MACRO: " << sig << endl;
}
int main() {
signal(SIGINT, myFunc);
while (1) {
cout << "Infinite Loop \n";
sleep(1); // sleep for 1 sec
}
}
```

Output(s): When the user pressed Ctrl + C, an interrupt signal is generated and it is handled by the signal handler, i.e., myFunc.

```
Infinite Loop
Infinite Loop
^CInterrupt signal is received: MACRO: 2
Infinite Loop
Infinite Loop
Infinite Loop
^CInterrupt signal is received: MACRO: 2
Infinite Loop
Infinite Loop

....
```

Note that sleep() is defined in <windows.h> for windows compiler, and sleep() function is defined in <unistd.h> for linux. However, if the header <csignal> is included, they can be omitted.

Example-12.2: Signal handler can perform default action as well. The default action SIG_DFL terminated the program.

Code 12.4
```
#include <iostream>
#include <csignal>

using namespace std;

int main() {
```

```
signal(SIGINT, SIG_DFL);

while (1) {

cout << "Infinite Loop" << endl ;
sleep(1);
}
}
```

Output(s): When Ctrl + C is pressed the signal handler performs the default action which is the termination of the program.

```
Infinite Loop
Infinite Loop
Infinite Loop
^C
...Program finished with exit code 0
```

Example-12.3: One of the default actions for SIGINT signal is the SIG_IGN which ignores the interrupt request.

Code 12.5
```
#include <iostream>
#include <csignal>

using namespace std;

int main() {

signal(SIGINT, SIG_IGN);

while (1) {

cout << "Infinite Loop" << endl;
sleep(1);
}
}
```

Output(s): When Ctrl + C is pressed the signal handler performs the default action SIG_IGN which disregards, i.e., ignores the signal action. The program goes on running.

```
Infinite Loop
Infinite Loop
Infinite Loop
^C
Infinite Loop
Infinite Loop

....
```

12.4 SIGQUIT

This signal macro is similar to **SIGINT**, however, the interrupt signal is generated when Ctrl + \ is pressed. Note Ctrl + \ means we press Ctrl and \ at the same time.

Example-12.4: Interrupt signal can be generated by Ctrl+C or Ctrl+ \ Some compilers support both of them some of them supports only Ctrl+C. In this example, we write a code which identifies whether Ctrl+C or Ctrl+ \ is pressed.

We first write the code for SIGINT signal as in Code-12.6 where interrupt is generated when Ctrl+C is pressed. Note Ctrl+C means we press Ctrl and C at the same time.

Code 12.6
```cpp
#include <iostream>
#include <csignal>

using namespace std;

void func1(int sig);

int main() {

signal(SIGINT, func1);

for(;;) {

cout << "Infinite Loop" << endl;
sleep(1);
}
}

void func1(int sig) {
cout << "\nCtrl+C is pressed \n";
}
```

Next, we add the signal handler for SIGQUIT which is generated when Ctrl + \ is pressed.

Code 12.7
```cpp
#include <iostream>
#include <csignal>

using namespace std;

void func1(int sig);
void func2(int sig);

int main() {

signal(SIGINT, func1);
```

```cpp
signal(SIGQUIT, func2);

for(;;) {

cout << "Infinite Loop \n";
sleep(1);
}
}

void func1(int sig) {

cout << "\nCtrl+C is pressed \n";
}

void func2(int sig) {

cout << "\nCtrl+ \\ is pressed \n";
}
```

Output(s):
Infinite Loop
Infinite Loop
Infinite Loop
Infinite Loop
^C
Ctrl+C is pressed
Infinite Loop
Infinite Loop
Infinite Loop
^\
Ctrl+ \ is pressed
Infinite Loop
Infinite Loop
Infinite Loop
...

12.5 Artificial Signal Generation

Interrupt signals can be generated by hardware, such as Ctrl+C press, or they can be generated by software as well. The raise() function can be used to generate interrupt signals. The prototype of the raise() function is

int raise(int sig);

Example-12.5: In the previous examples the interrupt signal SIGINT is generated by pressing Ctrl + C. In this example, we generate the signal SIGINT using the raise() function.

Code 12.8

```cpp
#include <iostream>
#include <csignal>
using namespace std;
void myFunc(int sig) {
cout << "Received SIGINT Signal. Signal MACRO: "
<< sig << endl;
}
int main(void) {
signal(SIGINT, myFunc);
cout << "Generating SIGINT Signal. Signal MACRO: "
<< SIGINT << endl;
raise(SIGINT);
cout << "Quits Program. \n";
}
```

Output(s):

Generating SIGINT Signal. Signal MACRO: 2

Received SIGINT Signal. Signal MACRO: 2

Quits Program.

SIG_ERR

It indicates an error in signal handling.

SIG_ACK

It indicates sucessfull signal handling.

Example-12.6: In this example we improve the previous example using the SIG_ERR and return value of raise() function.

Code 12.9

```cpp
#include <iostream>
#include <csignal>
using namespace std;
void myFunc(int sig) {
cout << "Has received the signal SIGTERM";
}
int main(void) {
if (signal(SIGTERM, myFunc) == SIG_ERR) {
cout << "Error while handling the signal.\n";
exit(0);
```

```cpp
}
cout << "Generating the signal SIGTERM.\n";
if (raise(SIGTERM) != 0) {
cout << "Error while generating the signal SIGTERM.\n";
exit(0);
}
}
```

Output(s):

```
Generating the signal SIGTERM.
Has received the signal SIGTERM
```

12.6 Some of the most used signals are:

SIGHUP: HUP is an abbreviation for "hang up". This signal is generated when the process terminates abruptly. The SIGHUP signal is generated when a remote connection is lost.

SIGABRT: The SIGABRT is generated when an error is detected by the program and abort() function is called.

SIGFPE: This signal is generated when overflow, division by zero, etc occurs in arrithmetic operations.

SIGSEGV: This name is an abbreviation for signal segmentation violation. When a program tries to read or write to a forbidden location, this signal is generated.

SIGALRM: This is a a timeout signal that is sent by alarm() . SIGALRM is sent when the timer expires after acertain amount of time.

SIGILL: It is an abbrviation for signal for illegal instruction . This signal is generated when code is corrupted or an attempt is made to execute data, or the program loads a corrupted dynamic library.

SIGUSR1 and **SIGUSR2:** The signals SIGUSR1 and SIGUSR2 may be used as you wish. It is useful to write a signal handler for them in the program that receives the signal for simple inter-process communication.

SIGTERM: This signal is used to quit the program in a clean manner while SIGKILL is an abnormal termination signal.

Problems

1) Explain the use of **raise** function in C++ signals.

2) How many ways are available to call the signal handler?

3) Write a C++ program which increments the value of a global variable every time Ctrl+C is pressed. The program stays inside an infinite loop, and whenver the global value reaches 10 the program terminates.

4) Write a C++ program which raises another interrupt signal whenever Ctrl+C is pressed.

Chapter-13

Classes

Abstract: In this chapter, we explain classes used in C++ programming. Classes can be considered as the extension of structures. Classes are the heart of object oriented programming. For this reason, it is essential to comprehend the subjects explained in this chapter very well to understand the subjects in the incoming chapters.

13.1 Classes

A class is a group of data types and functions. The elements of a class may have different types. Furthermore, some elements of a class may be functions, including operators.

The syntax of class declaration is shown in Code-13.1.

Code 13.1
```
class className {

public:
// public parameters and methods

private:
// private parameters and methods

protected:
// protected parameters and methods

}; // don't forget to put semicolon here
```

In Code-13.1, parameters are variables, and methods are functions belonging to a class.

As shown in Code-13.1, a class can have three different sections which are public, private and protected sections.

Let's define a class step by step. For this purpose, we first write the reserved word **class** as in Code-13.2.

Code 13.2

```
class
```

Next, we give a name to the class, in Code-13.3 the class name is the letter A, more complex names can be given such as myClass, etc.

Code 13.3

```
class A
```

We include the header files before the class definition as in Code-13.4.

Code 13.4

```
#include <iostream>
using namespace std;

class A {

}
```

Don't forget to put a semicolon after class definition as in Code-13.5. Semicolon is in yellow color.

Code 13.5

```
#include <iostream>
using namespace std;

class A {

};
```

We write an access specifier. In Code-13.6, public access specifier is used to define the public section.

Code 13.6

```
#include <iostream>
using namespace std;

class A {

public:

};
```

And variables can be written in public section as in Code-13.7.

Code 13.7

```cpp
class A {

public:
float x = 5.4;
};
```

It is possible to initialize the variables as in Code-13.8.

Code 13.8

```cpp
#include <iostream>
using namespace std;

class A {

public:
float x = 5.4;
};

int main() {

}
```

For the defined class we can define an object as in Code-13.9.

Code 13.9

```cpp
#include <iostream>
using namespace std;

class A {

public:
float x = 5.4;
};

int main() {

A myObj;

}
```

In Code-13.10, the value of the object parameter is displayed.

Code 13.10

```cpp
#include <iostream>
using namespace std;

class A {
```

```cpp
public:
float x = 5.4;
};

int main() {

A myObj;

cout << "x is " << myObj.x << endl;
}
```

13.2 Access Specifiers

A class has three different access specifiers which are public, private and protected.

13.2.1 Public Section

The member in the public section, i.e., variables and methods can be accessed outside class declaration.

Example-13.1: In Code-13.11, the objects parameters are accessed and printed in the main() function.

Code 13.11
```cpp
#include <iostream>
using namespace std;

class A {

public:
float x = 5.4;
float y = 8.9;
};

int main() {

A myObj;

cout << "x is " << myObj.x << endl;
cout << "y is " << myObj.y << endl;
}
```

Output(s):
```
x is 5.4
y is 8.9
```

Example-13.2: In this example, the defined class has a data parameter and a function, i.e., method. The method is called in the main() function. The method can access the public members.

Code 13.12
```cpp
#include <iostream>
using namespace std;

class A {

public:
float x = 1.8;

void disp() {

cout << "x is " << x << endl;
}
};

int main() {
```

```
A myObj;

myObj.disp();
}
```

Output(s): x is 1.8

13.2.2 More than One Public Section

Although it is not a good programming style, it is possible to use more than one public section.

Example-13.3: In this example, we show that more than one public section can be used.

Code 13.13
```cpp
#include <iostream>
using namespace std;

class A {

public:
float x = 1.8;
float y = 4.5;

public:
int z = 7;
};

int main() {

A myObj;

cout << "x is " << myObj.x << endl;
cout << "y is " << myObj.y << endl;
cout << "z is " << myObj.z << endl;
}
```

Output(s):
```
x is 1.8
y is 4.5
z is 7
```

13.2.3 Private Section

Members of private section cannot be accessed outside class declaration. That is, in main() function of the program we cannot directly use the values of parameters of the private section, or call the functions of the private section.

If access specifier is not indicated, then the default access specifier, which is private, is used by the compiler. Code-13.14 is the same as Code-13.15.

Code 13.14
```cpp
class A {

private:
float x = 1.8;
};
```

is the same as

Code 13.15
```cpp
class A {

float x = 1.8;

};
```

Example-13.4: In Code-13.16, myObj.x expression is the value of x variable in the private section, reading values of private section parameters are not allowed.

Code 13.16
```cpp
#include <iostream>
using namespace std;

class A {

private:
float x = 1.8;
};

int main() {

A myObj;

// error, private members are not accessible
// outside class declaration

cout << "x is " << myObj.x << endl;
}
```

Output(s): error: 'float A::x' is private within this context

Then, how to access to the variables of private section? This is indirectly possible, we can write functions in public section and these functions can access to the private section parameters. We can call public section functions inside main part.

Example-13.5: The method in the public section in Code-13.17 access the private section member, and the method is called in the main() function.

Code 13.17
```cpp
#include <iostream>
using namespace std;

class A {

private:
float x = 1.8;

public:
void disp() {

cout << "x is " << x << endl;
}
};

int main() {

A myObj;

myObj.disp();
}
```

Output(s): x is 1.8

The class declaration in Code-13.17 can be written as in Code-13.18 where we omitted the access specifier **private**. It is already private by default.

Code 13.18
```cpp
class A {

float x = 1.8; // private by default

public:
void disp() {

cout << "x is " << x << endl;
}
};
```

As in the case of public access specifier, we can use more than one **private** access specifier in class declaration.

Note that private members can include variables and functions in private section. Private functions are also not accessible outside the class declaration.

Example-13.6: The method in the private section in Code-13.19 cannot be called in the main() function.

Code 13.19

```cpp
#include <iostream>
using namespace std;

class A {

private:
float x;

void display() {

cout << "x is " << x << endl;
}

};

int main() {

A myObj;

myObj.display();
}
```

Output(s): error: 'void A::display()' is private within this context

13.2.4 Protected Section

Members of protected section cannot be accessed outside class declaration. The difference between private section members and protected section members is that the protected section members can be used by the derived classes; however, private section members cannot be used by derived classes. We will cover derived classes in details in Chapter-14.

We can access the protected members indirectly possible using public section functions.

Example-13.7: Protected members are not accessible outside the class declaration.

Code 13.20

```cpp
#include <iostream>
using namespace std;

class A {

protected:
float x = 1.8;
};

int main() {

A myObj;

// error, protected members are not accessible
// outside class declaration

cout << "x is " << myObj.x << endl;
}
```

Output(s): error: 'float A::x' is protected within this context

Example-13.8: Protected members can be accessed by the methods of the public section, and public section methods can be called in the main() function.

Code 13.21

```cpp
#include <iostream>
using namespace std;

class A {

protected:
float x = 1.8;

public:
void disp() {

cout << "x is " << x << endl;
```

```
}
};

int main() {

A myObj;

myObj.disp();
}
```

Output(s): x is 1.8

As in the case of public section, we can use more than one **protected** section in class declaration.

13.2.5 Scope Resolution Operator ::

The methods of a class can be implemented outside the class using scope resolution operator ::
Let's write the body of the function in Code-13.22 outside the class declaration.

Code 13.22
```cpp
#include <iostream>
using namespace std;

class A {

public:
float x = 1.8;

void disp() {

cout << "x is " << x << endl;
}
};

int main() {

A myObj;

myObj.disp();
}
```

For this purpose, we first copy all the function and paste it outside the class as in Code-13.23, and leave some space between function name and its return type. We leave the prototype of the function inside the class.

Code 13.23
```cpp
#include <iostream>
using namespace std;

class A {

public:
float x = 1.8;

void disp();

};

void disp() {

cout << "x is " << x << endl;

}

int main() {

A myObj;
```

```
myObj.disp();
}
```

In the next step, we write the class name with the scope resolution operator, i.e., **A::**, in front of the function name as in Code-13.24.

Code 13.24

```
#include <iostream>
using namespace std;

class A {

public:
float x = 1.8;

void disp();
};

void A::disp() {

cout << "x is " << x << endl;

}

int main() {

A myObj;

myObj.disp();
}
```

The function can be written inside the class declaration as in Code-13.25

Code 13.25

```cpp
#include <iostream>
using namespace std;

class A {

public:
float x = 1.8;

void disp() {

cout << "x is " << x << endl;
}
};

int main() {

A myObj;

myObj.disp();
}
```

The Codes-13.25 and 13.26 are equaivalent to each other.

Code 13.26

```cpp
#include <iostream>
using namespace std;

class A {

public:
float x = 1.8;

void disp();
};

void A::disp() {

cout << "x is " << x << endl;

}

int main() {

A myObj;

myObj.disp();
}
```

13.3 Separating Class Definition from Implementation

A C++ program can be written using three different files which are header, implementation and test files.

Code 13.27
```cpp
#include <iostream>
using namespace std;

class A {

private:
float x;

public:
void display();
};

void A::display() {

cout << "x is " << x <<endl;
}

int main() {

A myObj;

myObj.display();
}
```

The Code-13.27 can be participated into three parts as Code-13.28, Code-13.29, and Code-13.30.

Code 13.28
```cpp
// File name is A.h

class A {

private:
float x;

public:
void display();
};
```

Code 13.29
```cpp
// File name is A.cpp

#include <iostream>
```

```cpp
#include "A.h"
using namespace std;

void A::display() {

cout << "x is " << x <<endl;
}
```

Code 13.30
```cpp
// File name is test.cpp

#include "A.h"

int main() {

A myObj;

myObj.display();
}
```

13.4 Preventing Multiple Inclusions

The same header file can be included in a program multiple times, and this is a common mistake. To prevent the inclusion of a header file multiple times, we use the directive

#ifndef directiveName
#define directiveName

// header file codes

#endif

The header file in Code-13.30 can be written as in Code-13.31.

Code 13.31
```
// File name is A.h

#ifndef A_H
#define A_H

class A {

private:
float x;

public:
void display();
};

#endif
```

13.5 Constructors

A constructor is a function of a class that is called automatically when an object is defined. The constructor function is used to initialize the members of an object. The name of the constructor must be the same as the name of the class, and a constructor has no return type.

Constructors must be written in the **public** section of the class declaration.

Constructors can be divided into two main categories which are default and non-default constructors.

13.5.1 Default Constructors

Default constructors have no arguments. In Code-13.32, default constructor name is shown in yellow.

Code 13.32
```cpp
#include <iostream>
using namespace std;

class A {

private:
float x;

public:

A() { // default constructor
x = 6.5;
}

void display() {

cout << "x is " << x <<endl;
}

};
```

The default constructor and the display() function in Code-13.32 can be implemented outside the class declaration using scope resolution operator :: as in Code-13.33.

Code 13.33
```cpp
#include <iostream>
using namespace std;

class A {

private:
float x;

public:
A();
void display();
};

A::A() { // default constructor
x = 6.5;
}
```

```
void A::display() {

cout << "x is " << x << endl;
}
```

The entire program involving the default constructor is shown in Code-13.34.

Code 13.34
```
#include <iostream>
using namespace std;

class A {
private:
float x;

public:
A();
void display();
};
A::A() { // default constructor
x = 6.5;
}
void A::display() {

cout << "x is " << x <<endl;
}
int main() {

A myObj;
myObj.display();
}
```

When Code-13.34 is run, we get the output "x is 6.5".

The program in Code-13.34 can be written in three different files as in Code-13.35, Code-13.36 and Code-13.37.

Code 13.35
```
// File name is A.h

#ifndef A_H
#define A_H

class A {

private:
```

```
float x;

public:
A();
void display();
};
```

#endif

Code 13.36
```
// File name is A.cpp

#include <iostream>
#include "A.h"
using namespace std;

A::A() { // default constructor

x = 6.5;
}

void A::display() {

cout << "x is " << x <<endl;
}
```

Code 13.37
```
// File name is test.cpp

#include "A.h"

int main() {

A myObj;

myObj.display();
}
```

We can create a project and add the three files in Code-13.35, Code-13.36, and Code-13.37. When the test file in Code-13.37 is run we get the output "x is 6.5".

13.5.2 Non-Default Constructor

Non-default constructors are also called constructors with arguments.

Example-13.9: In Code-13.38, non-default constructor prototype is shown in yellow color.

Code 13.38

```cpp
// File name is A.h

#ifndef A_H
#define A_H

#include <iostream>
using namespace std;

class A {

private:
float x;

public:
A(); // default constructor

A(float v); // non-default constructor

float getX();
};

#endif
```

The implementation of the constructors and method is given in Code-13.39.

Code 13.39

```cpp
// File name is A.cpp

#include <iostream>
#include "A.h"
using namespace std;

A::A() { // default constructor
x = 6.5;
}

A::A(float v) { // non-default constructor
x = v;
}

float A::getX() {
```

```
    return x;
    }
```

Code-13.38 and Code-13.39 can be tested using Code-13.40. In Code-13.40 non-default constructor is called. All three files can be included in a C++ project, and when the test file is run, we get the output "x is 8.9".

Code 13.40
```cpp
// File name is testA.cpp
#include "A.h"
int main() {
A myObj(8.9); // non-default constructor is called
cout <<"x is " << myObj.getX() <<endl;
}
```
The test file can be written as in Code-13.41.

Code 13.41
```cpp
// File name is testA.cpp
#include "A.h"
int main() {
A myObj1; // default constructor is called
A myObj2(8.9); // non-default constructor is called
cout <<"x is " << myObj1.getX() <<endl;
cout <<"x is " << myObj2.getX() <<endl;
}
```
When Code-13.41 is run, we get the outputs

x is 6.5

x is 8.9

Example-13.10: The parameters of a non-default constructor can be initialized at the constructor header. If all the parameters are initialized, the constructor can be called as a default constructor. In this case, if the default constructor is also available, calling the non-default constructor with its default initial values created a conflict and error arises.

Code 13.42
```cpp
#include <iostream>
using namespace std;

class A {

private:
int x { };
int y { };

public:

A() { };
```

```cpp
A(int a, int b = 9 ) {
x = a; y = b;
}
};

int main() {

A a ; // OK
}
```

Code 13.43

```cpp
#include <iostream>
using namespace std;

class A {

private:
int x { };
int y { };

public:

A() { };

A(int a = 2 , int b = 9 ) {
x = a; y = b;
}
};

int main() {

A a ; // ERROR
}
```

13.6 Header Initialization for Constructors

It is possible to perform header initialization instead of the body initialization for constructors. The constructor initialization

```
className(arguments) {

param1 = value1;
param2 = value2;
...

};
```

can also be achieved using header initialization as

```
className(arguments): param1(value1), param2(value2)... {
// Additional statements if needed
}
```

If constructors are implemented outside class declaration as

```
className::className(arguments) {

param1 = value1;
param2 = value2;
...

};
```

then, header initialization can be done as

```
className::className(arguments): param1(value1), param2(value2)... {
// Additional statements if needed
}
```

Example-13.11: The default constructor in Code-13.44 can be written as in Code-13.45.

Code 13.44
```
A() {

x = 6.5
}
```

Code 13.45

```
A() : x(6.5) {

}
```

Example-13.12: The non-default constructor in Code-13.46 can be written as in Code-13.47.

Code 13.46
```
A(float v) {

    x = v;
}
```

Code 13.47
```
A(float v) : x(v) {

}
```

Example-13.13: The implementation of a non-default constructor of a class is given as in Code-13.48. Convert the constructor initialization in Code-13.48 to header initialization.

Code 13.48
```
A::A(int a, float b, double d) {

    w = a;
    x = b;
    y = d;
}
```

First, we move the assignment statements inside Code-13.48 to the header as in Code-13.49 where assignment statements are comma separated.

Code 13.49
```
A::A(int a, float b, double d) : w = a, x = b, y = d {



}
```

In the second step, we remove the = sign and put the values on the right hand side of = into parenthesis as in Code-13.50.

Code 13.50
```
A::A(int a, float b, double d) : w(a), x(b), y(d) {



}
```

Curly parentheses can be used instead of the rounded parentheses as in Code-13.51.

Code 13.51
```
A::A(int a, float b, double d) : w{a}, x{b}, y{d} {


}
```

13.6.1 Compulsory Header Initialization

There are some class members which must be initialized at the constructor header. These members are
- objects from other classes which do not have default constructor
- base class members of a derived class
- when constructor's argument name is same as class member name
- non-static constant data members, e.g., const int a;
- reference members, e.g., int& a;
- for better performance

Now, let's see some examples about these initializations.

Example-13.14: In Code-13.52, constant member in private section is initialized at constructor header.

Code 13.52

```cpp
#include<iostream>
using namespace std;
class A {
private:
const int x; // constant member
public:
A(int a) : x(a) { } // constant members
// are initialized at the header
int getX() { return x; }
};
int main() {
A myObj(6);
cout << "x is " << myObj.getX() << endl;
}
```

Output(s): x is 6

Example-13.15: In Code-13.53, reference member in private section is initialized at constructor header.

Code 13.53

```cpp
#include<iostream>
using namespace std;
class A {
private:
int& x; // reference member
public:
A(int& a) : x(a) { } // reference members
// are initialized at the header
int getX() { return x; }
};
int main() {
int a = 6;
A myObj(a);
cout << "x is " << myObj.getX() << endl;
```

```cpp
a = 8;
cout << "x is " << myObj.getX() << endl;
}
```

Output(s):

```
x is 6
x is 8
```

Example-13.16: In Codes-13.54, 13-55, and 13-56, header and body initializations are done.

Code 13.54

```cpp
#include <iostream>
using namespace std;

class A {

private:

int x;
const int y;
int& z;

public:

A(int a) {
x = a; // ok
y = a; // error
z = a; // error
};

};

int main() {

A a(6);
}
```

Code 13.55

```cpp
#include <iostream>
using namespace std;

class A {

private:

int x;
const int y;
int& z = x;
```

```
public:

 A(int a) : y(a), z (x) { // ok

 x = a; // ok
 };
 };

 int main() {

 A a(6);
 }
```

Code 13.56
```
#include <iostream>
using namespace std;

class A {

private:

int x;
const int y;
int& z = x;

public:

A(int a) : y(a), z (x) { // ok

x = a; // ok
};
};

int main() {

A a(6);
}
```

Example-13.17: In Code-13.57, in class B, object of class-A is initialized at the constructor header.

Code 13.57
```
#include<iostream>
using namespace std;
class A {
private:
int x;
public:
```

```cpp
A(int a) {
x = a;
cout << "Inside constructor for class-A" << endl;
cout << "x = " << x << endl << endl;
}
};
class B {
private:
A o; // object for class A
public:
B(int b): o(b) { // objects are initialized
// at constructor header
cout << "Inside constructor for class-B" << endl;
}
};
int main() {
B myObj(7);
}
```

Output(s):

```
Inside constructor for class-A
x = 7
Inside constructor for class-B
```

Example-13.18: In Code-13.58, base class constructor for class A is called at the header of constructor of class B.

Code 13.58

```cpp
#include<iostream>
using namespace std;
class A {
private:
int x;
public:
A(int a) {
x = a;
cout << "Inside constructor for class-A" << endl;
cout << "x = " << x << endl << endl;
}
};
class B : public A {
public:
B(int b) : A(b) { // base class costructor
// is called at the header
cout << "Inside constructor for class-B" << endl;
}
};
```

```cpp
int main() {
B myObj(7);
}
```

Output(s):

Inside constructor for class-A

x = 7

Inside constructor for class-B

Example-13.19: We initilaliz the members of the class having the same name as passing arguments as in Code-13.59.

Code 13.59

```cpp
#include<iostream>
using namespace std;
class A {
private:
int x; // member name is x
public:
A(int x) : x(x) { } // if argument name is the same as the
// the member name, then
// header initialization is used
int getX() { return x; }
};
int main() {
A myObj(6);
cout << "x is " << myObj.getX() << endl;
}
```

Output(s): x is 6

Header initialization has better performance regarding the total number of processes performed.

13.7 Destructors

A constructor is called when an object of a class is created and written to memory. Similarly, when an object is removed from memory, another special member function called destructor is automatically called.

Every class has exactly one destructor. **Destructors are written inside the public section** of a class. Note that a class can have more than one constructor, whereas a **class has only one destructor**.

If A is the name of the class, its destructor is written inside class declaration as

```
~A(){

// statements

}
```

and it is written outside class declaration as

```
A::~A(){

// statements

}
```

Example-13.20: This example illustrates the use of class destructor.

Code 13.60
```
#include <iostream>
using namespace std;
class A {
private:
string s;
public:
A(string st);
~A();
};
A::A(string st) {
s = st;
cout << "Inside constructor for " << st << endl;
}
A::~A() {
cout << "Inside destructor for " << s <<endl;
}
int main() {
A myObj1("myObj1"); // constructor for myObj1 is called here
} // destructor for myObj1 is called here
```
Output(s):
```
Inside constructor for myObj1
```

Inside destructor for myObj1

Example-13.21: This example illustrates the sequence of constructor and destructor calls.

Code 13.61

```cpp
#include <iostream>
using namespace std;
class A {
public:
A() { cout << "Inside constructor \n"; }
~A() { cout << "Inside destructor \n"; }
};


int main()
{
A myObj1; // constructor for myObj1 is called here
{
A myObj2; // constructor for myObj2 is called here
} // destructor for myObj2 is called here
} // destructor for myObj1 is called here
```

Output(s):

Inside constructor

Inside constructor

Inside destructor

Inside destructor

Example-13.22: This is another example illustrating the sequence of constructor and destructor calls.

Code 13.62

```cpp
#include <iostream>
using namespace std;
class A {
private:
string s;
public:
A(string st);
~A();
};
A::A(string st) {
s = st;
cout << "Inside constructor for " << st << endl;
}
A::~A() {
cout << "Inside destructor for " << s <<endl;
}
```

```cpp
int main() {
A myObj1("myObj1"); // constructor for myObj1 is called here
{ // local scope
A myObj2("myObj2"); // constructor for myObj2 is called here
} // destructor for myObj2 is called here
} // destructor for myObj1 is called here
```

Output(s):

Inside constructor for myObj1

Inside constructor for myObj2

Inside destructor for myObj2

Inside destructor for myObj1

Example-13.23: We create three objects belonging to the same class in Code-13.63.

Code 13.63

```cpp
#include <iostream>
using namespace std;

class A {
private:
string s;

public:
A(string st);

~A();
};

A::A(string st) {
s = st;
cout << "Inside constructor for " << st << endl;
}

A::~A() {
cout << "Inside destructor for " << s <<endl;
}

int main() {
A myObj1("myObj1");
A myObj2("myObj2");
A myObj3("myObj3");
}
```

Output(s):

Inside constructor for myObj1

Inside constructor for myObj2
Inside constructor for myObj3
Inside destructor for myObj3
Inside destructor for myObj2
Inside destructor for myObj1

13.8 Default and Delete Specifiers (Since C++ 11)

13.8.1 Deleted Functions

Deleted function declaration is introduced in the C++11 standard. A deleted function is declared by appending the "=delete" specifier to the end of the function declaration. Once a function is declared as a deleted function, the compiler disables the usage of the deleted function.

Implicitly defined functions can also be declared as deleted functions if you want to prevent its usage. For example, copy assignment operator and copy constructor of a class as can be declared as deleted functions.

Example-13.24: In this example, we show that calling a deleted non-default constructor creates error.

Code 13.64
```cpp
class A {

private:
float x;

public:
A(int a) { x = a; }
};

int main() {

A myObj1(5); // ok

// float to int conversion
A myObj2(3.4); // ok
}
```

Code 13.65
```cpp
class A {

private:
float x;

public:
A(int a) { x = a; }
A(double) = delete;
};

int main() {

A myObj1(5); // ok

A myObj2(3.4); // error
}
```

Output(s): error: use of deleted function 'A::A(double)'

Example-13.25: In this example, copy constructor is declared as a deleted function.

Code 13.66

```
class A {
private:
int x;
public:
A(int a) : x(a) {}
A(const A&) = delete; // The copy constructor is declared
// as a deleted function
};
int main(){
A g(32);
A h(g); // Error, the copy constructor is disabled
}
```

Output(s): error: use of deleted function 'A::A(const A&)'

Example-13.26: In this example, the default constructor is declared as a deleted function.

Code 13.67

```
class A {
private:
int x;
public:
A(int a) : x(a) {}
A() = delete; // The default constructor is declared
// as a deleted function
};
int main(){
A g(32);
A h; // error
}
```

Output(s): error: use of deleted function 'A::A()'

13.8.2 Defaulted Functions

Explicit defaulted function declaration is introduced in the C++11 standard. A defaulted function is declared by appending the "=default" specifier to the end of a function.

For explicit defaulted functions, the compiler employs the default implementations, which are more efficient than user implementations. An explicitly defaulted function must have **no default arguments**. Using explicitly defaulted functions we can save time and effort.

Example-13.27:

Code 13.68

```cpp
class A {
private:
int x;
public:
A() = default; // defaulted constructor
A(int a) : x(a) {}
A(const A&);
~A() = default; // defaulted destructor
};
A::A(const A&) = default; // defaulted copy constructor
```

Example-13.28:

Code 13.69

```cpp
class A {
public:
int func() = default; // Error, func is not a special
// member function.
A(double, int) = default; // Error, A(double, int) is not
// a member function.
A(double = 0) = default; // Error, A(double = 0) has a
// default argument.
};
```

13.9 Delegating Constructor

Delegating constructors call the other constructors of the same class to do the initialization. Delegating constructors are introduced in C++11. The syntax for constructor delegation is as

```cpp
className(arguments) : className(arguments) {
// statements
}
```

Example-13.29: Another example for delegate constructors.

Code 13.70

```cpp
class A {
int x, y, z; // private by default
public:
A() : A(4) { }
A(int a) : A(a, 0, 1) { }
A(int a, int b, int c) : x(a), y(b), z(c) { }
};
```

Example-13.30: This example illustrates the use of the delegated constructors.

Code 13.71

```cpp
#include<iostream>
using namespace std;
class A {
private:
const int x;
public:
A(int a, int b, int c) : A(a + b + c) { }
A(int a, int b) : A(a * b) {}
A(int a) : x(a) { } // header initialization
// is a must for constant members
void disp() {
cout << "x is " << x << endl;
}
};
int main(){
A myObj1(55, 11);
myObj1.disp();
A myObj2(6, 7, 9);
myObj2.disp();
}
```

Output(s):

```
x is 605
x is 22
```

Example-13.31: In this example, we show how to convert a non-default constructor to a delegated constructor.

Code 13.72

```cpp
class A {

int w, x, y;

public:

A() {
w = x = y = 0;
}

A(int a) {
w = 0;
x = 0;
y = a;
}
};
```

Code 13.73

```cpp
class A {

int w, x, y;

public:

A() {
w = x = y = 0;
}

A(int a) : A(){ // delegation
y = a;
}
};
```

Example-13.32: If a class contains objects from other classes as members, when the class instance is defined, constructors of the member objects run first.

Code 13.74

```cpp
#include <iostream>
using namespace std;
class A {
public:
A() { cout << "Inside default constructor-A" <<endl; }
~A() { cout << "Inside destructor-A" <<endl; }
};
class B {
private:
A a1;
```

```
public:
B() {cout << "Inside default constructor-B" <<endl; }
~B() { cout << "Inside destructor-B" <<endl; }
};
int main() {
B b;
cout << "Check point" <<endl;
}
```

Class B has an object a1, when B b is defined; first the constructor of a1 is run.

Output(s):

```
Inside default constructor-A
Inside default constructor-B
Check point
Inside destructor-B
Inside destructor-A
```

13.10 Copy Constructor

Copy constructors are used to copy the values an object to another object of the same class. The prototype of the copy constructor can be as

className (className& obj);

or as

className (const className& obj);

The **const** can be used to prevent the accident changes on the parameters of **obj**.

If you do not provide a copy constructor for a class, the compiler automatically employs one.

Let A be a class, and 'a' be an object of class A, the copy constructor is called in one of the cases

1)

A b(a); // copy constructor is called

2)

A b = a; // copy constructor is called

3)

void myFunc(A a) { // copy constructor is called

.....

}

4)

A myFunc(){

.....

return a; // copy constructor is called

}

Let's provide examples for these cases.

Example-13.33: In Code-13.75, copy constructor is called at the yellow highlighted code.

Code 13.75
```cpp
#include <iostream>
using namespace std;

class A {
public:
A() {
cout << "Inside default constructor" <<endl;
}

A(const A& a) {
cout << "Inside copy constructor" <<endl;
}
};
int main() {

A o1; // calls default constructor
A o2(o1); // calls copy constructor
```

```
}
```

Output(s):
Inside default constructor
Inside copy constructor
Example-13.34: In Code-13.76, copy constructor is called at the yellow highlighted code.
Code 13.76
```cpp
#include <iostream>
using namespace std;
class A {
public:
A() {
cout << "Inside default constructor" <<endl;
}
A(const A& a) {
cout << "Inside copy constructor" <<endl;
}
};
int main() {
A o1; // calls default constructor
A o2 = o1; // calls copy constructor
}
```

Output(s):
Inside default constructor
Inside copy constructor
If we have
```cpp
A o1;
A o2;
```
then
```cpp
o3 = o1;
```
does **NOT** call copy constructor, it uses assignment operator.

13.11 Objects as Function Arguments

When class objects are used as function arguments, constructors are called.

Assume that we have a class A, and we create an object and call the function as

A a;

myFunc(a);

When the function is called, copy constructor for the object is called since, function is called by pass by value method, and the object values are copied to the object at the function prototype which is given as

void myFunc(A b) { // copy constructor is called

// statements

} // destructor is called for b

// when function quits

and when the function quits, destructor is called for object b.

What happens if a function returns an object of a class?

Assume that the function has is as

A myFunc(A b) {

return b;

}

Due to pass by value, copy constructor is called, at the header of the function

A myFunc(A b) { // copy constructor is called

return b;

}

Inside function an object is returned, and the values of the header object are copied to this object, so copy constructor is called at return statement as in

A myFunc(A b) { // copy constructor is called

return b; // copy constructor is called

} // destructor is called for b

// destructor is called for b

and for the two objects.

If function argument involves a reference, then copy constructor is not called at header as shown in

A myFunc(A& b) { // copy constructor is NOT called

return b; // copy constructor is called

} // destructor is called for b

Example-13.35: In this example, it is illustrated how the constructors and destructors are called in a program which contains a function with object argument.

Code 13.77

```cpp
#include <iostream>
using namespace std;
class A {
public:
A() { cout << "Inside default constructor" << endl; }
```

```
A(const A& a) { cout << "Inside copy constructor" << endl; }
~A() { cout << "Inside destructor" << endl; }
};
void myFunc(A b) {
} // destructor is called for b
// when function quits
int main() {
A a; // default constructor is called for a
myFunc(a); // copy constructor is called, pass by value
cout << "Check point" << endl;
} // destructor is called for a
```
Output(s):
```
Inside default constructor
Inside copy constructor
Inside destructor
Check point
Inside destructor
```

Example-13.36: In this example, it is illustrated how the constructors and destructors are called in a program which contains a function which has an object argument and the function returns an object.

Code 13.78
```
#include <iostream>
using namespace std;
class A {
public:
A() { cout << "Inside default constructor" <<endl; }
A(const A& a) { cout << "Inside copy constructor" <<endl; }
~A() { cout << "Inside destructor" <<endl; }
};
A myFunc(A b) {
cout << "Inside myFunc" <<endl;
return b; // copy constructor is called
} // two destructors for b's are called here
// one b is at function arg, the next one is at return statement


int main() {
    A a; // default constructor is called for a
    myFunc(a); // copy constructor is called
    cout << "Check point" << endl;
} // destructor is called for a
```
Output(s):
```
Inside default constructor
Inside copy constructor
Inside myFunc
```

Inside copy constructor

Inside destructor

Inside destructor

Check point

Inside destructor

The program in Code-13.78 is modified as in Code-13.79 where a non-default constructor is used.

Code 13.79

```cpp
#include <iostream>
using namespace std;
class A {
public:
int y;
A(int x = 1) : y{x} {
cout << "Inside default constructor " << y << endl; }
A(const A& a) {
Y = a.y; cout << "Inside copy constructor " << "y = "
<< a.y << endl; }
~A() { cout << "Inside destructor" << " y = " << y << endl; }
};
A myFunc(A b) {
cout << "Inside myFunc" << " by = " << b.y << endl;
return b; // copy constructor is called
} // two destructors for b's are called here
// one b is at function arg, the next one is at return statement


int main() {
    A a(4); // default constructor is called for a
    myFunc(a); // copy constructor is called
    cout << "Check point" << endl;
} // destructor is called for a
```

When the program is run, we get the outputs

Output(s):

Inside default constructor 4

Inside copy constructor y = 4

Inside myFunc by = 4

Inside copy constructor y = 4

Inside destructor y = 4

Inside destructor y = 4

Check point

Inside destructor y = 4

Example-13.37: In this example, it is illustrated how the constructors and destructors are called in a program which contains a function which has an object argument and the function returns an object.

Code 13.80

```cpp
#include <iostream>
using namespace std;
class A {
public:
A() { cout << "Inside default constructor" <<endl; }
A(const A& a) { cout << "Inside copy constructor" <<endl; }
~A() { cout << "Inside destructor" <<endl; }
};
A myFunc(A& b) {
cout << "Inside myFunc" <<endl;
return b; // copy constructor is called
} // destructor for b is called here


int main() {
    A a; // default constructor is called for a
    myFunc(a);
    cout << "Check point" <<endl;
} // destructor is called for a
```

Output(s):
```
Inside default constructor
Inside myFunc
Inside copy constructor
Inside destructor
Check point
Inside destructor
```

Example-13.38: In this example, we illustrate how the constructors and destructors are called in a program which contains a function which has an object argument, and the function returns an object.

Code 13.81

```cpp
#include <iostream>
using namespace std;
class A {
public:
A() { cout << "Inside default constructor" <<endl; }
A(const A& a) { cout << "Inside copy constructor" <<endl; }
~A() { cout << "Inside destructor" <<endl; }
};
A myFunc(A& b) {
cout << "Inside myFunc" <<endl;
return b; // copy constructor is called
} // destructor for b is called here
```

```cpp
int main() {
    A a; // default constructor is called for a
    myFunc(a);
    cout << "Check point" <<endl;
} // destructor is called for a
```

Output(s):

```
Inside default constructor
Inside myFunc
Inside copy constructor
Inside destructor
Check point
Inside destructor
```

13.12 Assignment Operator

Although assignment operator and copy constructor performs similar things, they are completely different concepts.

Example-13.39: In yellow highlighted part in Code-13.82 copy constructor is **not** called.

Code 13.82

```cpp
#include <iostream>
using namespace std;
class A {
public:
A() {
cout << "Inside default constructor" <<endl;
}
A(const A& a) {
cout << "Inside copy constructor" <<endl;
}
};
int main() {
A o1; // calls default constructor
A o2; // calls default constructor
o2 = o1; // NO call for copy constructor
}
```

Output(s):

```
Inside default constructor
Inside default constructor
```

13.13 Rvalue references

l-value is used to refer to a memory location which holds an object and every memory location has an address.

r-value is used to refer to the value stored at an address in memory which is used for an object.

r-value is used on the right hand side of an assignment whereas l-value can be used on the left and right side of an assignment.

There are to reference types, and these are

    l-value reference
    r-value reference

l-value reference is defined as

```
int b = 100;
int& a = b; // lvalue reference
```

whereas r-value reference is defined as

```
int&& a = 100; // rvalue reference
```

we cannot define an r-value reference initialized to a variable as

```
int&& a = b; // error
```

In addition, on the right hand side of an l-value reference we cannot use a value as in

```
int& a = 100; // Error
```

however with constant qualifier it is possible to have a value on the right hand side of a l-value reference as in

```
const int& a = 100; // OK
```

Example-13.40: In this example, we define a function with r-value reference argument, and inspect the calling the function with different parameters.

```
Code 13.83
#include <iostream>
using namespace std;

void disp(int&& x) {

cout <<"x is " << x << endl;
}

int main() {

int a { 45 };
```

```cpp
int&& b { 50 };

//disp(a); // error
disp(45); // ok
disp(move(a)); // ok

// disp(b); //error
disp(move(b)); // ok
}
```

Example-13.41: In this example, we have two functions with the same name, one has l-value argument and the other has r-value argument.

Code 13.84

```cpp
#include <iostream>
using namespace std;
void myFunc(const int& x) { // l-value arguments
cout << "x is " << x << endl;
}
void myFunc(int&& x) { // r-value arguments
cout << "x is " << x << endl;
}
int main() {
int x {43};
myFunc(x); // calls function with l-value argument
myFunc(67); // calls function with r-value argument
}
```

Output(s):

```
x is 43
x is 67
```

Example-13.42: In this example, we print the address of an r-value both inside the main() function and inside a user defined function.

Code 13.85

```cpp
#include <iostream>
using namespace std;

void myFunc(int&& b) {

cout << "b is " << b << endl;
cout << "&b is " << &b << endl;
}

int main() {

int&& a = 10;
```

```cpp
cout << "a is " << a << endl;
cout << "&a is " << &a << endl;

myFunc(move(a));
}
```

Output(s):
a is 10
&a is 0x7ffcd589185c
b is 10
&b is 0x7ffcd589185c

Example-13.43: The difference of this example from the previous one is that the function has l-value argument.

Code 13.86
```cpp
#include <iostream>
using namespace std;

void myFunc(int b) {

cout << "b is " << b << endl;
cout << "&b is " << &b << endl;
}

int main() {

int a = 10;

cout << "a is " << a << endl;
cout << "&a is " << &a << endl;

myFunc((a));
myFunc(move(a));
}
```

Output(s):
a is 10
&a is 0x7fff7cd363c4
b is 10
&b is 0x7fff7cd363ac
b is 10
&b is 0x7fff7cd363ac

13.14 Move Constructor

Copy constructor and copy assignment operator creates a copy of the original object, whereas, the move constructor or move assignment operator changes the ownership of the values from one object to the other. Using move semantics, duplicate copy of the same object is prevented and resources are efficiently used. Move operation can be considered as destructive copying.

Non-constant r-value reference arguments are used in move semantics.

Move semantics improves the system performance. Since, it may be time consuming to make a copy of large objects; however, changing the ownership objects is an immediate process. Besides, move semantics prevent unnecessary copies, for instance when functions are called by value, copy constructors are used, which may be an unnecessary operation for some function calls. The syntax of the move constructor is

```
className(className&& rValue) {
// statements
}
```

Example-13.44: This example illustrates the use of the move constructor.
Code 13.87

```cpp
#include <iostream>
using namespace std;
class A {
public:
string name;
A() {
name = "Ilhan";
cout << "Inside default constructor" << endl;
}
A(const A& a) {
name = a.name;
cout << "Inside copy constructor" << endl;
}
A(A&& a){
name = move(a.name);
cout << "Inside move constructor" << endl;
}
};
int main() {
A o1 ;
cout << "Before move, o1.name = " << o1.name <<endl;
A o2(move(o1)); // move constructor is called
// it passes r-value reference
cout << "After move, o1.name = " << o1.name <<endl;
cout << "o2.name = " << o2.name <<endl;
}
```

Output(s):
Inside default constructor
Before move, o1.name = Ilhan
Inside move constructor
After move, o1.name =
o2.name = Ilhan
Example-13.45: The program in previous example can be written as Code-13.88.
Code 13.88

```cpp
#include <iostream>
using namespace std;
class A {
public:
string name;
A() {
name = "Ilhan";
cout << "Inside default constructor" << endl;
}
A(const A& a) {
name = a.name;
cout << "Inside copy constructor" << endl;
}
A(A&& a){
name = move(a.name);
cout << "Inside move constructor" << endl;
}
};
int main() {
A o1 ;
cout << "Before move, o1.name = " << o1.name <<endl;
A o2 = move(o1); // passes r-value reference
cout << "After move, o1.name = " << o1.name <<endl;
cout << "o2.name = " << o2.name <<endl;
}
```

Output(s):
Inside default constructor
Before move, o1.name = Ilhan
Inside move constructor
After move, o1.name =
o2.name = Ilhan
Example-13.46:
Code 13.89

```cpp
#include <iostream>
using namespace std;
class A {
```

```cpp
public:
string name;
A() {
name = "Ilhan";
cout << "Inside default constructor" << endl;
}
A(const A& a) {
name = a.name;
cout << "Inside copy constructor" << endl;
}
A(A&& a){
name = move(a.name);
cout << "Inside move constructor" << endl;
}
};
A myFunc(A a) {
return a; // calls copy/move constructor
}
int main() {
A o1 ;
cout << "Before move, o1.name = " << o1.name <<endl;
A o2 = myFunc(move(o1)); // move constructor is called
// it passes r-value reference
cout << "After move, o1.name = " << o1.name <<endl;
cout << "o2.name = " << o2.name <<endl;
}
```

Output(s):

```
Inside default constructor
Before move, o1.name = Ilhan
Inside move constructor
Inside move constructor
After move, o1.name =
o2.name = Ilhan
```

13.15 Conversion Constructor in C++

Consider the expression

$$int\ a = 3.14;$$

the floating point number 3.14 is implicitly converted to integer 3, and the value of a equals 3.

Now consider a class with name A, and assume that it has a parametric constructor given as

```
A(double a) {

// statements

}
```

The object of this class can be created either as

$$A\ obj(5.6);\ A\ obj\{5.6\};$$

Now what happens if we write

$$A\ obj = 5.6;$$

In this case, the compiler implicitly converts 5.6 to class object, and the above statement is interpreted as

$$A\ obj = A(5.6);$$

which is equal to

$$A\ obj(5.6);$$

The compiler performs implicit class-type conversions using constructors. The conversions are made by invoking the corresponding constructor which has the same argument values with the assigned ones.

Example-13.47: This example illustrates the use of the conversion constructor.

Code 13.90

```cpp
#include <iostream>
using namespace std;
class A {
private:
double x;
public:
A(double a) {
x = a;
cout << "Inside constructor, x is " << x << endl;
}
};
int main() {
A a1 = 4.5;
A a2 = A(4.7); // A a2 = A{4.7}
A a3(6.9);
}
```

Output(s):

```
Inside constructor, x is 4.5
Inside constructor, x is 4.7
```

Inside constructor, x is 6.9

In a similar manner assume that the class A has a parametric constructor given as

A(double a, double b) {

// statements

}

Then, the assignment

$$A\ obj = \{5.6, 7.8\};$$

equals to one of

$$A\ obj = A(5.6, 7.8);\ A\ obj = A\{5.6, 7.8\};$$
$$A\ obj(5.6, 7.8);\ A\ obj\{5.6, 7.8\};$$

13.15.1 Explicit conversion

Consider the expression

$$int\ a = (double)\ 3.14;$$

where explicit cast is used and the floating number 3.14 is converted to integer using explicit cast. Now, consider the expression

$$A\ obj = (A)\ 2.5;$$

In this expression explicit cast is used and this expression equals to one of

$$A\ obj\ (2.5);\ A\ obj\ \{2.5\};\ A\ obj = A(2.5);\ A\ obj = A\{2.5\};$$

In a similar manner, the expression

$$A\ obj = (A)\ \{2.5, 6.7\};$$

equals to one of

A obj (2.5, 6.7); A obj {2.5, 6.7};

A obj = A(2.5, 6.7); A obj = A{2.5, 6.7};

Example-13.48:

Code 13.91

```cpp
#include <iostream>
using namespace std;
class A {
private:
double x;
public:
A(double a, double b) {
x = a + b;
cout << "Inside constructor, x is " << x << endl;
}
};
int main() {
A a1 = {4.5, 7.8};
A a2 = A{4.5, 7.8};
A a3 = (A){4.5, 7.8};
A a4 = A(4.5, 7.8);
A a5{4.5, 7.8};
A a6{4.5, 7.8};
}
```

Output(s):

```
Inside constructor, x is 12.3
Inside constructor, x is 12.3
Inside constructor, x is 12.3
```

Inside constructor, x is 12.3

Inside constructor, x is 12.3

Inside constructor, x is 12.3

Implicit or explicit class conversions can be used at function calls or at function returns. For example, implicit cast is used in function returns as in

```cpp
class A {
// statements
};
A myFunc(double a, double b){

return {a, b}; // the same as return A{a, b}
}
```

and implicit cast is used in function calls as in

```cpp
void disp(A obj) {
// statements
}
disp( {5.6, 7.8} ); // the same as disp( A{5.6, 7.8} )
```

Example-13.49:

Code 13.92

```cpp
#include <iostream>
using namespace std;
class A {
private:
double x;
public:
A(double a, double b) {
x = a + b;
cout <<"Inside constructor, x is " << x << endl;
}
};
A myFunc(double a, double b) {
cout << "Inside function" << endl;
return {a, b};
}
int main() {
double a = 4.5, b = 6.7;
A obj = myFunc (a, b);
}
```

Output(s):

Inside function

Inside constructor, x is 11.2

Example-13.50:

Code 13.93

```cpp
#include <iostream>
using namespace std;
class A {
public:
double x;
A(double a, double b) {
x = a + b;
cout << "Inside constructor, x is " << x << endl;
}
};
void disp(A obj) {
cout << "Inside disp(), x is " << obj.x <<endl;
}
int main() {
disp( {5.6, 7.8} ); // the same as disp( A{5.6, 7.8} )
}
```

Output(s):

Inside constructor, x is 13.4

Inside disp(), x is 13.4

13.16 Explicit Specifier in C++

In the previous section we explained the implicit and explicit conversions used for constructors. In this section we will see how to disable the implicit conversion property. The explicit keyword is used to disable the implicit conversion for class constructors.

Example-13.51: In Code-13.94, implicit conversion is used for A a = 4.5; In Code-13.95, the implicit conversion is disabled using the keyword **explicit** as shown in yellow in Code-13.95. Code-13.94 compiles whereas Code-13.95 gives error.

Code 13.94
```cpp
#include <iostream>
using namespace std;

class A {

private:
double x;

public:

A(double a) {
x = a;
}
};

int main() {

A a = 4.5; // OK
}
```

Code 13.95
```cpp
#include <iostream>
using namespace std;

class A {

private:
double x;

public:

explicit A(double a) {
x = a;
}
};
```

```cpp
int main() {

A a = 4.5; // ERROR
}
```

13.17 Constant Member Functions

It is forbidden for the constant member functions to change the values of the data members of their class. Constant member function are defined by appending the keyword **const** to the end of the function definition header.

The prototype of a constant member function is as

returnDataType functionName(arguments) const;

If the function is implemented inside class, it is written as

returnDataType functionName(arguments) const {

// statements

}

If the function is implemented outsie class, it is written as

returnDataType **className::**functionName(arguments) const {

// statements

}

Example-13.52: In Code-13.96, declaration and implementation templates of a constant function are given.

Code 13.96

```cpp
int getX() const;

int getX() const {

// statements

}

int A::getX() const {

// statements

}
```

Example-13.53: Constant functions of a class cannot modify data values.

Code 13.97

```cpp
#include<iostream>
using namespace std;

class A {

private:
int x;

public:
A(int a) : x(a) {}

int getX() const {
```

```
x = 12; // error, constant function
// cannot change member values
return x;
}
};

int main() {

A myObj(6);

cout << "x is " << myObj.getX() << endl;
}
```

Example-13.54: Non-constant member functions can modify data.

Code 13.98
```
#include<iostream>
using namespace std;

class A {

private:
int x;

public:
A(int a) : x(a) { }

void setX(int b) { x = b; }

int getX() const { return x; }
};

int main() {

A myObj(6);

cout << "x is " << myObj.getX() << endl;

myObj.setX(65);

cout << "x is " << myObj.getX() << endl;
}
```

Output(s):
```
x is 6
x is 65
```

13.18 Static Members of Classes

We can have static variables in the public section as shown in Code-13.99. Static variables cannot be initialized in their declarations as indicated in Code-13.99

Code 13.99
```cpp
#include <iostream>
using namespace std;

class A {
public:

static float x = 5.7; // not allowed
};
```

Static variables of a class must be initialized with scope resolution operator as shown in Code-13.100.

Code 13.100
```cpp
#include <iostream>
using namespace std;
class A {
public:
static float x;
};
float A::x = 1.8; // no static word in front of A::
```

Example-13.55: In Code-13.101, we create and object having static variable, and print static value.

Code 13.101
```cpp
#include <iostream>
using namespace std;

class A {

public:

static float x;

};

float A::x = 1.8;

int main() {

A myObj;

cout << "x is: " << myObj.x << endl;
}
```

Output(s):
x is: 1.8

Once static variable is initialized with scope resolution operator, its value can be changed using the object of the class.

Example-13.56: We can change the static variable as in Code-13.102.

Code 13.102

```cpp
#include <iostream>
using namespace std;
class A {
public:
static float x;
};
float A::x = 1.8; // no static word in front of A::
int main() {
A myObj;
cout << "x is: " << myObj.x << endl;
myObj.x = 4.5;
cout << "x is: " << myObj.x << endl;
}
```

Output(s):

x is: 1.8

x is: 4.5

Example-13.57: Static value can be changed using the scope resolution operator as in Code-13.103.

Code 13.103

```cpp
#include <iostream>
using namespace std;

class A {

public:
static float x;
};
float A::x = 1.8;

int main() {

cout << "x is: " << A::x << endl;

A myObj;
myObj.x = 4.5;
cout << "x is: " << A::x << endl;

A::x = 6.7;
cout << "x is: " << A::x << endl;
}
```

Output(s):

x is: 1.8

x is: 4.5

x is: 6.7

Static variables are stored in a common memory location. The objects of the same class are affected if one object changes the value of a static variable.

Example-13.58: Static variables are the shared variables. The objects of the same class share the same static variables.

Code 13.104

```cpp
#include <iostream>
using namespace std;
class A {
public:
static float x;
};
float A::x = 1.8;
int main() {
cout << "x is: " << A::x << endl;
A myObj1;
A myObj2;
myObj1.x = 4.5;
cout << "x is: " << A::x << endl;
A::x = 6.7;
cout << "x is: " << A::x << endl;
cout << "myObj1.x is: " << myObj1.x << endl;
cout << "myObj2.x is: " << myObj2.x << endl;
}
```

Output(s):

x is: 1.8

x is: 4.5

x is: 6.7

myObj1.x is: 6.7

myObj2.x is: 6.7

13.18.1 Static Functions

Static functions are used to return the values of static varaibles and static functions can be called without creating an instance of the class.

Example-13.59: In Code-13.104B, we call static function using the scope resolution operator.

Code 13.104B

```cpp
#include <iostream>
using namespace std;

class A {
public:
static int N;
static int getObjNum() {return N;}
A() { N++; };
};

int A::N = 0;

int main() {

A myObj1;
cout << "N is " << A::getObjNum() << endl;

A myObj2, myObj3;
cout << "N is " << A::getObjNum() << endl;
cout << "myObj1.N is " << myObj2.N << endl;
}
```

Output(s):
N is 1
N is 3
myObj1.N is 3

If static functions are implemented outside the class declaration, then the word static is not used in front of the function name as illustrated in Code-13.105.

Code 13.105

```cpp
class A {

public:
static int N;
static int getObjNum();
A() { N++; };
};
```

```
int A::N = 0;
int A::getObjNum () {return N;} // ok
```

If we use the word **static** in front of the function implementation as in Code-13.106, error arises

Code 13.106

```
class A {
public:
static int N;
static int getObjNum();
A() { N++; };
};
int A::N = 0;
static int A::getObjNum () {return N;} // error, due to the static
                                       // word in front of
                                       // function return type
```

Problems

1) Find the mistake in the class declaration in Code-13.107.

Code 13.107
```cpp
class A {

public:
float x = 8.7;
}
```

2) Why does the program in Code-13.108 gives error?

Code 13.108
```cpp
#include <iostream>
using namespace std;

class A {

float x = 6.7;
};

int main() {

A myObj;

cout << "x is " << myObj.x << endl;
}
```

3) Declare a class which has public and private sections. The class has integer data variables in both public and private sections. Initialize the variables in the class declaration. Write a function in public section to display the values of the variables. In main() function write a test program which crates an object of the class and call the display function.

4) The Code-13.109 gives compile error. Find the mistake in the Code-13.109.

Code 13.109
```cpp
#include <iostream>
using namespace std;

class A {

protected:
float x = 8.9;
};

int main() {
```

```
A myObj;

cout << "x is " << myObj.x << endl;
}
```

5) Write the program in Code-13.110 using the scope resolution operator ::

Code 13.110
```
#include <iostream>
using namespace std;

class A {

public:
float x = 7.9;

void disp() {

cout << "x is " << x << endl;
}
};

int main() {

A myObj;

myObj.disp();
}
```

6) Write the program in Code-13.110 as the composition of three sub-programs.

7) The default constructor of a class is given in Code-13.111. Change the constructor such that variables are initialized at the constructor header.

Code 13.111
```
A(int a, int b, int c) {

w = a;
x = b;
y = c;
}
```

8) Which data members of a class should be initialized at the costructor header?

9) What is the output of Code-13.112?

Code 13.112
```
#include <iostream>
using namespace std;
```

```cpp
class A {

private:
int x;

public:
A(int a);
~A();
};

A::A(int a) {
x = a;
cout << "Inside constructor, x = " << x << endl;
}
A::~A() {
cout << "Inside destructor, x = " << x << endl;
}

int main() {

{A myObj1(6);}
A myObj2(9);
A myObj3(7);
}
```

Chapter-14

Inheritance

Abstract: In this chapter we explain inheritance subject. Inheritance is the heart of object oriented programming. Using inheritance, we can declare new classes using the already declared ones. It is like building new floors over the existing ones. Access specifiers play a critical role in inheritance. Newly declared classes can inherit the members of an existing class in different ways using the access specifiers. For this reason, it is important to know the functions of access specifiers very well to comprehend the inheritance subject well.

14.1 Short Review of Access Specifiers

A class can have three sections which are **public, protected** and **private**.

The **public** members are accessible by all the class functions and they are also accessible in the main program as well. Public members are accessible by derived class functions.

The **private** members are accessible by all the class functions and they are **NOT** directly accessible in the main program. **Private** members are **NOT** accessible by derived class functions.

The **protected** members are accessible by all the class functions and they are **NOT** directly accessible in the main program. **Protected** members are accessible by derived class functions.

Example-14.1: In this example, accessibility of public, protected and private members outside class declaration is illustrated.

Code 14.1

```cpp
#include <iostream>
using namespace std;
class A {
public:
int a;
protected:
int b;
private:
int c;
public:
A() : a {1}, b {2}, c {3} {} // defaut constructor
};
int main() {
A obj;
cout << "a = " << obj.a << endl; // ok
cout << "b = " << obj.b << endl; // error
cout << "c = " << obj.c << endl; // error
}
```

14.2 Inheritance

In object-oriented programming, new classes can be defined using existing classes. This is called inheritance.

In C++, a derived class D is extended from another class B, which is called a base class.

Base class can also be called as a **parent class** or a **superclass**, and a derived class can also be called as a **child class** or a **subclass**.

A derived class inherits accessible data fields and functions from its base class and may also add new data fields and functions. There are three types of derivation from a base class, and these derivation types are **public, private** and **protected**. In Codes-14.2, 14.3 and 14.4 class derivation using different access specifiers is illustrated.

Code 14.2
```cpp
class Base {

// statements

};

class Derived: public Base {

// statements

};
```

Code 14.3
```cpp
class Base {

// statements

};

class Derived: private Base {

// statements

};
```

Code 14.4
```cpp
class Base {

// statements

};

class Derived: protected Base {

// statements

};
```

14.3 Public Derivation

In public derivation, all the public and protected members of the base class can be accessed by the functions of the derived class. Public and protected members of the base class are inherited as the public and protected members of the derived class. In Code-14.5, the public inheritance is explained.

Code 14.5

```cpp
class Base {

public:
int x;
protected:
int y;
private:
int z;
};

class PublicDerived: public Base {

/*
x is public
y is protected
z is not accessible from PublicDerived
*/
};
```

Example-14.2: The object of a derived class can access the public members of both base and derived classes.

Code 14.6

```cpp
#include <iostream>
using namespace std;

class Base {

public:
void dispB() {

cout << "Inside base class" << endl;
}
};

class Derived : public Base {

public:
void dispD() {
```

```cpp
cout << "Inside derived class" << endl;
}
};

int main() {

Derived obj;

obj.dispB();

obj.dispD();
}
```

Output(s):
Inside base class
Inside derived class

Example-14.3: Private and protected members of base and derived classes cannot be accessed by derived class object in main function.

Code 14.7

```cpp
#include <iostream>
using namespace std;
class Base {
public:
int w = 2, x = 5;
protected:
int y = 7;
};
class Derived : public Base {
public:
int z = 13;
void disp() {
cout << "y = " << y << endl;
}
protected:
int k = 15;
};
int main() {
Derived obj;
cout << obj.w << endl; // w is accessible
cout << obj.y << endl; // error, y is not accesible
obj.disp(); // output: y = 7
cout << obj.k << endl; // error, k is not accesible
}
```

Example-14.4: The methods of a derived class can access to the protected members of a base class.

Code 14.8

```cpp
#include <iostream>
using namespace std;
class Base {
public:
void disp_pblB() { cout << "Inside public/Base" << endl; }
protected:
void disp_prtB() { cout << "Inside protected/Base" << endl; }
private:
void disp_prvB() { cout << "Inside private/Base" << endl; }
};
class Derived : public Base {
public:
void disp_pblD() {
cout << "Inside public/Derived" << endl;
}
void disp() { disp_prtB(); } // can access protected
// members of base class
};
int main() {
Derived obj;
obj.disp_pblB(); // output: "Inside public/Base"
obj.disp(); // output: "Inside protected/Base"
}
```

Output(s):

```
Inside public/Base
Inside protected/Base
```

Example-14.5: Protected members of a base class are not directly accessible outside base class declaration.

Code 14.9

```cpp
#include <iostream>
using namespace std;
class Base {
protected:
void disp_prtB() { cout << "Inside protected/Base" << endl; }
};
class Derived : public Base {
public:
void disp2() {
disp_prvB();
```

```cpp
}
};
int main() {
Derived obj;
obj.disp_prtB(); // error, protected members are not
// directly accessible outside class
}
```

Example-14.6:

Code 14.10

```cpp
#include <iostream>
using namespace std;
class Base {
private:
void disp_prvB() { cout << "Inside private/Base" <<endl; }
};
class Derived : public Base {
public:
void disp() { disp_prvB(); }
private:
void disp_prvD() {
cout << "Inside private/Derived" << endl;
}
};
int main() {
Derived obj;
obj.disp();// error, inside it calls base private member
obj.disp_prvB(); // error, base private member is
// never accessible
obj.disp_prvD(); // error, derived private member is not
// accessible outside class
}
```

14.4 Protected Derivation

In protected derivation, all the public and protected members of the base class become protected members of the derived class. Private members of the base class are not accessible in the derived class.

The accessibility of the members of the base class in the protected derived class is illustrated in Code-14.11.

Code 14.11
```cpp
class Base {

public:
int x;
protected:
int y;
private:
int z;
};

class ProtectedDerived: protected Base {

/*
x is protected
y is protected
z is not accessible from ProtectedDerived
*/
};
```

Example-14.7: Private members of base class are not accessible by the derived class methods. Protected members of base class are not directly accessible in the main() function.

Code 14.12
```cpp
#include <iostream>
using namespace std;
class Base {
public:
int x = 1;
protected:
int y = 2;
private:
int z = 3;
};
class Derived : protected Base {
public:
void disp1() {
```

```cpp
cout << "x is " << x << endl; // x is protected, ok
}
void disp2() {
cout << "y is " << y << endl; // y is protected,ok
}
void disp3() {
cout << "z is " << z << endl; // error, z is not accessible
}
};
int main() {
Derived obj;
cout << obj.x; // error, x is protected
// member of derived class
}
```

Example-14.8: In this example, we have three classes having the relation Base->Derived1->Derived2

Code 14.13

```cpp
#include <iostream>
using namespace std;
class Base {
public:
int x = 1;
};
class Derived1 : protected Base {
public:
int y = 2;
};
class Derived2 : protected Derived1 {
public:
void disp1() {
cout << "x is " << x << endl; // x is protected, ok
}
void disp2() {
cout << "y is " << y << endl; // y is protected, ok
}
};
int main() {
Derived2 obj;
cout << obj.x; // error, x is protected
// member of Derived2
cout << obj.y; // error, y is protected
// member of Derived2
obj.disp1(); // ok
obj.disp2(); // ok
}
```

14.5 Private Derivation

In private derivation, all the public and protected members of the base class become private members of the derived class. Private members of the base class are not accessible in the derived class.

The accessibility of the members of the base class in the private derived class is illustrated in Code-14.14.

Code 14.14
```cpp
class Base {
public:
int x;
protected:
int y;
private:
int z;
};

class PrivateDerived: private Base {

/*
x is private
y is private
z is not accessible from PrivateDerived
*/
};
```

If the private keyword is removed in class derivation, by default private derivation is use by the compiler. Codes-14.15 and 14.16 are equivalent codes.

Code 14.15
```cpp
class Derived: private Base {

// statements
};
```

Code 14.16
```cpp
class Derived: Base {

// statements
};
```

Example-14.9: Private derivation makes all the accessible members of base class private to the derived class.

Code 14.17
```cpp
#include <iostream>
using namespace std;
```

```cpp
class Base {

public:
int x = 5;

protected:
int y = 7;

private:
int z = 9;
};

class Derived : private Base {

// x is private, y is private
// z is not accessible in class Derived
};

int main() {

Derived obj;
cout << obj.x; // error, x is private
// for objects of class Derived
}
```

Summary

The derived classes with different access specifiers and the accessibility of the inherited members are summarized in Code-14.18.

Code 14.18

```cpp
class Base {
public:
int x;
protected:
int y;
private:
int z;
};
class PublicDerived: public Base {
/*
x is public
y is protected
z is not accessible from PublicDerived
*/
};
class ProtectedDerived: protected Base {
```

```cpp
    /*
    x is protected
    y is protected
    z is not accessible from ProtectedDerived
    */
};

class PrivateDerived: private Base {
    /*
    x is private
    y is private
    z is not accessible from PrivateDerived
    */
};
```

14.6 Constructor and Destructor Chaining

When a derived class object is created, first the base class's constructor is invoked, then the derived class's constructor is invoked.

Example-14.10: In this example, the invoke order of the base and derived classes is illustrated.

Code 14.19

```cpp
#include <iostream>
using namespace std;
class Base {
public:
Base() {
cout << "Inside base-class constructor " << endl;
}
};
class Derived : public Base {
public:
Derived() {
cout << "Inside derived-class constructor " << endl;
}
};
int main() {
Derived d;
}
```

Output(s):

```
Inside base-class constructor
Inside derived-class constructor
```

14.7 Explicit call of the default Base constructor

First base class default constructor is called, and then the derived class constructor is called. Base class default constructor can be called explicitly as in Code-14.20.

Code 14.20
```
Derived(parameterList): Base() {

// statements
}
```

If the base-class default constructor is not explicitly called, it is called automatically as illustrated in Codes-14.21 and 14.22.

Code 14.21
```
class Derived : public Base {

public:

Derived() {

// statements
}
};
```

Code 14.22
```
class Derived : public Base {

public:

Derived() : Base() {

// statements
}
};
```

If multiple base classes are used, then the default constructors of the base classes can be called as in Code-14.23.

Code 14.23
```
Derived(parameterList): Base1(), Base2(), Base3(),... {
// statements
}
```

Base-class non-default constructor can be called as in Code-14.24.

Code 14.24
```
Derived(parameterListD): Base(parameterListB) {

// statements
```

```cpp
}
```

Example-14.11:

Code 14.25

```
#include <iostream>
using namespace std;
class Base {
public:
Base() {
cout << "Inside base class constructor" << endl;
}
};
class Derived : public Base {
public:
Derived() : Base() { // explicit call of base class
// default constructor
cout << "Inside derived class constructor" << endl;
}
};
int main() {
Derived d;
}
```

Output(s):

```
Inside base class constructor
Inside derived class constructor
```

Example-14.12: In this example, non-default constructor call order for base and derived classes is illustrated.

Code 14.26

```
#include <iostream>
using namespace std;

class Base {

public:

int x;

Base(int a) : x(a) {

cout << "Inside base constructor" << endl;
cout << "x is " << x << endl << endl;
}
};

class Derived : public Base {

public:
```

```cpp
int y;

Derived(int a, int b) : y(b), Base(a) {

cout << "Inside derived constructor " << endl;
cout << "y is " << y << endl;
}
};

int main() {

Derived d(1,3);
}
```

Output(s):
```
Inside base constructor
x is 1
Inside derived constructor
y is 3
```

14.8 This pointer in Constructors

If the constructor parameters of a class have the same name as the members of the class, then **'this'** pointer is used to distinguish the parameters having the same name.

Code 14.27
```cpp
#include <iostream>
using namespace std;

class Base {

public:
int x;

Base(int a) {

x = a; // the same as
// this -> x = a;
}
};
```

Code 14.28
```cpp
#include <iostream>
using namespace std;

class Base {

public:
int x; // this -> x refers
// to this variable

Base(int x) {

this -> x = x;
}
};
```

Example-14.13: The Code-14.26 can be written using **this** pointer as Code-14.29.

Code 14.29
```cpp
#include <iostream>
using namespace std;
class Base {
public:
int x;
Base(int x) {
this -> x = x;
```

```cpp
cout << "Inside base constructor " << endl;
cout << "x is " << this -> x << endl;
}
};
class Derived : public Base {
public:
int y;
Derived(int x, int y): Base(x) {
this -> y = y;
cout << "Inside derived constructor " << endl;
cout << "y is " << this -> y <<endl;
}
};
int main() {
Derived d(1,3);
}
```

14.9 Multiple Inheritance

A derived class can have more than one base class, and this is called multiple inheritance. For example,

```cpp
class Derived: public Base1, public Base2 {
// statements
};
```

Example-14.14:

Code 14.30

```cpp
#include <iostream>
using namespace std;
class Base1 {
public:
Base1() {
cout << "Inside Base1 constructor" << endl;
}
};
class Base2 {
public:
Base2() {
cout << "Inside Base2 constructor" << endl;
}
};
class Derived : public Base1, public Base2 {
public:
Derived() {
cout << "Inside Derived constructor" << endl;
}
};
int main() {
Derived obj;
}
```

Output(s):

Inside Base1 constructor
Inside Base2 constructor
Inside Derived constructor
The constructor in Code-14.31

Code 14.31

```cpp
class Derived : public Base1, public Base2 {
public:
Derived() {
cout << "Inside Derived constructor" << endl;
}
};
```

is the same as the constructor in Code-14.32.

Code 14.32

```
class Derived : public Base1, public Base2 {
public:
Derived() : Base1(), Base2() {
cout << "Inside Derived constructor" << endl;
}
};
```

If the order of the base class constructors are written as in Code-14.33

Code 14.33

```
class Derived : public Base1, public Base2 {
public:
Derived() : Base2(), Base1() {
cout << "Inside Derived constructor" << endl;
}
};
```

then the output of the program does not change. However, if the header of the class is written as in Code-14.34

Code 14.34

```
class Derived : public Base2, public Base1 {
public:
Derived() : Base1(), Base2() {
cout << "Inside Derived constructor" << endl;
}
};
```

then the output of the program becomes as

```
Inside Base2 constructor
Inside Base1 constructor
Inside Derived constructor
```

Example-14.15: Ambiguity can arise if a derived class has the same base class more than once, and this happens in case of multiple inheritance.

Code 14.35

```
#include <iostream>
using namespace std;

class Base {

public:

void disp() {

cout << "Hello World";
}
};

class Derived1 : public Base {
```

```cpp
};

class Derived2 : public Base {

};

class Derived : public Derived1, public Derived2 {

};

int main() {

Derived obj;

obj.disp();
}
```

The class Derived inherits the same base method twice and the compiler cannot distinguish between methods which has the same name.

Output(s):

error: request for member 'disp' is ambiguous

To avoid the ambiguity we can use the scope resolution operator :: while calling the function as in Code-14.36.

Code 14.36

```cpp
int main() {

Derived obj;

obj.Derived1::disp();
}
```

14.10 Virtual Keyword

Virtual keyword can be used in different purposes in C++. In this section, we explain the use of virtual keyword for different scenarios.

14.10.1 Use of Virtual Keyword to Prevent Duplicate Inclusion of Base Class

In multiple inheritance, we can use virtual keyword to prevent double inclusion of the same base class in the derived class.

Example-14.16:

Code 14.37

```cpp
#include <iostream>
using namespace std;

class Base {

public:
void disp() {
cout << "Hello World!";
}
};

class Derived1 : virtual public Base {
};

class Derived2 : public virtual Base {
};

class Derived : public Derived1, public Derived2 {
};

int main() {
Derived obj;
obj.disp();
}
```

Output(s):
Hello World!

14.10.2 Redefining Functions and Virtual Functions

A function with the same name can be implemented both in base and derived classes. This is called polymorphism. To distinguish these two functions from each other we use the virtual keyword in front of the function name in base class.

Example-14.17: We use the same function in base and derived classed in Code-14.38.

Code 14.38
```cpp
#include <iostream>
using namespace std;

class Base {

public:
void A() {
cout << "Inside Base::A()\n";
}

};

class Derived : public Base {

public:
void A() {
cout << "Inside Derived::A()\n";
}
};

int main() {

Base b;
Derived d;

b.A(); // prints Inside Base::A()
d.A(); // prints Inside Derived::A()
}
```

When Code-14.38 is run we get the outputs:
Output(s):
Inside Base::A()
Inside Derived::A()
The test part of the Code-14.38 is modified as in Code-14.39.

Code 14.39
```cpp
#include <iostream>
using namespace std;
```

```cpp
class Base {

public:

void A() {
cout << "Inside Base::A()\n";
}
};

class Derived : public Base {

public:

void A() {
cout << "Inside Derived::A()\n";
}
};

int main() {

Base b;
Derived d;

Base* ptr;

ptr = &b;
ptr->A(); // prints Inside Base::A()

ptr = &d;
ptr->A(); // prints Inside Base::A()
}
```

When Code-14.39 is run we get the outputs:
Output(s):
Inside Base::A()
Inside Base::A()
It is seen that the same output is obtained for both calls.
Now we write the keyword **virtual** to the front of the function header as in Code-14.40.

Code 14.40
```cpp
#include <iostream>
using namespace std;

class Base {

public:
```

```cpp
virtual void A() {
cout << "Inside Base::A()\n";
}
};

class Derived : public Base {

public:

void A() {
cout << "Inside Derived::A()\n";
}
};

int main() {

Base b;
Derived d;

Base* ptr;

ptr = &b;
ptr->A(); // prints Inside Base::A()

ptr = &d;
ptr->A(); // prints Inside Derived::A()
}
```

Output(s):
Inside Base::A()
Inside Derived::A()
The use of **virtual** keyword enables the compiler to distinguish between base class function and derived class function.

Example-14.18: In this example, two different derived classes having the same base class are passed to the argument of a function.

Code 14.41
```cpp
#include <iostream>
using namespace std;

class Base {

public:
virtual void A() {
cout << "Inside Base::A()\n";
}
};
```

```cpp
class Derived1 : public Base {

public:
void A() {
cout << "Inside Derived1::A()\n";
}
};

class Derived2 : public Base {

public:
void A() {
cout << "Inside Derived2::A()\n";
}
};

void disp(Base* p) {

p->A();

}

int main() {

Derived1 d1;
Derived2 d2;

disp(&d1);
disp(&d2);
}
```

Output(s):
Inside Derived1::A()
Inside Derived2::A()

14.10.3 Virtual Destructors

It is necessary to define the base class destructors with virtual attribute if a base class pointer points to a dynamically created derived class object.

Example-14.19: In Code-14.42, we have base and derived classes, and in the main part of the program we have a base class pointer pointing to a derived class object which is dynamically created using new() function.

Code 14.42

```cpp
#include<iostream>
using namespace std;
class Base {
public:
Base() {
cout << "Inside Base Constructor" << endl;
}
~Base() {
cout << "Inside Base Destructor" << endl;
}
};
class Derived: public Base {
public:
Derived() {
cout << "Inside Derived Constructor" << endl;
}
~Derived() {
cout << "Inside Derived Destructor" << endl;
}
};
int main(void) {
Base* ptr = new Derived();
delete ptr;
}
```

When Code-14.42 is run, we get the output(s)

Inside Base Constructor

Inside Derived Constructor

Inside Base Destructor

It is seen that the destructor of the derived class is not called. To eliminate this problem, we modify our program as in Code-14.43 where base class has a virtual destructor.

Code 14.43

```cpp
#include<iostream>
using namespace std;
class Base {
public:
Base() {
```

```cpp
cout << "Inside Base Constructor" << endl;
}
virtual ~Base() {
cout << "Inside Base Destructor" << endl;
}
};
class Derived: public Base {
public:
Derived() {
cout << "Inside Derived Constructor" << endl;
}
~Derived() {
cout << "Inside Derived Destructor" << endl;
}
};
int main(void) {
Base* ptr = new Derived();
delete ptr;
}
```

When Code-14.43 is run we get the outputs:

Inside Base Constructor

Inside Derived Constructor

Inside Derived Destructor

Inside Base Destructor

Example-14.20: If a virtual function in base class is not redefined in derived class, and if a base class pointer pointing to a derived class object calls the function, then the virtual function of the base class is executed. In this example, we illustrate this scenario.

Code 14.44

```cpp
#include<iostream>
using namespace std;

class Base {
public:

virtual void disp() {

cout << "Inside Base::disp()" << endl;
}
};

class Derived : public Base {

// no code
};
```

```
int main() {

Base* ptr = new Derived();

ptr->disp();
}
```

Output(s): Inside Base::disp()

14.10.4 Pure Virtual Functions and Abstract Classes

Pure virtual functions have no body parts and they are initialized to zero, e.g.,

$$virtual\ void\ disp() = 0;$$

The classes that have pure virtual functions are called abstract classes, and we cannot create an object for an abstract class. Then, why an abstract class is used?

It is used for step-wise code development. That is, assume that you want to develop a code but you don't know how to start. The solution to this problem is that you first define the prototypes of the methods you want to write and you organize these methods in a class as virtual methods.

In the next step you implement these methods, and for this purpose you define a derived class and implement these methods in the derived class. And consider that at a different time it comes to your mind that you can implement the virtual methods in a different way, then you derive another class and you do the implementations of the methods in a different way. That is why we use abstract classes.

Example-14.21: Objects can not be defined for abstract classes.

Code 14.45

```cpp
#include<iostream>
using namespace std;
class Base { // abstract class
public:
virtual void disp() = 0; // abstract virtual function
};
int main() {
Base obj; // error
}
```

Output(s): error: cannot declare variable 'obj' to be of abstract type 'Base'

Example-14.22: An abstract class can contain a normal method as in Code-14.46, however, an object for an abstract class cannot be defines whether it contains a normal method or not.

Code 14.46

```cpp
#include<iostream>
using namespace std;
class Base {
public:
virtual void disp1() = 0; // abstract virtual method
void disp2() { // normal method
cout << "Hello World!" << endl;
}
};
int main() {
Base obj; // error
}
```

Output(s): error: cannot declare variable 'obj' to be of abstract type 'Base'

Example-14.23: In this example, we illustrate how to write a C++ program in a stepwise manner. Assume that you want to write a program that calculated the area and circumference of a circle. You think that you need two methods for your class, and you don't know the formulas used for the calculation of the area and the circumference of a circle. You start writing your program, first you write and abstract class as in Code-14.47.

Code 14.47

```cpp
#include<iostream>
using namespace std;
class Base {
public:
virtual float getArea() = 0; // area
virtual float getCircumference() = 0; // circumference
};
```

In the next step, you find a formula and learn the formulas for the calculation of area and circumference of a circle. You define a derived class called Circle, and implement the virtual methods for the derived class as in Code-14.48.

Code 14.48

```cpp
#include<iostream>
using namespace std;
class Base {
public:
virtual float getArea() = 0; // area
virtual float getCircumference() = 0; // circumference
};
class Circle : public Base {
private:
float r;
public:
Circle (float a = 1 ) {
r = a;
}
float getArea() {
return 3.14 * r * r;
};
float getCircumference() {
return 2 * 3.14 * r;
}
};
```

The main function for Code-14.48 can be written as in Code-14.49.

Code 14.49

```cpp
int main() {
Circle obj = 2;
cout << "Area is " << obj.getArea() << endl;
cout << "Circumference is " << obj.getCircumference() << endl;
}
```

When Codes-14.48 and 14.49 are concatenated and run we get the output
Area is 12.56
Circumference is 12.5

14.10.5 Ambiguities in Class Derivation

If the same names are used in base and derived classes for some members, then ambiguity arises. Ambiguity is not an error. It is just fuzziness.

We can solve ambiguity using scope resolution (::) operator.

Consider Code-14.50 where we have two base classes and one derived class. All the classes have a member with the same name "num".

Code 14.50

```cpp
#include<iostream>
using namespace std;
class Base1 {
public:
int num = 1;
};
class Base2 {
public:
int num = 2;
};
class Derived : public Base1, public Base2 {
public:
int num = 3;
};
```

In Code-14.51, we have a test program for the classes defined in Code-14.50.

Code 14.51

```cpp
int main() {
Derived obj;
Derived* ptr = &obj;
ptr -> num = 10;
cout << "Base1::num = " << ptr-> Base1::num << endl;
cout << "Base2::num = " << ptr-> Base2::num << endl;
cout << "Derived::num = " << ptr-> Derived::num << endl;
}
```

When Code-14-51 is run we get the outputs

```
Base1::num = 1
Base2::num = 2
Derived::num = 10
```

Hence, it is clear that in the expression ptr -> num = 10; "num refers to the member of the derived class. If we want to change the value of the same parameter in the base classes, we can use the scope resolution operator (::) as in Code-14.52.

Code 14.52

```cpp
int main() {
Derived obj;
Derived* ptr = &obj;
ptr -> Base1::num = 5;
```

```cpp
ptr -> Base2::num = 7;
ptr -> Derived::num = 12; // or ptr -> num = 12;
cout << "Base1::num = " << ptr-> Base1::num << endl;
cout << "Base2::num = " << ptr-> Base2::num << endl;
cout << "Derived::num = " << ptr-> num << endl;
}
```

Base1::num = 5
Base2::num = 7
Derived::num = 12

14.10.6 Pure Virtual Destructor

It is possible to define pure virtual destructors in C++. A class containing pure virtual destructor is an abstract class. The body a pure virtual destructor must be written although for abstract classes, objects cannot be defined.

Example-14.24: When the program in Code-14.53 is executed, we get error since the virtual destructor of the base class is not implemented.

Code 14.53
```cpp
#include <iostream>
using namespace std;
class Base {
public:
virtual ~Base() = 0;
};
class Derived : public Base {
public:
~Derived() {
cout << "~Derived() is called";
}
};
int main() {
Derived obj;
}
```

To eliminate the erroneous situation in Code-14.53, we implement the virtual destructor of the base class as in Code-14.54 which is error free.

Code 14.54
```cpp
#include <iostream>
using namespace std;
class Base {
public:
virtual ~Base() = 0;
};
Base::~Base() {
cout << "~Base() is called";
}
class Derived : public Base {
public:
~Derived() {
cout << "~Derived() is called \n";
}
};
int main() {
Derived obj;
}
```

Problems

1) Find the error in Code-14.55.

Code 14.55
```cpp
#include <iostream>
using namespace std;
class A {
int a;
public:
int b = 6;
};
int main() {
A obj;
cout << "a = " << obj.a << endl;
cout << "b = " << obj.b << endl;
}
```

2) Fill the dots in Code-14.56 with one of the words, public, protected, private or not accessible.

Code 14.56
```cpp
class Base {

public:
int x;
protected:
int y;
private:
int z;
};

class PublicDerived: public Base {

/*
x is ...
y is ...
z is ...
*/
};
```

3) What is the output of Code14.57?

Code 14.57
```cpp
#include <iostream>
using namespace std;

class Base {
```

```cpp
public:
int x = 2;

protected:
int y = 7;

};

int main() {

Base obj;
cout << obj.x << endl;
cout << obj.y << endl;
}
```

4) Write a base class which has public and private sections, and in these sections the class has two integer variables.

Write a derived class which inherits the base class members.

Derived class has a method which modifies the accessible members of the base class and displays the modified values.

Write a test program and create a derived class object an using the object call the display method of the derived class.

5) What is the main difference between private and protected members of a base class?

6) Are the protected members of a base class are directly accessible outside base class declaration?

7) Fill the dots in Code-14.58 with one of the words, public, protected, private or not accessible.

Code 14.58
```cpp
class Base {

public:
int x;
protected:
int y;
private:
int z;
};
class ProtectedDerived: protected Base {

/*
x is ...
y is ...
z is ...
*/
};
```

8) Find the errors in Code-14.59.

Code 14.59

```cpp
#include <iostream>
using namespace std;

class Base {

public:
int x = 1;

protected:
int y = 2;
};

class Derived : protected Base {

};
int main() {

Derived obj;

cout << obj.x;
cout << obj.y;
}
```

Chapter-15

Operator Overloading

Abstract: In this chapter we explain operator overloading in C++. Operator overloading is the extension of the capabilities of arithmetic and logical operators for objects. For instance, we can sum two integers, but we cannot sum two objects. However, extending the capability of the + operator it is possible to sum two objects.

15.1 Introduction

Consider Code-15.1 where there are two integers x, y and we sum these two integers and equate it to z

Code 15.1
```
int x = 1;
int y = 5;
int z;

z = x + y;
```

Now, consider Code-15.2 where we declare a class and define two objects of this class and sum these two objects and equate it to another object. When Code-15.2 is run, the compiler issues an error. Is there a way to avoid such an error and enable the compiler such that it can perform the addition of two objects? The answer of this question is yes and the solution passes through extending the capabilities of the + operator for the defined class.

Code 15.2
```
#include <iostream>
using namespace std;

class Point {

public:
int x = 1;
int y = 2;
}

int main() {

Point p1;
Point p2;

Point ps = p1+p2 // ??
}
```

We can extend the capability of $+$ operator and define it for classes as well, and this is called operator overloading. Hence, extending the capabilities of the operators is called operator overloading.

15.1.1 Syntax for C++ Operator Overloading

The syntax of the operator overloading is shown in Code-15.3.

Code 15.3
```
class className {

public

returnType operator symbol (arguments) {

// statements
}

};
```

In Code-15.3,
returnType is the return type of the function,
operator is a keyword,
symbol is the operator we want to overload, like: +, <, -, ++, etc.,
arguments are the arguments passed to the function

15.2 Overloading + Operator

In this section, we will overload the + operator for the class in Code-15.4.

Code 15.4
```cpp
class Point {

public:

int x = 1;
int y = 3;

void display() {

cout << "x is " << x;
cout << ", y is " << y <<endl;
}
};
```

The template of the operator overloading function is
```cpp
returnType operator symbol (arguments) {
// statements
}
```
which can be written for the class in Code-15.4 as
```cpp
Point operator + (const Point& obj) {
// statements
}
```
where the returnType is a Point class object. The statements inside the function can be filled as in
```cpp
Point operator + (const Point& obj) {
Point t;
t.x = x + obj.x;
t.y = y + obj.y;
return t
}
```
Using the overloaded function for the class in Code-15.4, we can write the complete program as in Code-25.5. Note that the operator overloading method is written **inside the public** section of the class.

Code 15.5
```cpp
#include <iostream>
using namespace std;

class Point {

public:

int x = 1;
```

```cpp
int y = 3;

// written inside the public section
Point operator + (const Point& obj) {

Point t;

t.x = x + obj.x;
t.y = y + obj.y;

return t;
}

void display() {

cout << "x is " << x;
cout << ", y is " << y <<endl;
}
};

int main() {

Point p1;
Point p2;

p1.display();

Point ps = p1.operator + (p2);

ps.display();
}
```

In Code-15.5,

$$\text{Point ps = p1.operator + (p2);}$$

can be written as

$$\text{Point ps = p1 + p2;}$$

When Code-15.5 is run, we get the outputs

x is 1, y is 3

x is 2, y is 6

The operator overloading function of Code-15.5 is shown in Code-15.6 for the reminder.

Code 15.6

```cpp
Point operator + (const Point& obj) {

Point t;

t.x = x + obj.x;
```

```
    t.y = y + obj.y;

    return t;
}
```

The function in Code-15.6 returns a Point object. We can write the operator overloading function for + as in Code-15.7 where the function returns a reference to the object, and inside Code-15.7 we use **this** pointer.

Code 15.7

```
Point& operator + (const Point& obj) {

    this -> x = this -> x + obj.x;

    this -> x = this -> y + obj.y;

    return *this;
}
```

If we use Code-15.7 for the overloading operator, then the main function of program in Code-15.5 can be written as in Code-15.8.

Code 15.8

```
int main() {

    Point p1;
    Point p2;

    p1.display();

    p1 + p2; // the same as p1.operator + (p2);

    p1.display();
}
```

15.3 Overloading << Operator

In this section we will overload the output operator <<.

In Code-15.9, we use the output operator << to print the value of an integer variable to the screen.

Code 15.9

```
int x = 1;

cout << " x is " << x << endl;
```

Now, consider the class Point in Code-15.10. If we compile Code-15.10, compiler error arises. Then, it is possible to display class parameters using **cout << ... ?**

Code 15.10
```
#include <iostream>
using namespace std;

class Point {

public:
int x = 1;
int y = 2;
}

int main() {

Point p;
cout << p; // is this possible ??
}
```

The answer of the question yes, if we overload the operator <<, i.e., extent the operator capabilities, for the class Point we can print the parameters of the class object.

The general syntax of operator overloading
```
returnType operator symbol (arguments) {
// statements
}
```
for << operator has three forms, one of them is

```
void operator << (ostream& os) {
// statements
}
```
and the second form is

```
ostream & operator << (ostream &out, const Point &c) {
// statements
}
```

and the third form is

```
friend ostream & operator << (ostream &out, const Point &c) {
// statements
}
```

The use of the first form is not very common compared to the second and third forms.

The parameters of the class object for the first form are printed as

$$obj.\textbf{operator} << (cout);$$

and for the second and third forms, the object parameters are printed using

$$cout << obj;$$

If there are private parameters of the object, then the second form creates a problem, since private members are not accessible by the functions outside the class.

The operator overloading function for the << operator is written outside the class declaration.

Let's write a << overloading function for the class in Code-15.11.

Code 15.11
```cpp
#include <iostream>
using namespace std;

class Point {

public:

int x = 1;
int y = 3;
};
```

First, we write the function skeleton as in Code-15.12. Note that << operator overloading function is written **outside** class declaration.

Code 15.12
```cpp
#include <iostream>
using namespace std;

class Point {

public:

int x = 1;
int y = 3;
};

ostream & operator << (ostream &os, const Point &c) {

// statements
```

```
}
```

In the next step, the body of the operator overloading function is written as in Code-15.13.

Code 15.13
```cpp
#include <iostream>
using namespace std;

class Point {

public:

int x = 1;
int y = 3;
};

ostream & operator << (ostream &os, const Point &c) {

os << "x is: " << c.x <<endl;
os << "y is: " << c.y <<endl;

return os;
}
```

Finally, we can add the main function as in Code-15.14.

Code 15.14
```cpp
#include <iostream>
using namespace std;
class Point {
public:
int x = 1;
int y = 3;
};
ostream & operator << (ostream &os, const Point &c) {
os << "x is: " << c.x << endl;
os << "y is: " << c.y << endl;
return os;
}
int main() {
Point p;
cout << p;
}
```

The class in Code-15.14 does not contain a private section. Let's add a private section to the class in Code-15.14 and rewrite the operator overloading function as in Code-15.15.

Code 15.15
```cpp
#include <iostream>
```

```cpp
using namespace std;

class Point {
private:
int z;

public:
int x = 1;
int y = 3;
};
ostream & operator << (ostream &os, const Point &c) {

os << "x is: " << c.x << endl;
os << "y is: " << c.y << endl;
os << "z is: " << c.z << endl;
return os;
}

int main() {

Point p;
cout << p; // error
}
```

When the Code-15.15 is run we get "error: 'int Point::z' is private within this context"

That is overloaded operator function cannot access to the private members of the class. To solve this problem we need to introduce the overloaded function as the friend function for the class as in Code-15.16. When Code-15.16 is run, we get no error.

Code 15.16

```cpp
#include <iostream>
using namespace std;
class Point {
private:
int z;
public:
int x = 1;
int y = 3;
friend ostream & operator << (ostream&, const Point&);
};
ostream & operator << (ostream &os, const Point &c) {
os << "x is: " << c.x <<endl;
os << "y is: " << c.y <<endl;
os << "z is: " << c.z <<endl;
return os;
}
```

```
int main() {
Point p;
cout << p; // ok
}
```

The friend function shown in Code-15.16 can be written in any section inside the class declaration, i.e., it can be written in the private section as well. It is also possible to write all the function body inside the class as in Code-15.17.

Code 15.17

```
#include <iostream>
using namespace std;
class Point {
private:
int z;
public:
int x = 1;
int y = 3;
friend ostream & operator << (ostream &os, const Point &c) {
os << "x is: " << c.x <<endl;
os << "y is: " << c.y <<endl;
os << "z is: " << c.z <<endl;
return os;
}
};
```

We can write the overloading function for << using the second form as in Code-15.18.

Code 15.18
```cpp
void operator << (ostream& os) {

os << "x is: " << x << endl;
os << "y is: " << y << endl;
os << "z is: " << z << endl;

}
```

The complete program with alternative overloading function is shown in Code-15.19.

Code 15.19
```cpp
#include <iostream>
using namespace std;

class Point {

private:

int z = 5;

public:

int x = 1;
int y = 3;

void operator << (ostream& os);

};

void Point::operator << (ostream& os) {

os << "x is: " << x << endl;
os << "y is: " << y << endl;
os << "z is: " << z << endl;

}

int main() {

Point p;

p.operator << (cout); // ok
}
```

15.4 Overloading >> Operator

In Code-15.20, we get a value from user using **cin** object.

Code 15.20
```
int x;

cout << "Enter x value: " << endl;

cin >> x;
```

Now, consider the class Point in Code-15.21, can we get object parameters using **cin >> ... ?**

Code 15.21
```
#include <iostream>
using namespace std;

class Point {

public:
int x;
int y;
}

int main() {

Point p;

cout << "Enter class parameters x, y " << endl;

cin >> p;
}
```

If you compile Code-15.21, the compiler error arises.

We can extend the capability of >> operator and define it for classes as well, i.e., we can write an operator overloading function for >>.

The operator >> can be overloaded using two methods, the syntax of the first method is
```
void Point::operator >> (istream& is) {
// statements
}
```
and for this method we use the **cin** function as
$$obj.operator >> (cin);$$
The syntax of the second method is
```
friend istream & operator >> (istream& is, className& c) {
// statements
}
```

Example-15.1: In Code-15.22 we have a class declaration inside the prototype of the operator overloading function for >> is written.

Code 15.22
```cpp
#include <iostream>
using namespace std;

class Point {

public:
int x;
int y;

void operator >> (istream& is);
};
```

The body of the operator overloading function for >> in Code-15.22 can be written as in Code-15.23

Code 15.23
```cpp
void Point::operator >> (istream& is) {

cout << "Enter x value: ";

is >> x;

cout << "Enter y value: ";

is >> y;
}
```

The complete program is shown in Code-15.24.

Code 15.24
```cpp
#include <iostream>
using namespace std;

class Point {

public:
int x;
int y;

void operator >> (istream& is);
};

void Point::operator >> (istream& is) {

cout << "Enter x value: ";
```

```cpp
is >> x;

cout << "Enter y value: ";

is >> y;
}

int main() {

Point p;

cout << "Enter class parameters x, y " << endl;

p.operator >> (cin);

cout << "You entered " << p.x << " for x" << endl;
cout << "You entered " << p.y << " for y" << endl;
}
```

Output(s):
```
Enter class parameters x, y
Enter x value: 56
Enter y value: 78
You entered 56 for x
You entered 78 for y
```
Example-15.2: In this example, we overload the >> operator using the first syntax.

Code 15.25
```cpp
#include <iostream>
using namespace std;
class Point {
public:
int x;
int y;
friend istream & operator >> (istream& is, Point &c);
};


istream & operator >> (istream& is, Point &c) {
    cout << "Enter x value: ";
    is >> c.x;
    cout << "Enter y value: ";
    is >> c.y;
    return is;
}
int main() {
Point p;
```

```cpp
cout << "Enter class parameters x, y " << endl;
cin >> p;
cout << "You entered " << p.x << " for x" << endl;
cout << "You entered " << p.y << " for y" << endl;
}
```

Output(s):

```
Enter class parameters x, y
Enter x value: 56
Enter y value: 45
You entered 56 for x
You entered 45 for y
```

Example-15.3: In this example, we use operator overloading for both << and >>.

Code 15.26

```cpp
#include <iostream>
using namespace std;
class Point {
public:
int x;
int y;
friend ostream & operator << (ostream&, const Point&);
friend istream & operator >> (istream&, Point&);
};
istream & operator >> (istream& is, Point &c) {
cout << "Enter x value: ";
is >> c.x;
cout << "Enter y value: ";
is >> c.y;
return is;
}
ostream & operator << (ostream &os, const Point &c) {
os << "x is " << c.x <<endl;
os << "y is " << c.y <<endl;
return os;
}
int main() {
Point p;
cout << "Enter class parameters x, y " << endl;
cin >> p;
cout << p;
}
```

Output(s):

```
Enter class parameters x, y
Enter x value: 23
Enter y value: 67
```

```
x is 23
y is 67
```

15.5 Overloading the Subscript Operator []

The subscript operator [] is used to access and modify a data field or an element in an object.

The prototype of the overloading operator is

dataType& operator[] (**int** index)

where the reference symbol & is necessary to be able to assign new values to the class elements.

Example-15.4: Consider Code-15.27, when it is compiled we get

"error: no match for 'operator[]' (operand types are 'Point' and 'int')"

Thus, we need to define subscript operator for this class.

Code 15.27
```cpp
#include <iostream>
using namespace std;

class Point {

public:
int x = 1, y = 3, z = 5;
};

int main() {

Point p;

p[0] = 8; p[1] = 5; p[2] = 12; // error
}
```

We define subscript operator as in Code-15.28.

Code 15.28
```cpp
#include <iostream>
using namespace std;

class Point {

public:
int x = 1, y = 3, z = 5;
int& operator [] (int indx);
};

int& Point::operator [] (int indx) {

if(indx == 0)
return x;

else if(indx == 1)
```

```cpp
  return y;

else if(indx == 2)
return z;

else {
cout << "Indx is out of range!" << endl;
exit(1);
}

}

int main() {

Point p;

p[0] = 8; p[1] = 5; p[2] = 12; // ok
}
```

If we use

$$\text{int Point::}\mathbf{operator}\ [\ ]\ (\text{int indx})$$

in Code-15.28 instead of

$$\text{int\& Point::}\mathbf{operator}\ [\ ]\ (\text{int indx})$$

then we get error at the line

$$p[0] = 8; p[1] = 5; p[2] = 12;$$

Since L-values are needed to assign new values to the parameters.
We can add the overloading function for << as in Code-15.29.

Code 15.29

```cpp
#include <iostream>
using namespace std;
class Point {
public:
int x = 1, y = 3, z = 5;
friend ostream& operator << (ostream& os, const Point &c);
int& operator [] (int indx);
};
ostream& operator << (ostream& os, const Point& c) {
os << "x is: " << c.x;
os << ", y is: " << c.y;
os << ", z is: " << c.z << endl;
return os;
}
int& Point::operator [] (int indx) {
if(indx == 0)
return x;
else if(indx == 1)
```

```cpp
    return y;
    else if(indx == 2)
    return z;
    else {
    cout << "Indx is out of range!" << endl;
    exit(1);
    }
    }
    int main() {
    Point p;
    cout << p;
    p[0] = 8; p[1] = 5; p[2] = 12;
    cout << p;
    }
```

When Code-15.29 is run, we get the output

```
x is: 1, y is: 3, z is: 5
x is: 8, y is: 5, z is: 12
```

15.6 Overloading Augmented Assignment Operators

C++ has augmented assignment operators

$$+= \quad -= \quad *= \quad /= \quad \textbf{and} \quad \%=$$

for adding, subtracting, multiplying, dividing, and modulus a value in a variable.

These operators can be overloaded for a class. The general template for augmented operator overloading is

```
className& operator symbol (const className& obj) {
// statements
return *this;
}
```

The template use for += operator is as

```
className& operator += (const className& obj) {
// statements
return *this;
}
```

For the other augmented operators similar expressions are available.

Example-15.5: In Code-15.30, the operator += is overloaded for the class Point.

Code 15.30

```
class Point {

public:

int x = 1, y = 3, z = 5;

Point& operator += (const Point& obj);
};

Point& Point::operator += (const Point& obj) {

x = x + obj.x;
y = y + obj.y;
z = z + obj.z;

return *this;
}
```

In Code-15.31 overloaded function for << is included. In the main() function of the program, two objects are summed using augmented addition operator and the result is printed.

Code 15.31

```
#include <iostream>
using namespace std;
class Point {
public:
int x = 1, y = 3, z = 5;
```

```cpp
Point(int a, int b, int c) {x = a; y = b; z = c;};
friend ostream & operator << (ostream &out, const Point &c);
Point& operator += (const Point& obj);
};
ostream & operator << (ostream& os, const Point &c) {
os << "x is: " << c.x <<endl;
os << "y is: " << c.y <<endl;
os << "z is: " << c.z <<endl;
return os;
}
Point& Point::operator += (const Point& obj) {
x = x + obj.x;
y = y + obj.y;
z = z + obj.z;
return *this;
}
int main() {
Point p1(2,3,5);
cout << p1 << endl;
Point p2(4,4,4);
cout << p2 << endl;
p1 += p2;
cout << p1 << endl;
}
```

Output(s):

```
x is: 2
y is: 3
z is: 5
x is: 4
y is: 4
z is: 4
x is: 6
y is: 7
z is: 9
```

15.7 Overloading the Unary Operators

Since the unary operator - operates on the calling object itself, the unary function operator has no parameters

The operator overloading prototype for unary operator - is as

className **operator** - ()

Example-15.6: In Code-15.32, the unary operator - overloaded for the class Point.

Code 15.32
```
class Point {

public:
int x = 1, y = 3, z = 5;

Point(int a, int b, int c) {

x = a; y = b; z = c;
};

Point operator - ();
};

Point Point::operator - () {

return Point(-x,-y,-z);
}
```

The unary operator – is tested in Code-15.33

Code 15.33
```
#include <iostream>
using namespace std;
class Point {
public:
int x = 1, y = 3, z = 5;
Point(int a, int b, int c) {x = a; y = b; z = c;}};
friend ostream & operator << (ostream& os, const Point &c);
Point operator - ();
};
ostream & operator << (ostream& os, const Point &c) {
os << "x = " << c.x;
os << ", y = " << c.y;
os << ", z = " << c.z;
return os;
}
Point Point::operator - () {
return Point(-x,-y,-z);
```

```cpp
}
int main() {
Point p1(2,3,5);
cout << p1 << endl;
cout << -p1 << endl;
Point p2 = -p1;
cout << p2 << endl;
}
```

Output(s):

```
x = 2, y = 3, z = 5
x = -2, y = -3, z = -5
x = -2, y = -3, z = -5
```

15.8 Overloading the ++ and—Operators

The pre-increment, pre-decrement, post-increment, and post-decrement operators can be overloaded.

The ++ and—operators can be used as prefix or postfix.

In the prefix operations 1 is added or subtracted from the variable and this has the higher priority than the assignment operator.

In the postfix operations 1 is added or subtracted from the variable and this has lower priority than the assignment operator.

How does C++ distinguish the prefix ++ or—operators from the postfix ++ or—operators?

For postfix operators, a special **dummy** parameter of the **int** type is used as overloaded function argument, and for the prefix operator no argument is used for the overloaded function.

Prefix increment syntax

The prefix operators are Lvalue operators. The template for prefix operator ++ is as

className& operator ++ ()

Postfix increment syntax

The postfix operators are NOT Lvalue operators. The template for postfix operator ++ is as

className operator ++ (int dummy)

Example-15.7:

Code 15.34

```cpp
#include <iostream>
using namespace std;
class Point {
public:
int x = 1, y = 3, z = 5;
Point(int a, int b, int c) {x = a; y = b; z = c;};
friend ostream & operator << (ostream &out, const Point &c);
Point& operator ++ (); // prefix increment
Point operator ++ (int dumy); // postfix increment
};
ostream & operator << (ostream &os, const Point &c) {
os << "x is: " << c.x;
os << ", y is: " << c.y;
os << ", z is: " << c.z <<endl;
return os;
}
Point& Point::operator ++ () { // prefix increment
x = x + 1; y = y + 1; z = z + 1;
return *this;
}
Point Point::operator ++ (int dumy) { // postfix increment
Point p(x,y,z);
x = x + 1; y = y + 1; z = z + 1;
return p;
```

```cpp
}
int main() {
Point p1(2,3,5);
cout << p1;
Point p2 = p1++;
cout << p2;
cout << p1;
Point p3 = ++p1;
cout << p1;
cout << p3;
}
```

Output(s):

x is: 2, y is: 3, z is: 5
x is: 2, y is: 3, z is: 5
x is: 3, y is: 4, z is: 6
x is: 4, y is: 5, z is: 7
x is: 4, y is: 5, z is: 7

15.9 friend Functions and friend Classes

Private members of a class cannot be accessed from outside the class. However, it is possible to allow some trusted functions and classes to access a class's private members, and this is achieved using the friend keyword. Functions and classes introduced as friend functions or classes inside another class can access another class's private members.

Example-15.8: The function p() in Code-15.35 is introduced as a friend function, and for this reason the function p() can access the private members of the class.

```
Code 15.35
#include <iostream>
using namespace std;

class A {

public:

A() : x(3), y(4) {};
A(int a, int b): x(a), y(b) {};
friend void p();

private:
int x, y;
};
void p() {

A obj(5,7);
cout << "x is " << obj.x <<endl;
cout << "y is " << obj.y <<endl;
}

int main() {

p();
}
```

Output(s):
x is 5
y is 7

Example-15.9: In Code-15.36, class B is introduced as a friend of class A, and this means that the methods of class B can access all the members of class A.

```
Code 15.36
#include <iostream>
using namespace std;

class A {
```

```cpp
public:

A() : x(3), y(4) {};
A(int a, int b): x(a), y(b) {};
friend class B;

private:
int x, y;
};

class B {

public:

A obj = A(5,6);
void p();
void g();
};

void B::p() {
cout << "x is " << obj.x <<endl;
}

void B::g() {
cout << "y is " << obj.y <<endl;
}

int main() {

B obj;

obj.p();
obj.g();
}
```

Output(s):
x is 5
y is 7

15.10 Operator Overloading Using Friend Functions

Operator overloading can be performed using **friend** functions. In this case, usually operator functions take two input parameters. For instance, the operator + can be overloaded using the friend function as in

friend Point **operator** + (const Point& p1, const Point& p2);

Note that, in Code-15.5 it is overloaded as

Point **operator** + (const Point& obj);

Example-15.10:

Code 15.37

```cpp
#include <iostream>
using namespace std;



class Point {
    private:
    int x = 1, y = 3, z = 5;
    public:
    Point(int a, int b, int c) : x{a}, y{b}, z{c} { };
    friend ostream& operator << (ostream& os, const Point& c);
    friend Point operator + (const Point &p1, const Point& p2);
    };
    ostream & operator << (ostream& os, const Point& c) {
    os << "x is: " << c.x << ", ";
    os << "y is: " << c.y << ", ";
    os << "z is: " << c.z;
    return os;
    }
    Point operator + (const Point& p1, const Point& p2) {
    return Point(p1.x + p2.x, p1.y + p2.y, p1.z + p2.z);
    }
    int main() {
    Point p1(2,3,5);
    cout << p1 << endl;
    Point p2(6,6,6);
    cout << p2 << endl;
    Point ps = p1+p2;
    cout << ps << endl;
    }
```

Output(s):

```
x is: 2, y is: 3, z is: 5
x is: 6, y is: 6, z is: 6
x is: 8, y is: 9, z is: 11
```

If private members are not accessed by the operator function, non-member functions can also be used for operator overloading, for instance Code-15.37 can also be written as Code-15.38.

Code 15.38

```cpp
#include <iostream>
using namespace std;
class Point {
public: // only public section is available
int x = 1, y = 3, z = 5;
Point(int a, int b, int c) : x{a}, y{b}, z{c} { };
friend ostream & operator << (ostream& out, const Point& c);
};
ostream & operator << (ostream& os, const Point& c) {
os << "x is: " << c.x << ", ";
os << "y is: " << c.y << ", ";
os << "z is: " << c.z;
return os;
}
Point operator+(const Point& p1, const Point& p2) {
return Point(p1.x + p2.x, p1.y + p2.y, p1.z + p2.z);
}
int main() {
Point p1(2,3,5);
cout << p1 << endl;
Point p2(6,6,6);
cout << p2 << endl;
Point ps = p1 + p2;
cout << ps << endl;
}
```

Output(s):

```
x is: 2, y is: 3, z is: 5
x is: 6, y is: 6, z is: 6
x is: 8, y is: 9, z is: 11
```

Note that in Code-15.38, we did not define the operator overloading function as a **friend** function in the class, since it does not access to the **private** members, no need to define it as a friend function.

If the operator overloading function uses the **private** members, it must be defined as **friend** function as in Code-15.39.

Code 15.39

```cpp
#include <iostream>
using namespace std;
class Point {
private:
int x = 1, y = 3, z = 5;
public:
Point(int a, int b, int c) : x{a}, y{b}, z{c} { };
friend ostream & operator << (ostream& os, const Point& c);
friend Point operator+(const Point& p1, const Point& p2);
```

```cpp
};
ostream & operator << (ostream &os, const Point &c) {
os << "x is: " << c.x << ", ";
os << "y is: " << c.y << ", ";
os << "z is: " << c.z;
return os;
}
Point operator+(const Point& p1, const Point& p2) {
return Point(p1.x + p2.x, p1.y + p2.y, p1.z + p2.z);
}
int main() {
Point p1(2,3,5);
cout << p1 << endl;
Point p2(6,6,6);
cout << p2 << endl;
Point ps = p1 + p2;
cout << ps << endl;
}
```

15.11 Converting Classes to Primitive Data Types

Operator overloading can be used to convert classes to other data types such as **double, int, float,** etc

Syntax: operator data_type();

Example-15.11: If the expression **operator double**() is overloaded for a class, the class object is converted to a double.

Example-15.12: In Code-15.40, the class object is converted to an integer using **operator int**() which is overloaded for the class Point.

```
Code 15.40
#include <iostream>
using namespace std;

class Point {

public:
int x = 1;
Point(int a) : x{a} { };
operator int();
};
Point::operator int() {
return x;
}
int main() {

Point p(2);
int num = p;
cout << "Number is " << num << endl;
}
```

Example-15.13: In Code-15.41, the class object is converted to a double using **operator double**() which is overloaded for the class Point.

```
Code 15.41
#include <iostream>
#include <typeinfo>
using namespace std;
class Point {
public:
int x = 1, y = 5;
Point(int a, int b) {x=a; y=b;};
operator double();
};
Point::operator double() {
return double(x*x+y*y);
}
```

```cpp
int main() {
Point p(2,3);
double num=p;
cout << "Number is: " << num << endl;
cout << typeid(num).name() << endl; // d means double
}
```

15.12 Operators that can be Overloaded

The set of the operators that can be overloaded in C++ can be listed as in

```
+ - */% ^ & | ~
! = < > += -= *= /= %=
^= &= |= << >> <<= >>= == !=
<= >= && || ++ — , ->* ->
( ) [ ] new delete new[] delete[]
```

15.13 Operators that CANNOT be overloaded

The set of the operators that cannot be overloaded in C++ are

?: . .* ::

Problems

1) Overload the + operator for the class A in Code-15.42. Write a test program to test the + operator.

Code 15.42
```cpp
class A {

public:

double x = 4.5;
double y = 2.3;
};
```

2) Find the mistake in Code-15.43.

Code 15.43
```cpp
class A {

public:
int x = 1;

private:
A operator + (const A& obj) {
A t;
t.x = x + obj.x;
return t;
}
};
```

3) Fill in the dots in Code-15.44, and then write a test program in main() function to test the Code-15.44.

Code 15.44
```cpp
class A {

public:
int x = 1;

private:
A& operator + (const A& obj) {

...x = ...x + obj.x;

return ...;
}
};
```

4) Overload the << operator for the class A in Code-15.45. Write a test program to test the << operator.

Code 15.45

```cpp
class A {

public:

float x = 7.5;
int y = 6;
};
```

5) Find the mistakes in Code-15.46.

Code 15.46

```cpp
ostream operator << (ostream os, const B& b) {

os << "x is: " << b.x <<endl;
return &os;
}
```

6) Overload the >> operator for the class A in Code-15.47. Write a test program to test the >> operator.

Code 15.47

```cpp
class A {

public:

char x = 'A';
int y = 8;
};
```

7) Find the mistakes in Code-15.48.

Code 15.48

```cpp
class A {

public:

char x = 'A';
int y = 8;
};

A::operator >> (istream is) {

cout << "Enter x value: ";

is >> x;
}
```

8) Fill the dots in Code-15.49, and then write a test program in main() function to test the Code-15.49.

Code 15.49
```cpp
class A {

public:
int x = 8, y = 3;
... operator [] (...);
};

... A::operator [] (...) {

// ... write here some statements

}
```

9) Define a class whose constructor dynamically allocates memory for its public members, and overload the assignment operator = for this class.

Chapter-16

Concurrency in C++

Abstract: In this chapter we explain the topic of concurrency in C++ programming. Parallel processing is achieved using concurrency, and concurrent programs are written using threads. Threads are used to execute a number of functions is to be run in parallel. Compiler resources are shared parallel among a number of functions, and each function performs its operation independently from other functions. If common memory location is shared by a number of functions, race problem arises. In this chapter, we also explain how to avoid the race problem in parallel processing.

16.1 Thread Object

Threads are created using the object **thread** which is defined in the header file <thread>.

Theread object is created as

thread thread_object(threadFunction, parameters);

where the parameters are passed to the thread function,

Example-16.1: In Code-16.1 we create a thread object and print its size.

Code 16.1

```
#include <iostream>
#include <thread>
using namespace std;
int main() {
thread thr;
cout << "Size of thread is " << sizeof(thread) << endl;
}
```

Output(s):

Size of thread is 8

Size of the thread object is the same as the size of the unsigned long int.

Example-16.2: In Code-16.2, we create a thread object with a thread function and parameter.

Code 16.2

```
#include <iostream>
#include <thread>
using namespace std;
void myFunc(int value) {
cout << "Inside thread, value is " << value << endl;
}
int main() {
thread thr (myFunc, 1);
}
```

When Code-16.2 is executed, we get the output

terminate called without an active exception

Thus, the coded did not execute as we expected. Since the compiler does not wait for the completion of the thread execution. To solve this issue we can use a sleep function as in Code-16.3.

Code 16.3

```
#include <iostream>
#include <thread>
using namespace std;
void myFunc(int value) {
cout << "Inside thread, value is " << value << endl;
}
int main() {
thread thr (myFunc, 1);
sleep(1);
//thr.detach();
```

```
}
```

When Code-16.3 is executed, we get the output

Inside thread, value is 1

terminate called without an active exception

Although we got the expected output, we still have the unfriendly message apearing after the expected output.

The message "terminate is called without an active exception" appears when a thread destructor is called before calling detach() or join() in the defined thread.

To solve this issue, we can use the detach() function as in Code-16.4.

Code 16.4

```cpp
#include <iostream>
#include <thread>
using namespace std;
void myFunc(int value) {
cout << "Inside thread, value is " << value << endl;
}
int main() {
thread thr (myFunc, 1);
sleep(1);
thr.detach();
}
```

When Code-16.4 is executed, we get the output "Inside thread, value is 1"

That is fixed now.

16.2 join() Function

Join function is defined in the thread clas, i.e., we have

thread::join

join() function does not terminate the main() function until the thread finishes its execution.

Example-16.3: Code-16.4 can be written as Code-16.5 where no sleep function is used, since join() function guarantees the completion of the thread execution.

Code 16.5

```cpp
#include <iostream>
#include <thread>
using namespace std;
void myFunc(int value) {
cout << "Inside thread, value is " << value << endl;
}
int main() {
thread thr (myFunc, 1);
thr.join();
}
```

Output(s):

Inside thread, value is 1

Example-16.4: In Code-16.6, we have a thread function which has an infinite loop. Two threads use the same function.

Code 16.6

```cpp
#include <iostream>
#include <thread>
using namespace std;
void myFunc(int value) {
while(1){
cout << "Inside thread, value is " << value << endl;
sleep(1);
}
}
int main() {
thread thr1 (myFunc, 1);
thread thr2 (myFunc, 2);
thr1.join();
thr2.join();
}
```

Output(s):

Inside thread, value is 1
Inside thread, value is 2
Inside thread, value is 1
Inside thread, value is 2

Inside thread, value is 1
Inside thread, value is 2

......

Example-16.5: In Code-16.7 we use two different thread functions for two threads, and use join() function for both threads.

Code 16.7

```cpp
#include <iostream>
#include <thread>
using namespace std;
void myFunc1(int);
void myFunc2(int);
int main() {
thread thr1 (myFunc1, 3);
thread thr2 (myFunc2, 4);
thr1.join();
thr2.join();
}
void myFunc1(int value) {
while(1) {
cout << "Inside thread-1, value is " << value << endl;
sleep(1);
}
}
void myFunc2(int value) {
while(1) {
cout << "Inside thread-2, value is " << value << endl;
sleep(1);
}
}
```

Output(s):

Inside thread-1, value is 3
Inside thread-2, value is 4
Inside thread-1, value is 3
Inside thread-2, value is 4
Inside thread-1, value is 3
Inside thread-2, value is 4

.....

16.2 Thread ID

Every thread has a uniue thread identidy number, i.e., ID number. The thread ID can be found using get_id() function whose prototype is

$$\text{id get\_id() const noexcept;}$$

and this function returns a default constructed id object if there is no thread, otherwise it gets the ID of the running thread.

Example-16.6: In Code-16.8, we get the thread IDs and print them.

Code 16.8

```cpp
#include <iostream>
#include <thread>

using namespace std;

void myFunc1();
void myFunc2();

int main() {

thread thr1 (myFunc1);
thread thr2 (myFunc2);

thread::id tid1 = thr1.get_id();
thread::id tid2 = thr1.get_id();

cout << "Thread ID1 = " << tid1 << endl;
cout << "Thread ID2 = " << tid2 << endl;

thr1.join();
thr2.join();
}

void myFunc1() {}

void myFunc2() {}
```

Output(s):
Thread ID1 = 139797066266176
Thread ID2 = 139797066266176

16.3 jthread Class

jthread class owns the properties of thread class with some additional properties. jthread objects are cooperatively interruptible and join by default.

Example-16.7: In Code-16.9, we define a jthread object. Since it is joined by default, we did not use join() function explicitly.

Code 16.9

```cpp
#include <chrono>
#include <iostream>
#include <thread>
using namespace std::chrono_literals;
using namespace std;
void myFunc();
int main() {
jthread thr{myFunc};
cout << "Thread ID is: " << hex << thr.get_id() << endl;
}
void myFunc() {
this_thread::sleep_for(100ms);
}
```

Output(s): Thread ID is: 7fdd3ed0a640

Example-16.8: We have to use join() function for the thread objects to guarantee the completion of their execution.

Code 16.10

```cpp
#include <chrono>
#include <iostream>
#include <thread>
using namespace std::chrono_literals;
using namespace std;
void myFunc(int x) {
cout << "Inside thread, x = " << x << endl;
this_thread::sleep_for(chrono::seconds(1));
}
int main() {
thread thr1(myFunc, 3);
thread thr2(myFunc, 8);
//thr1.join();
//thr2.join();
cout << "Terminating the main() \n";
}
```

When Code-16.10 is run we get the ouput

Terminating the main()

terminate called without an active exception

If we use jthread class for the thread objects, they are automatically join by default. When Code-16.10 is written as in Code-16.11 using jthread class, we get the output

```
Terminating the main()
Inside thread, x = 8
Inside thread, x = 3
```

Code 16.11

```cpp
#include <chrono>
#include <iostream>
#include <thread>

using namespace std::chrono_literals;
using namespace std;

void myFunc(int x) {

cout << "Inside thread, x = " << x << endl;
this_thread::sleep_for(chrono::seconds(1));
}
int main() {

jthread thr1(myFunc, 3);
jthread thr2(myFunc, 8);

//thr1.join();
//thr2.join();

cout << "Terminating the main() \n";
}
```

If we use the join() function for the jthread objects as in Code-16.12, then the output of the program becomes as

```
Inside thread, x = 3
Inside thread, x = 8
Terminating the main()
```

where the message " Terminating the main()" is displayed last, i.e., main thread, that is main function is terminated last.

Code 16.12

```cpp
#include <chrono>
#include <iostream>
#include <thread>

using namespace std::chrono_literals;
using namespace std;

void myFunc(int x) {

cout << "Inside thread, x = " << x << endl;
this_thread::sleep_for(chrono::seconds(1));
```

```cpp
}

int main() {

jthread thr1(myFunc, 3);
jthread thr2(myFunc, 8);

thr1.join();
thr2.join();

cout << "Terminating the main() \n";
}
```

16.4 joinable() Function

The joinable() function is used to check whether a thread can join to the main thread or not.

The prototype of the joinable() function is as

$$\text{bool joinable() const noexcept;}$$

The function returns the result of

$$\text{get\_id() != id().}$$

where id() returns a value if no thread is associated, and get_id() returns a value if there is an associated thread, otherwise get_id() returns the same value as id().

That is a defined thread which is not active is not joinable. A thread, that has finished its execution, is still considered an active thread and is therefore joinable.

Example-16.9: In Code-16.13 we test the joinable() function for different scenarios.

Code 16.13

```cpp
#include <chrono>
#include <iostream>
#include <thread>
using namespace std::chrono_literals;
using namespace std;
void myFunc();
int main() {
jthread thr;
cout << "Thread is not running, joinable: " << thr.joinable() << endl;
thr = jthread{myFunc};
cout << "Thread is running, joinable: " << thr.joinable() << endl;
cout << "Thread ID is: " << thr.get_id() << endl;
thr.join();
cout << "After thread joining, joinable: " << thr.joinable() << endl;
cout << "Thread ID is: " << thr.get_id() << endl;
thr = jthread{myFunc}; // assign thread again
cout << "Thread ID is: " << thr.get_id() << endl;
thr.detach();
cout << "After thread detaching, joinable: " << thr.joinable() << endl;
}
void myFunc() {
this_thread::sleep_for(100ms);
}
```

Output(s):

```
Thread is not running, joinable: 0
Thread is running, joinable: 1
Thread ID is: 140720069908032
After thread joining, joinable: 0
Thread ID is: thread::id of a non-executing thread
Thread ID is: 140720069908032
After thread detaching, joinable: 0
```

16.5 detach() Function

The prototype of the detach() function is as

void detach();

With detach() function, thread of execution is disassembled from the jthread object, and execution continues independently. Upon the termination of thread, allocated resources are freed.

The detached thread becomes free, and runs on its own. It becomes a daemon process.

Example-16.10: In this example, we explain the use of the detach() function. Consider Code-16.14.

Code 16.14

```cpp
#include <chrono>
#include <iostream>
#include <thread>

using namespace std::chrono_literals;
using namespace std;

void myFunc(int x) {

cout << "Inside thread, x = " << x << endl;
this_thread::sleep_for(chrono::seconds(1));
}
int main() {

thread thr1(myFunc, 3);
thread thr2(myFunc, 8);

thr1.join();
thr2.join();

cout << "Terminating the main() \n";
}
```

When Code-16.14 is run, we get the output

```
Inside thread, x = 3
Inside thread, x = 8
Terminating the main()
```

Now, let's add the detach() functions to the program as shown in Code-16.15. When detach () functions are added to the program, the threads become daemon processes and they become independent of the main thread, and without the use of sleep() function, if is not possible to see the outputs of the threads due to the termination of the main thread. However, the threads continue running at the background even the main thread terminates.

Code 16.15

```cpp
#include <chrono>
```

```cpp
#include <iostream>
#include <thread>

using namespace std::chrono_literals;
using namespace std;

void myFunc(int x) {

cout << "Inside thread, x = " << x << endl;
this_thread::sleep_for(chrono::seconds(1));
}

int main() {

thread thr1(myFunc, 3);
thread thr2(myFunc, 8);

thr1.detach();
thr2.detach();

sleep(2);

cout << "Terminating the main() \n";
}
```

When Code-16.15 is run with a C++ compiler of C++20 or higher version, we get the output

```
Inside thread, x = 8
Inside thread, x = 3
Terminating the main()
```

If we do not use the sleep() function in the main part of the Code-16.x, we can get a possible output

```
Terminating the main()
```

Example-16.11: detach() and join() functions cannot be used together.

Code 16.16

```cpp
#include <chrono>
#include <iostream>
#include <thread>
using namespace std::chrono_literals;
using namespace std;
void myFunc(int x) {
cout << "Inside thread, x = " << x << endl;
this_thread::sleep_for(chrono::seconds(1));
}
int main() {
```

```cpp
    thread thr1(myFunc, 3);
    thread thr2(myFunc, 8);
    thr1.join();
    thr2.join();
    thr1.detach();
    thr2.detach();


cout << "Terminating the main() \n";
    }
```

Output(s):

Inside thread, x = 3
Inside thread, x = 8
terminate called after throwing an instance of 'std::system_error'
what(): Invalid argument

16.6 sleep_for () Function

The sleep_for function suspends the execution of a thread for a certain period of time. Its prototype is as

```cpp
template< class Rep, class Period >
void sleep_for( const std::chrono::duration<Rep, Period>& sleep_duration );
```

This duration can be from nanoseconds to hours i.e.

```cpp
std::chrono::nanoseconds
std::chrono::microseconds
std::chrono::milliseconds
std::chrono::seconds
std::chrono::minutes
std::chrono::hours
```

Example-16.12: In this example, we illustare the use if the sleep_for() function.

Code 16.17

```cpp
#include <iostream>
#include <thread>
using namespace std;
int main() {
this_thread::sleep_for(10s);
// suspends the execution for 10sec
this_thread::sleep_for(chrono::milliseconds( 10 ) );
// suspends the execution for 10sec
this_thread::sleep_for(10ms);
// suspends the execution for 10ms
this_thread::sleep_for(chrono::milliseconds( 10 ) );
// suspends the execution for 10ms
this_thread::sleep_for(10ns);
// suspends the execution for 10ns
this_thread::sleep_for(chrono::milliseconds( 10 ) );
// suspends the execution for 10ns
}
```

Example-16.13: In the previous example, we did not use std:: before this_thread::sleep_for() function, in this example we use std:: before this_thread::sleep_for() function.

Code 16.18

```cpp
#include <iostream>
#include <thread>
using namespace std;
int main() {
std::this_thread::sleep_for(10s);
// suspends the execution for 10sec
std::this_thread::sleep_for(std::chrono::milliseconds( 10 ) );
```

```cpp
    // suspends the execution for 10sec
    std::this_thread::sleep_for(10ms);
    // suspends the execution for 10ms
    std::this_thread::sleep_for(std::chrono::milliseconds( 10 ) );
    // suspends the execution for 10ms
    std::this_thread::sleep_for(10ns);
    // suspends the execution for 10ns
    std::this_thread::sleep_for(std::chrono::milliseconds( 10 ) );
    // suspends the execution for 10ns
}
```

16.7 sleep_until() Function

The sleep_until() function suspends the execution of a thread until a defined time. Its prototype is as

```
template< class Clock, class Duration >
void sleep_until( const std::chrono::time_point<Clock,Duration>& sleepTime );
```

Example-16.14: In this example, we illustrate the use of the sleep_unti() function.

Code 16.19

```cpp
#include <iostream>
#include <thread>
using namespace std;
int main() {
auto a = chrono::steady_clock::now();
this_thread::sleep_until(a + 200ms);
auto b = chrono::steady_clock::now();
chrono::duration<double, std::milli> time {b - a};
cout << "Paused for " << time.count() << " miliseconds" << endl;
}
```

Output(s): Paused for 200.109 miliseconds

16.8 yield () Function

This function signals the thread scheduler such that other threads can also run. The current thread may suspend its operation or continue running

inline void yield() noexcept;

In fact, the exact behavior of this function depends on the operating system scheduler in use. For example, a first-in-first-out realtime scheduler may halt the current thread and change its order in the queue taking account the priorities of the other tasks.

Example-16.15: In this example, we illustrate the use of the yield() function.

Code 16.20

```cpp
#include <iostream>
#include <thread>
using namespace std;
void myFunc() {
std::this_thread::yield(); // Let the other threads take priority,
// because this thread is dummy
for(int indx = 0; indx < 10; indx++) { sleep(1); }
std::cout << "Hello World!";
}
int main() {
thread thr{ myFunc };
thr.join();
}
```

16.9 Killing a Thread in C++

The

```
class stop_source;
```

has some methods which are used to issue a stop request, check whether the thread can be stopped or not etc.

The methods of the stop_source class can be divided into two parts which are **modifiers and observers**. The **modifier methods** are

```
request_stop() swap()
```

The request_stop() function is used to stop a request for a running thread. The swap() function is used to swap to objects of stop_source class.

The **observer methods** are

```
get_token() stop_requested() stop_possible()
```

get_token()
It returns a token for the related thread. It returns a stop_token **for** the associated stop-state

stop_requested()
It checks whether a stop request is issued for a corresponding thread or not.

stop_possible()
It checks whether a thread can be stopped or not.


```
class stop_token;
```

The methods of the **class stop_token** are used with a **stop_source** object, and the methods of
the **class stop_token** are used to query whether a **stop request** is made.

And this is achieved using **stop_requested method**, or, **stop_possible method**, for an associated stop_source object.

Example-16.16: In this example, we check whether a thread can be stopped or not.

Code 16.21

```cpp
#include <iostream>
#include <thread>
using namespace std;
jthread thr;
void myFnc() {
cout << "Inside the thread!";
}
int main() {
thr = jthread(myFnc);
stop_source ss = thr.get_stop_source();
stop_token st = ss.get_token();
bool r1 = st.stop_possible();
bool r2 = st.stop_requested();
cout << "Stop possible: " << r1 << endl;
cout << "Stop requested: " << r2 << endl;
thr.join();
```

```
}
```

Output(s):

Stop possible: 1

Stop requested: 0

Inside the thread!

Example-16.17: In this example, we send a stop request to a thread which has a while-loop and the thread terminates when it receives the stop request.

Code 16.22

```cpp
#include <iostream>
#include <thread>

using namespace std;
using namespace std::chrono_literals;

jthread thr;

void myFnc(stop_token st) {

while (!st.stop_requested()) {

cout << "Inside thread function." << endl;
this_thread::sleep_for(chrono::seconds(1));
}

cout << "Thread is cancelled" << endl;
}
int main() {

thr = jthread(myFnc);

this_thread::sleep_for(chrono::seconds(2));

stop_source ss = thr.get_stop_source();

thr.request_stop();
stop_token st = thr.get_stop_token();
//stop_token st1 = ss.get_token();

if (!st.stop_requested())
cout << "Still waiting for the thread" << endl;

else {
cout << "Stop request is made now" << endl;
thr.request_stop();
}
```

```
    thr.join();
  }
```

Output(s):

Inside thread function.
Inside thread function.
Stop request is made now
Thread is cancelled

16.10 Mutex Functions in C++

A mutex objext is created as

mutex obj;

Race condition is prevented using mutex lock() and unlock() functions whose prototypes are

void lock(); void unlock();

These functions should be written to the beginning of end of thread function to prevent race condition. If a thread locks the mutex object, then shared resources cannot be used by other threads.

Consider Code-16.23,

Code 16.23

```cpp
#include <iostream>
#include <thread>
#include <mutex>

using namespace std;

int glb_var = 0;

void myFunc1();
void myFunc2();

int main() {

thread thr1(myFunc1), thr2(myFunc2);

thr1.join();
thr2.join();

cout << "Inside main " << endl;
cout << "glb_var = " << glb_var << endl;
}

void myFunc1() {

for(long unsigned indx = 0; indx < 100; indx++) {
glb_var++;
}
}
void myFunc2() {

for(long unsigned indx = 0; indx < 100; indx++) {
glb_var—;
}
}
```

When Code-16.23 is run, we always get the output

Inside main

glb_var = 0

Lets increase the loop execution number as shown in yellow in Code-16.24.

Code 16.24

```cpp
void myFunc1() {
for(long unsigned indx = 0; indx < 10000000; indx++) {
glb_var++;
}
}
void myFunc2() {
for(long unsigned indx = 0; indx < 10000000; indx++) {
glb_var—;
}
}
```

When Code-16.x is run there times, we get the outputs

Inside main

glb_var = -1698093

Inside main

glb_var = -61627

Inside main

glb_var = 30178

That is due to race issue, we get a different output at each run.

To prevent race problem, we use define mutex object and use mutex lock() and unlock() functions as shown in Code-16.25.

Code 16.25

```cpp
#include <iostream>
#include <thread>
#include <mutex>
using namespace std;
int glb_var = 0;
mutex mtx;
void myFunc1();
void myFunc2();
int main() {
thread thr1(myFunc1), thr2(myFunc2);
thr1.join();
thr2.join();
cout << "Inside main " << endl;
cout << "glb_var = " << glb_var << endl;
}
void myFunc1() {
mtx.lock();
for(long unsigned indx = 0; indx < 100; indx++) {
```

```
glb_var++;
}
mtx.unlock();
}
void myFunc2() {
mtx.lock();
for(long unsigned indx = 0; indx < 100; indx++) {
glb_var—;
}
mtx.unlock();
}
```

When Code-16.25 is run, we always get the output

Inside main

glb_var = 0

16.10.1 try_lock() mutex function

try_lock() function atempts to obtain ownership of the mutex without blocking. The function
lock() will block if the mutex is not available, and it waits until mutex is available, while try_lock() returns even
if the mutex is not available.

The prototype of the try_lock() function is as

$$\text{bool try\_lock();}$$

The function tries to lock the mutex, and if this process is successful it returns true, otherwise, it returns false.

Code 16.26

```cpp
#include <iostream>
#include <thread>
#include <mutex>
using namespace std;
int glb_var_shared = 0;
int glb_var_exclusive = 0;
mutex mtx;
void myFunc1();
void myFunc2();
int main() {
thread thr1(myFunc1), thr2(myFunc2);
thr1.join();
thr2.join();
cout << "Inside main " << endl;
cout << "glb_var_shared = " << glb_var_shared << endl;
cout << "glb_var_exclusive = " << glb_var_exclusive << endl;
}
void myFunc1() {
if (mtx.try_lock()) {
for(long unsigned indx = 0; indx < 1000000000; indx++) {
glb_var_shared++;
}
mtx.unlock();
}
for(long unsigned indx = 0; indx < 1000000000; indx++) {
glb_var_exclusive++;
}
}
void myFunc2() {
mtx.lock();
for(long unsigned indx = 0; indx < 1000000000; indx++) {
glb_var_shared—;
}
mtx.unlock();
```

```
}
```

At one run we get the output

```
Inside main
glb_var_shared = -1000000000
glb_var_exclusive = 1000000000
```

At another run we get the output

```
Inside main
glb_var_shared = 0
glb_var_exclusive = 1000000000
```

16.10.2 recursive_mutex

Recursive mutex is used in recursive functions and inside loops.

Example-16.18:

Code 16.27

```cpp
#include <iostream>
#include <thread>
#include <mutex>
using namespace std;
recursive_mutex mtx;
int main() {


for(int indx = 0; indx < 4; indx++) {
    mtx.lock();
    cout << "mutex is locked: " << indx << endl;
    }


for(int indx = 0; indx < 4; indx++) {
    mtx.unlock();
    cout << "mutex is unlocked: " << indx << endl;
    }
    }
```

Output(s):

```
mutex is locked: 0
mutex is locked: 1
mutex is locked: 2
mutex is locked: 3
mutex is unlocked: 0
mutex is unlocked: 1
mutex is unlocked: 2
mutex is unlocked: 3
```

Example-16.19:

Code 16.28

```cpp
#include <iostream>
#include <thread>
#include <mutex>

using namespace std;
```

```cpp
void recFunc(int N);

recursive_mutex mtx;

int main() {

thread thr(recFunc, 2);

thr.join();
}

void recFunc(int N) {

if(N <= 0)
return;

mtx.lock();
cout << "Mutex is locked " << endl;

recFunc(—N);

mtx.unlock();
cout << "Mutex is unlocked " << endl;
}
```

Output(s):
Mutex is locked
Mutex is locked
Mutex is unlocked
Mutex is unlocked

16.10.3 lock guard

Mutex lock and unlock function can be automatically implemented using lock_guard() function. The thread function in Code-16.29 can be written as Code-30.

Code 16.29

```cpp
mutex mtx;

void myFunc() {
mtx.lock();
// statements
mtx.unlock();
}
```

Code 16.30

```cpp
mutex mtx;

void myFunc() {
lock_guard<mutex> lock(mtx);
// statements
}
```

Example-16.20: The program in Code-16.26 can be written as in Code-16.31.

Code 16.31

```cpp
#include <iostream>
#include <thread>
#include <mutex>

using namespace std;

int glb_var = 0;
mutex mtx;

void myFunc1();
void myFunc2();

int main() {

thread thr1(myFunc1), thr2(myFunc2);

thr1.join();
thr2.join();

cout << "Inside main " << endl;
```

```cpp
cout << "glb_var = " << glb_var << endl;
}
void myFunc1() {

lock_guard<mutex> lock(mtx);

for(long unsigned indx = 0; indx < 100; indx++) {
glb_var++;
}
}

void myFunc2() {

lock_guard<mutex> lock(mtx);

for(long unsigned indx = 0; indx < 100; indx++) {
glb_var—;
}
}
```

16.11 Atomic Operations

Atomic variables are used to avoid the race condition eliminating the use of the mutex functions.

The atomic integral data types are defined either as

```
atomic_char char
atomic_schar signed char
atomic_uchar unsigned char
atomic_short short
atomic_ushort unsigned short
atomic_int int
atomic_uint unsigned int
atomic_long long
atomic_ulong unsigned long
atomic_llong long long
atomic_ullong unsigned long long
atomic_char16_t char16_t
atomic_char32_t char32_t
atomic_wchar_t wchar_t
```

or as in

```
atomic<char> char
atomic<schar> signed char
atomic<u_char> unsigned char
atomic<short> short
atomic<u_short> unsigned short
atomic<int> int
atomic<u_int> unsigned int
atomic<long> long
atomic<u_long> unsigned long
atomic<char16_t> char16_t
atomic<char32_t> char32_t
atomic<wchar_t> wchar_t
```

Note that in atomic<...> definition list, we do not have atomic<llong> and atomic<ullong> types. Floating point atomic data types are defined as

```
atomic<float> float
atomic<double> double
atomic<long double> long double
```

Atomic data types for fixed width integers are defined as

Atomic **typedef** <inttypes.h> type

atomic_int_least8_t int_least8_t
atomic_uint_least8_t uint_least8_t
atomic_int_least16_t int_least16_t
atomic_uint_least16_t uint_least16_t
atomic_int_least32_t int_least32_t
atomic_uint_least32_t uint_least32_t
atomic_int_least64_t int_least64_t
atomic_uint_least64_t uint_least64_t
atomic_int_fast8_t int_fast8_t
atomic_uint_fast8_t uint_fast8_t
atomic_int_fast16_t int_fast16_t
atomic_uint_fast16_t uint_fast16_t
atomic_int_fast32_t int_fast32_t
atomic_uint_fast32_t uint_fast32_t
atomic_int_fast64_t int_fast64_t
atomic_uint_fast64_t uint_fast64_t
atomic_intptr_t intptr_t
atomic_uintptr_t uintptr_t
atomic_size_t size_t
atomic_ptrdiff_t ptrdiff_t
atomic_intmax_t intmax_t
atomic_uintmax_t uintmax_t

Example-16.21:

Code 16.32

```cpp
#include <iostream>
#include <atomic>

using namespace std;

int main() {

atomic_int x {10}; // 1st method
atomic<int> y {45}; // 2nd method
atomic_llong z {78}; // ok
// atomic<llong> z; // error, no such definition

cout << "Atomic x: " << x << endl;
cout << "Atomic y: " << y << endl;
cout << "Atomic z: " << z << endl;
}
```

Output(s):
Atomic x: 10
Atomic y: 45

Atomic z: 78

Example-16.22: Size of atomic data type can be calculated using sizeof() operator.

Code 16.33

```cpp
#include <iostream>
#include <atomic>
using namespace std;
int main() {
cout << "Size of int is: " << sizeof(int) << endl;
cout << "Size of atomic_int is: " << sizeof(atomic_int) << endl;
cout << "Size of atomic<int> is: " << sizeof(atomic<int>) << endl;
cout << "Size of atomic<float> is: " << sizeof(atomic<float>) << endl;
cout << "Size of atomic<double> is: " << sizeof(atomic<double>) << endl;
cout << "Size of atomic<long double> is: "
<< sizeof(atomic<long double>) << endl;
}
```

Output(s):

Size of int is: 4

Size of atomic_int is: 4

Size of atomic<int> is: 4

Size of atomic<float> is: 4

Size of atomic<double> is: 8

Size of atomic<long double> is: 16

Example-16.23: Size of atomic data type can be calculated using sizeof() operator.

Code 16.34

```cpp
#include <iostream>
#include <atomic>

using namespace std;

int main() {

cout << "Size of atomic_int_least8_t is: "
<< sizeof(atomic_int_least8_t) << endl;

cout << "Size of atomic_int_fast16_t is: "
<< sizeof(atomic_int_fast16_t) << endl;

cout << "Size of atomic_ptrdiff_t is: "
<< sizeof(atomic_ptrdiff_t) << endl;
}
```

Output(s):

Size of atomic_int_least8_t is: 1

Size of atomic_int_fast16_t is: 8

Size of atomic_ptrdiff_t is: 8

16.12 Atomic Pointers

Pointers are data types. As with any other data type, we can define atomic pointer data types as well.

Atomic Pointer to an Ordinary Data

Example-16.24: Atomic pointer to ordinary float data.

Code 16.35
```cpp
#include <iostream>
#include <atomic>

using namespace std;

int main() {

float a = 10.7;

atomic<float*> fp = &a;

cout << "*fp = " << *fp << endl;
}
```

Output(s): *fp = 10.7

Example-16.25: Atomic pointer to ordinary integer data.

Code 16.36
```cpp
#include <iostream>
#include <atomic>

using namespace std;

int main() {

int a = 45;

atomic<int*> ptr = &a;

cout << "*ptr = " << *ptr << endl;
}
```

Output(s): *ptr = 45

Atomic Pointer to Atomic Data

Example-16.26: Atomic pointer to atomic float data.

Code 16.37
```cpp
#include <iostream>
```

```cpp
#include <atomic>

using namespace std;

int main() {

atomic<float> a = 45.8;

atomic<atomic<float>*> ptr = &a;

cout << "*ptr = " << *ptr << endl;
}
```

Output(s): *fp = 45.8

Example-16.27: Atomic pointer to atomic integer data.

Code 16.38
```cpp
#include <iostream>
#include <atomic>

using namespace std;

int main() {

atomic_int a = 45;

atomic<atomic_int*> ptr = &a;

cout << "*ptr = " << *ptr << endl;
}
```

Output(s): *ptr = 45

16.13 Race Prevention by Atomic Variables

Atomic variables are used to prevent race conditions.

Example-16.28: In this example, we illustrate how the atomic variables eliminate the race condition. Let's define two global variables, one is atomic and the other is normal, as in Code-16.39.

Code 16.39
```cpp
#include <iostream>
#include <thread>
#include <atomic>

using namespace std;

int glb_var1 = 0;

atomic_int glb_var2 = 0;

void myFunc1();

int main() {

}
```

We add one thread function which increments the global variables as in Code-16.40.

Code 16.40
```cpp
#include <iostream>
#include <thread>
#include <atomic>
using namespace std;
int glb_var1 = 0;
atomic_int glb_var2 = 0;
void myFunc1();
int main() {
}
void myFunc1() {
for(long unsigned indx = 0; indx < 10000000; indx++) {
glb_var1++;
glb_var2++;
}
}
```

We add a second thread function which decrements the global variables as in Code-16.41.

Code 16.41
```cpp
#include <iostream>
#include <thread>
#include <atomic>
using namespace std;
```

```cpp
int glb_var1 = 0;
atomic_int glb_var2 = 0;
void myFunc1();
void myFunc2();
int main() {
}
void myFunc1() {
for(long unsigned indx = 0; indx < 10000000; indx++) {
glb_var1++;
glb_var2++;
}
}
void myFunc2() {
for(long unsigned indx = 0; indx < 10000000; indx++) {
glb_var1—;
glb_var2—;
}
}
```

We create two threads as in Code-16.42.

Code 16.42

```cpp
#include <iostream>
#include <thread>
#include <atomic>
using namespace std;
int glb_var1 = 0;
atomic_int glb_var2 = 0;
void myFunc1();
void myFunc2();
int main() {
thread thr1(myFunc1);
thread thr2(myFunc2);
}
void myFunc1() {
for(long unsigned indx = 0; indx < 10000000; indx++) {
glb_var1++;
glb_var2++;
}
}
void myFunc2() {
for(long unsigned indx = 0; indx < 10000000; indx++) {
glb_var1—;
glb_var2—;
}
}
```

We add the join() functions as in Code-16.43.

Code 16.43

```cpp
#include <iostream>
#include <thread>
#include <atomic>
using namespace std;
int glb_var1 = 0;
atomic_int glb_var2 = 0;
void myFunc1();
void myFunc2();
int main() {
thread thr1(myFunc1);
thread thr2(myFunc2);
thr1.join();
thr2.join();
cout << "glb_var1 is " << glb_var1 << endl;
cout << "glb_var2 is " << glb_var2 << endl;
}
void myFunc1() {
for(long unsigned indx = 0; indx < 10000000; indx++) {
glb_var1++;
glb_var2++;
}
}
void myFunc2() {
for(long unsigned indx = 0; indx < 10000000; indx++) {
glb_var1--;
glb_var2--;
}
}
```

Output(s): When the program is run, we get the output.

```
glb_var1 is -495813
glb_var2 is 0
```

From these outputs, it is seen that for non-atomic global variable, race condition exists, whereas, for atomic global variable race condition is eliminated.

Example-16.29: This example is an improved version of the previous example. In this example, we create 20 threads which use the same function. We have one global atomic integer, and a normal global integer variable. The thread function increments both variables.

Code 16.44

```cpp
#include <iostream>
#include <thread>
#include <atomic>
```

```cpp
using namespace std;
void myFunc();
atomic_int a_glb = 0;
int glb = 0;
int main() {
thread thrd[20];
for(int i = 0; i < 20; i++)
thrd[i] = thread(myFunc);
for(int i = 0; i < 20; i++)
thrd[i].join();
cout << "The value of atomic global variable a_glb is "
<< a_glb << endl;
cout << "The value of global variable glb is "
<< glb << endl;
}


void myFunc() {
    for(int indx = 0; indx < 10000; indx++) {
    a_glb++; // atomic operation
    glb++;
    }
}
```

Output(s): When the program is run, we get the outputs.
The value of atomic global variable a_glb is 200000
The value of global variable glb is 197760

The for-loop is run for 10000 times, and there are 20 threads. This means that global variables are incremented $20 \times 10000 = 200000$, and this value is displayed for atomic global variable, whereas, for non-atomic global variable a smaller number is displayed.

From the outputs, it is seen that race condition exists for non-atomic global variable.

Example-16.30: If **a** is a atomic integer, than **a++** is an atomic operation, whereas **a = a+1** is not an atomic operation. If the thread function in the previous example is replaced by the function in Code-16.45, race condition is not eliminated for atomic variable.

Code 16.45
```cpp
 void myFunc() {

 for(int indx = 0; indx < 10000; indx++) {
 a_glb = a_glb + 1; // NOT atomic operation

 glb = glb + 1;
 }
```

```
}
```

If the thread function in the Code.16.44 is replaced by the function in Code-16.45, we get the outputs:
The value of atomic global variable a_glb is 82939
The value of global variable glb is 134120

16.14 Lock-Free Atomic Types

Some hardware structures do not support atomic types, and when atomic types are met, parallel processing operations are performed using lock, unlock functions as in as mutex lock and unlock functions. Atomic operations are fast, but, parallel processing performed by lock, unlock function are slower compared to atomic operations.

Some atomic types are forced to be lock free, for instance atomic flags are all lock free.

To understand whether a data type is lock free or not we can use some built-in C++ functions whose prototypes are

bool atomic_is_lock_free(const volatile A *object) noexcept;

bool atomic_is_lock_free(const A *object) noexcept;

bool A::is_lock_free() const volatile noexcept;

bool A::is_lock_free() const noexcept;

To understand whether a atomic data type is lock free or not, we can check its correponding macro value. The macros of some atomic types are listed as

Atomic Type Lock Free Macro

atomic_bool ATOMIC_BOOL_LOCK_FREE

atomic_char ATOMIC_CHAR_LOCK_FREE

atomic_char16_t ATOMIC_CHAR16_T_LOCK_FREE

atomic_char32_t ATOMIC_CHAR32_T_LOCK_FREE

atomic_wchar_t ATOMIC_WCHAR_T_LOCK_FREE

atomic_short ATOMIC_SHORT_LOCK_FREE

atomic_int ATOMIC_INT_LOCK_FREE

atomic_long ATOMIC_LONG_LOCK_FREE

atomic_llong ATOMIC_LLONG_LOCK_FREE

atomic_intptr_t ATOMIC_POINTER_LOCK_FREE

Macros can have three different values which are

0 which indicates that atomic type is never lock-free,

1 which indicates that atomic type is sometimes lock-free,

2 which indicates that atomic type is always lock-free.

Example-16.31:

Code 16.46
```cpp
#include <atomic>
#include <iostream>

using namespace std;

int main() {

atomic_int a;

cout << boolalpha
```

```
    << "atomic_int is lock free? "
    << atomic_is_lock_free(&a) << endl

    << "atomic_int is lock free? "
    << a.is_lock_free() ;
  }
```

Output(s):

atomic_int is lock free? true

atomic_int is lock free? true

Example-16.32: We can check whether atomic integer type is lock-free or not in our computer using Code-16.47.

Code 16.47

```
#include <atomic>
#include <iostream>
using namespace std;
int main() {
if(ATOMIC_INT_LOCK_FREE==0) {
cout << "atomic_int type is never lock-free" << endl;
}
else if(ATOMIC_INT_LOCK_FREE==1) {
cout << "atomic_int type is sometimes lock-free" << endl;
}
else if(ATOMIC_INT_LOCK_FREE==2) {
cout << "atomic_int type is always lock-free" << endl;
}
}
```

Output(s): atomic_int type is always lock-free

16.15 Atomic Assignments, Operators and Functions

Some operators operating on atomic variables are race free, i.e., they are atomic operators. Not all the operators are atomic ones.

For instance;

```
atomic_int a = 0;
a++; // this is an atomic operation
a = a + 1; // this is NOT an atomic operation
```

The atomic operators are listed as:

```
a++ a-- --a ++a
a += b  a -= b  a *= b  a /= b  a %= b
a &= b  a |= b  a ^= b  a >>= b  a <<= b
```

16.16 Atomic Functions

In this section, we explain some of the atomic functions.

16.16.1 atomic_is_lock_free() Function

The prototype of this function is

bool atomic_is_lock_free(const volatile **A *obj**);

This function returns true if the atomic operations on all objects of the type A are lock-free.

Example-16.33:

Code 16.48

```cpp
#include <atomic>
#include <iostream>
using namespace std;
int main() {
atomic_int a;
cout << "atomic_int a is ";
cout << (atomic_is_lock_free(&a) ? "lock-free" : "not lock-free");
}
```

Output(s): atomic_int a is lock-free

16.16.2 atomic_fetch_key() Function

The prototype of this function is

C atomic_fetch_key(volatile **A* obj, M arg**);

where C, non atomic type, is the value held previously by the atomic object pointed to by obj, arg is the argument supplied.

This function performs arithmetic and bitwise computations. The operations are applicable on atomic integer type. The argument can have the expressions in

key op computation
add + addition
sub - subtraction
or | bitwise inclusive or
xor bitwise exclusive or
and & bitwise and

If key=add, then we have the addition function

C atomic_fetch_add(volatile **A* obj, M arg**);

Example-16.34: This example illustrates the use of atomic_fetch_add() function.

Code 16.49
```cpp
#include <atomic>
#include <iostream>

using namespace std;

int main() {

atomic_int a = 6;

int ret;

ret = atomic_fetch_add(&a, 8); // a = a+8

cout << "a = " << a << ",";
cout << "ret = " << ret;
}
```

Output(s): a = 14, ret = 6

Example-16.35: This example illustrates the use of atomic_fetch_sub() function.

Code 16.50
```cpp
#include <atomic>
#include <iostream>

using namespace std;
```

```cpp
int main() {

atomic_int a = 6;

int ret;

ret=atomic_fetch_sub(&a, 3); // a = a-3

cout << "a = " << a << ", ";
cout << "ret = " << ret;
}
```

Output(s): a = 3, ret = 6

Example-16.36: This example illustrates the use of atomic_fetch_xor() function.

Code 16.51

```cpp
#include <atomic>
#include <iostream>
using namespace std;
int main() {
atomic_uchar a = 0x0F;
atomic<u_char> b = 0xF0;
atomic_uchar ret;
ret = atomic_fetch_xor(&a, b); // a = a XOR b
cout << "a = " << hex << showbase << (int) a << ", ";
cout << "ret = " << hex << (int)ret;
}
```

Output(s): a = 0xff, ret = 0xf

Example-16.37: The function atomic_fetch_add() is race free. This example shows that if we perfom classical summation race conditon is not avoided, where performing summations using atomic_fetch_add() with an atomic variables avoids race problem.

Code 16.52

```cpp
#include <atomic>
#include <iostream>
#include <thread>
using namespace std;
atomic_int a = 0;
int b = 0;
void myFunc();
int main() {
thread thrd[20];
for(int i = 0; i < 20; i++)
thrd[i] = thread(myFunc);
for(int i = 0; i < 20; i++)
```

```cpp
thrd[i].join();
cout << "The value of atomic global variable a is "
<< a << endl;
cout << "The value of global variable b is "
<< b << endl;
}
void myFunc() {
for(int indx = 0; indx < 10000; indx++) {
atomic_fetch_add(&a, 8); // a = a+8, atomic operation
b = b + 8; // non atomic operation
}
}
```

Output(s):

The value of atomic global variable a is 1600000

The value of global variable b is 537744

The results show that when classical summation is performed by threads, race condition occurs, whereas the function atomic_fetch_add() avoids the race problem.

16.16.3 atomic_store() Function

The prototype of the function is

void **atomic_store**(volatile **A* obj** , **C desired**);

where A is an atomic data type and C is a normal, i.e., non-atomic data type.
This is a write operation, it atomically, i.e., race freely, performs the operation

***obj = desired**

Example-16.38: This example illustrates the use of atomic_store() function.

Code 16.53

```cpp
#include <atomic>
#include <iostream>

using namespace std;

int main() {

atomic_int a;
atomic_store(&a, 17); // atomic write operation

cout << "a = " << a;
}
```

Output(s): a = 17

16.16.4 atomic_load() Function

The prototype of the function is

C atomic_load(const volatile **A* obj**);

where A is an atomic data type and C non-atomic data type.

This is atomic read operation. It returns the current value of the atomic variable pointed by obj, i.e., it performs

C=*obj

Example-16.39: This example illustrates the use of atomic_load() function.

Code 16.54

```cpp
#include <atomic>
#include <iostream>

using namespace std;

int main() {

atomic_int a = 30;
atomic_int ret;

ret = atomic_load(&a); // atomic read operation

cout << "a = " << a;
}
```

Output(s): a = 30

16.16.5 atomic_exchange() Function

The prototype of the function is

C atomic_exchange(volatile **A* obj, C desired**);

where A is an atomic data type and C non-atomic data type.

This is atomic r read-modify-write operation. Tthe value pointed by obj is replaced with desired and the value obj held previously is returned.

Example-16.40: This example illustrates the use of atomic_exchange() function.

Code 16.55

```cpp
#include <atomic>
#include <iostream>
using namespace std;
int main() {
atomic_int a = 30;
int desired = 20;
int C;
cout << "Value of a is: " << a << endl;
C = atomic_exchange(&a, desired); // atomic operation
cout << "New value of a is: " << a << endl;
cout << "Old value of a is: " << C;
}
```

Output(s):

Value of a is: 30
New value of a is: 20
Old value of a is: 30

16.16.6 Comparison Functions

We have the atomic comparison functions

atomic_compare_exchange_weak()
atomic_compare_exchange_strong()

The prototypes of these functions are
bool atomic_compare_exchange_strong(volatile **A* obj**, \
C* expected, C desired);
bool atomic_compare_exchange_weak(volatile **A *obj**, \
C* expected, C desired);
The value pointed to by object is compared to the value pointed to by expected and
- if they are equal, the value pointed to by object is replaced with desired,
- if they are not equal, the value pointed to by expected is updated with the value pointed to by object.

Exchange weak is preferred in loops for better performance. Exchange weak sometimes return false if even values are equal to each other.

Example-16.41: This example illustrates the use of atomic comparison functions.

Code 16.56

```cpp
#include <atomic>
#include <iostream>
using namespace std;
int main() {
atomic_int a = 23;
atomic_int b = 26;
int expected = 23;
int desired = 56;
bool ret;
cout << "a is: " << a << endl;
cout << "expected is: " << expected << endl;
cout << "desired is: " << desired<< endl;
ret = atomic_compare_exchange_strong(&a, &expected, desired);
cout << "Comparison result is: " << ret << endl;
cout << "a is: " << a << endl;
cout << "expected is: " << expected << endl;
cout << "b is: " << b << endl;
cout << "expected is: " << expected << endl;
cout << "desired is: " << desired << endl;
ret = atomic_compare_exchange_strong(&b, &expected, desired);
cout << "Comparison result is: " << ret << endl;
cout << "b is: " << b<< endl;
cout << "expected is: " << expected << endl;
}
```

Output(s):

```
a is: 23                      b is: 26
expected is: 23               expected is: 23
desired is: 56                desired is: 56
Comparison result is: 1       Comparison result is: 0
a is: 56                      b is: 26
expected is: 23               expected is: 26
```

16.16.7 atomic_flag Macro

It is an atomic Boolean type. This atomic type is guaranteed to be lock-free. The atomic type atomic_bool can perform load and store operations whereas atomic_flag does not provide load or store operations. It has two states, set and clear.

The macro

ATOMIC_FLAG_INIT

initializes an atomic_flag variable to the clear state.

If an atomic_flag variable is not initialized, it is gets an indeterminate state.

The function

atomic_flag_test_and_set()

with prototype

bool atomic_flag_test_and_set(volatile **atomic_flag *object**);

sets an atomic_flag variable to true, and it returns the value of variable before the update.

The function

atomic_flag_clear()

with prototype

void **atomic_flag_clear**(volatile **atomic_flag *object**);

sets an atomic_flag variable to false. There is no return value for this function

Example-16.42: This example illustrates the use of atomic flag functions.

Code 16.57

```cpp
#include <atomic>
#include <iostream>
using namespace std;
int main() {
atomic_flag flg = ATOMIC_FLAG_INIT;
bool ret;
// cout << "Initial flag value is : " << flg.value();
ret = atomic_flag_test_and_set(&flg);
// cout << "After set, flag value is : " << flg;
// cout << "After set, returned value is : " << ret;
atomic_flag_clear(&flg);
//cout << "After clear, flag value is : " << flg;
}
```

Output(s):

Initial flag value is : 0

After set, flag value is : 1

After set, returned value is : 0

After clear, flag value is : 0

16.16.8 atomic_init() Function

The prototype of the function is

void atomic_init(volatile A *obj, C value);

where A is an atomic data type and C non-atomic data type.

This function initializes the atomic variable A by the value of V. Although this function initializes an atomic variable, it is **NOT a race-free** function.

Example-16.43: This example illustrates the use of atomic_init() function.

Code 16.58

```
#include <atomic>
#include <iostream>
using namespace std;
int main() {
atomic_int a;
int b = 18;
atomic_init(&a,b); // the same as: atomic_init(&a,18)
cout << "a = " << a;
}
```

Output(s): a = 18

16.17 Memory Order in C++

Before studying the memory order in C++, let's see some terminology

16.17.1 Acquire, Release, and Consume

Reading an atomic variable is called **acquire operation**, i.e., acquire operation is atomic read operation, and writing an atomic variable is called **release operation**, i.e., atomic write operation.

The word **load** can be used for read operation. In C, we have race-free atomic load function. In a similar manner we can use the word **store** for write operation.

The sentence

"Let's say that **a** is an atomic variable, and when a thread acquires **a**, it can see value of the **a** released in another thread."

means that

"Let's say that **a** is an atomic variable, and when a thread reads the value of atomic **a**, it can see value of the atomic **a** written in another thread."

In a C++ program, besides to atomic read and write operations, non-atomic read and write operations also exist.

Consume is a less-strict version of acquire. You cannot reorder anything before acquire operation. However, before consume operation you cannot reorder only those which depends on the loaded atomic value.

Fences

The word **fence** is used for non-atomic variables. Acquire of a non-atomic variable is called **fence acquire**, and similarly release of a non-atomic variable is called **fence release**.

16.17.2 Memory Order

The enumerated type **memory_order** is used to order memory accesses of regular non-atomic operations around an atomic operation. It is used to synchronize operations on distinct threads.

It is defined in <stdatomic.h> as

typedef enum {

memory_order_relaxed = **__ATOMIC_RELAXED,**

memory_order_consume = **__ATOMIC_CONSUME,**

memory_order_acquire = **__ATOMIC_ACQUIRE,**

memory_order_release = **__ATOMIC_RELEASE,**

memory_order_acq_rel = **__ATOMIC_ACQ_REL,**

memory_order_seq_cst = **__ATOMIC_SEQ_CST**

}memory_order;

By default for atomic operations sequentially consistent memory ordering is used by the compiler. However, default choice can hurt performance..

but the library's atomic operations can be given an additional memory_order argument to
specify the exact constraints, beyond atomicity, that the compiler and processor must enforce
for that operation.

The compiler can reorder memory access using selected member of **memory_order**

memory_order_relaxed

No order is guaranteed concerning locking and normal memory accesses.

memory_order_consume

Assume that an atomic load operation is performed, no reads or writes in the current thread that depend on the value being loaded can be done.

This is almost the same as memory_order_acquire, except for that the ordering is guaranteed only for dependent data.

memory_order_acquire

Assume that an atomic load operation is performed, no reads or writes in the current thread that depend on the value being loaded can be done.

memory_order_release

Assume that an atomic store operation is performed, no reads or writes in the current thread can be done after this store operation. This prevents ordinary loads and stores from being reordered after the store operation.

memory_order_acq_rel

This is a hybrid of memory_order_acquire and memory_order_release. Assume inside a thread one variable is loaded and another one is stored, no memory reads or writes in the current thread can be reordered before the load, or after the store. That is raed and write operations cannot be re-ordered around the operation.

memory_order_seq_cst

A load operation with this memory order performs an acquire operation, a store performs a release operation, and read-modify-write performs both an acquire operation and a release operation, plus a single total order exists in which all threads observe all modifications in the same order

Table 16-1 Supported memory orders for atomic functions.

Functions	Supported `memory_order` Values				
	relaxed	acquire	release	acq_rel	seq_cst
load	✓	✓	✗	✗	✓
store	✓	✗	✓	✗	✓
exchange compare_exchange_* fetch_*	✓	✓	✓	✓	✓
fence	✓	✓	✓	✓	✓

atomic_thread_fence

The prototype of this function is

void **atomic_thread_fence(memory_order order)**;

This function achieves a memory synchronization order for non-atomic and relaxed atomic accesses without an associated atomic operation.

atomic_signal_fence

The prototype of this function is

void **atomic_signal_fence(memory_order order)**;

The atomic_signal_fence() achieves synchronization of non-atomic and relaxed atomic accesses between a thread and a signal handler which are included in the same thread.

16.17.3 Atomic Functions with Memory Order

In the previous sections, we explained the functions

void **atomic_store**(volatile **A *object, C desired**);

C **atomic_load**(const volatile **A *object**);

C **atomic_exchange**(volatile **A *object, C desired**);

bool **atomic_compare_exchange_strong**(volatile **A *object, C *expected,**
C **desired**);

bool **atomic_compare_exchange_weak**(volatile **A *object, C *expected,**
C **desired**);

C **atomic_fetch_key**(volatile **A *object, M operand**);

bool **atomic_flag_test_and_set**(volatile **atomic_flag *object**);

void **atomic_flag_clear**(volatile **atomic_flag *object**);

These functions can be used with memory order property, the operation of the functions are the same and the prototypes of these functions with memory order input are as

void **atomic_store_explicit**(volatile **A *object, C desired,**
memory_order order);

C **atomic_load_explicit**(const volatile **A *object, memory_order order**);

```
    C atomic_exchange_explicit(volatile A *object, C desired,\
    memory_order order);
    bool atomic_compare_exchange_strong_explicit(volatile A *object,\
    C *expected,\
    C desired,\
    memory_order success, memory_order failure);



bool atomic_compare_exchange_weak_explicit(volatile A *object,\
    C *expected, C desired,\
    memory_order success,\
    memory_order failure);
    C atomic_fetch_key_explicit(volatile A *object, M operand,\
    memory_order order);
    bool atomic_flag_test_and_set_explicit(volatile atomic_flag *object,\
    memory_order order);
    void atomic_flag_clear_explicit(volatile atomic_flag *object,\
    memory_order order);
```

Problems

1) Fill in the dots in Code-16.59.

Code 16.59

```cpp
#include <iostream>
#include <thread>
using namespace std;
void myFunc(int value) {
while(1){
cout << "Inside thread, value is " << value << endl;
sleep(1);
}
}
int main() {
thread thr1 (...;
thread thr2 (...);
....join();
...join();
}
```

2) For the previous problem, using for-loop create 10 threads for myFunc in Code-15.59
3) What is the detach() function used for?
4) What can we do if we include the header line

using namespace std::chrono_literals;

in our program.
5) Fill in the dots in Code-16.60.

Code 16.60

```cpp
using namespace std;

void myFunc();

int main() {

thread thr (...);

thread::id tid = ...

cout << "Thread ID = " << tid << endl;

...join();
}
void myFunc() {}
```

6) Fill the dots in Code-16.61.

Code 16.61

```
mutex mtx;

void myFunc() {

mtx... // lock mutex here

for(long unsigned indx = 0; indx < 10000; indx++) {
// statements
}
mtx... // lock mutex here
}
```

7) Write Code-16.62 using lock_guard() function.

Code 16.62

```
mutex mtx;

void myFunc() {

mtx.lock();
// statements
mtx.unlock();
}
```

8) Why do we use atomic data types

9) Are the any differences between the use of atomic data types and mutex functions? Which one is preferable and why?

10) Define an atomic double variable.

11) Assume that a is an atomic variable, is the operation a = a+2 is an atomic operation?

12) What does lock free atomic type mean?

13) Explain the use of atomic_store() and atomic_load() functions.

Chapter-17

Templates in C++

Abstract: In this chapter, we will explain the templates used in C++ programming. Templates are used to write generic programs, and the use of templates decreases the number of program lines that must be written to achieve a specific task. Professional programmers always use templates while developing their codes.

17.1 Introduction

To understand the template need, let's first look at the following program.

```
Code 17.1
#include <iostream>
using namespace std;

int sum( int x, int y) {

return x + y;
}
float sum( float x, float y) {

return x + y;
}
double sum( double x, double y) {

return x + y;
}

int main() {

cout << "Sum : " << sum(5, 6) << endl;
cout << "Sum : " << sum(6.3, 7.2) << endl;
cout << "Sum : " << sum(7.24, 9.2874) << endl;
}
```

In Code-17.1, the same function is written for different arguments
We can prevent such situations using templates. There are two types of templates in C++, anf these are

function templates
class Templates

The keyword **template** is used to write generic codes. It can be used either as

$$\textbf{template} < class\ T >$$

or as

$$\textbf{template} < typename\ T >$$

17.2 The Use of Template for a Function

The example below illustrates the use of **template** to write a function that can accept both integer and double data types.

The Code-17.1 can be written using **template** use as Code-17.2.

Code 17.2
```cpp
#include <iostream>
using namespace std;

template <typename T>
T sum( T x, T y) {

return x + y;
}

int main() {

cout << "Sum : " << sum(5, 6) << endl;
cout << "Sum : " << sum(6.3, 7.2) << endl;
cout << "Sum : " << sum(7.24, 9.2874) << endl;
}
```

Example-17.1: In this example, we write a template function which finds the larger of two numbers and returns the larger one.

Code 17.3
```cpp
#include <iostream>
#include <string>
using namespace std;
template <class T>
T Max(T a, T b) {
return a < b ? b:a;
}
int main () {
int i = 39;
int j = 20;
cout << "Max(i, j): " << Max(i, j) << endl;
double f1 = 13.5;
double f2 = 20.7;
cout << "Max(f1, f2): " << Max(f1, f2) << endl;
}
```
Templates containing more than one parameter can also be written.

Example-17.2: In Code-17.4, we write a template function which uses two template parameters.

Code 17.4

```cpp
#include <iostream>
using namespace std;

template < typename T1, typename T2 >
// or template < class T1, class T2 >

T2 product(T1 x, T2 y) {

return (T2)(x * y);
}

int main() {

cout << product(3, 4.7) << endl;
cout << product(4, 5.6) << endl;
}
```

17.3 Class Template

Just as we can define function templates, we can also define class templates. The syntax of class template is shown in Code-17.5

Code 17.5

```
template <class T> // or template <typename T>
class class_name {

... .. ...

public:
T var;
T functionName(T arg);

... .. ...

};
```

Example-17.3: In Code-17.6, we define a class with template parameter T which is used in private and public sections.

Code 17.6

```
template <class T>
class A {
//Declaration of variables of the class
private:
T digit1, digit2;
public:
A(T d1, T d2); //non-default constructor of the class
T larger(); //Function declaration to find the larger
// number of the two
};
```

17.3.1 Implementation of Methods

A class method employing a single template parameter is implemented as in

```
T class_name <T> :: functionName(T arg) {

// statements
}
```

Example-17.4: The non-default constructor and larger() method in Code-17.6 are implemented as in Code-17.7.

Code 17.7
```
template <class T>
A <T> :: A(T d1, T d2) {
// statements
}

template <class T>
T A <T> :: larger() {
// statements
}
```

17.3.2 How to Create a Class Template Object?

The template to create an object for a class which uses template parameters is as

className<dataType1, dataType2,...> classObject;

Example-17.5: For the class defined in Code-17.6, objects can be created as in Code-17.8.

Code 17.8

```
A<int> o1;

A<float> o2;

A<string> o3;
```

Example-17.6: In Code-17.9, a complete example is provided to illustrate the use of the template for Point class.

Code 17.9

```cpp
#include <iostream>
#include <typeinfo>

using namespace std;

template <class T>

class Point{
private:
T x;
T y;

public:
Point(T a, T b);
T getX();
T getY();

void disp();
};

template <class T>
Point<T>::Point(T a, T b) {

x = a; y = b;
}

template <class T>
T Point<T>::getX() {

return x;
}

template <class T>
T Point<T>::getY() {
```

```cpp
return y;
}

template <class T>
void Point<T>::disp() {

cout << "x is:" << x <<endl;
cout << "y is:" << y <<endl;
cout <<" Data type of x is";
cout << typeid(x).name() << endl;
}

int main () {

int a = 3, b = 6;
double c = 6.5, d = 10.2;

Point<int> o1(a,b);
cout << "x is " << o1.getX() << endl;
cout << "Type of x is ";
cout << typeid(o1.getX()).name() <<endl;

Point<double> o2(c,d);
cout << "c is " << o2.getX() << endl;
cout << "Type of c is ";
cout << typeid(o2.getX()).name() <<endl;
}
```

Output(s):

x is 3
Type of x is i
c is 6.5
Type of c is d

Example-17.7: In Code-17.10 , we use two template parameters for illustrative purpose.

Code 17.10

```cpp
#include <iostream>
using namespace std;

template <class T, class U>

class A {
T x;
U y;

public:
A() { cout << "Constructor is called" << endl; }
};

int main() {
```

```
  A<char, char> a;
  A<int, double> b;
  }
```

Output(s):

Constructor is called

Constructor is called

Like normal parameters, we can specify default arguments to templates.

Example-17.8: In Code-17.11, the telmplate parameter **U** has the default data type **char**.

Code 17.11

```cpp
#include <iostream>
using namespace std;
template <class T, class U = char>
class A {
public:
T x;
U y;
A() { cout << "Constructor is called" << endl; }
};
int main() {
// This will call A<int, char>
A<int> obj;
// typeid(x).name()
cout <<"Type of y is " << typeid(obj.y).name() <<endl;
}
```

Output(s):

Constructor is called

Type of y is c

Example-17.9: In Code-17.12, we create a dynamic generic array, initilalize it and print its elements.

Code 17.12

```cpp
#include <iostream>
using namespace std;
template <typename T>
class myArray {
private:
T* ptr;
int size;
public:
myArray(T a [], int N);
void disp();
};
template <typename T> myArray<T>::myArray(T a[], int N) {
ptr = new T[N];
size = N;
for(int indx = 0; indx < size; indx++)
ptr[indx] = a[indx];
}
template <typename T> void myArray<T>::disp() {
for(int indx = 0; indx < size; indx++)
cout << ptr[indx] << " ";
cout << endl;
}
int main() {
int a [4] = { 6, 9, 23, 7 };
myArray< int > obj(a, 4);
obj.disp();
}
```

Output(s): 6 9 23 7

Problems

1) Write the program in Code-17.13 using templates.

```cpp
Code 17.13
#include <iostream>
using namespace std;

int disp(int x) {

cout << x << endl;
}
int disp(char y) {

cout << y << endl;
}
int disp(double z) {

cout << z << endl;
}

int main() {

cout << "x : " << disp(5) << endl;
cout << "y : " << << disp('A') << endl;
cout << "z : " << << disp(4) << endl;
}
```

2) For the class defined in Code-17.14, write the implementation of constructors outside the class definition.

```cpp
Code 17.14
template <class T>
class A {
public:
T digit1, digit2;
A(); // default constructor
A(T d1, T d2); //non-default constructor of the class
A(T d1); //non-default constructor of the class
};
```

3) Define objects for the class of problem-3.

4) Fill in the dots in Code-17.15

```cpp
Code 17.15
#include <iostream>
using namespace std;
```

```cpp
template <...>
class A {
T x;
U y;
public:
A() { cout << "Constructor is called" << endl; }
};
int main() {
A<...> a;
A<...> b;
}
```

Bibliography

1) Y. Daniel Liang, et. all, Introduction to Programming With C++, 2014, ISBN 10: 0-273-79324-1, Pearson Education

2) U Kirch-Prinz, P. Prinz, A Complete Guide to Programming in C++, 2002 by Jones and Bartlett Publishers, ISBN: 0-7637-1817-3

3) Behrouz A. Forouzan, Richard F. Gilberg, C++ Programming: An Object-Oriented Approach, Published by McGraw-Hill Education, 2020, ISBN 978-0-07-352338-5